*Australian
Pioneer Women*

Australian Pioneer Women

EVE POWNALL

VIKING O'NEIL

To
the first, the lonely ones
who made the paths we follow

Viking O'Neil
Penguin Books Australia Ltd
487 Maroondah Highway, PO Box 257
Ringwood, Victoria 3134, Australia
Penguin Books Ltd
Harmondsworth, Middlesex, England
Viking Penguin Inc.
40 West 23rd Street, New York, N.Y. 10010, U.S.A.
Penguin Books Canada Ltd
2801 John Street, Markham, Ontario, Canada L3R 1B4
Penguin Books (N.Z.) Ltd
182-190 Wairau Road, Auckland 10, New Zealand

First published as *Mary of Maranoa* 1959
Second edition published by Lloyd O'Neil Pty Ltd 1980
Reprinted 1983, 1986
This edition published by Penguin Books Australia Ltd 1988
Copyright © Text: Eve Pownall, 1959

All rights reserved. Without limiting the rights under
copyright reserved above, no part of this publication may
be reproduced, stored in or introduced into a retrieval system,
or transmitted, in any form or by any means (electronic,
mechanical, photocopying, recording or otherwise) without
the prior written permission of both the copyright owner
and the above publisher of this book.

Produced by Viking O'Neil
56 Claremont Street, South Yarra, Victoria 3141, Australia
A division of Penguin Books Australia Ltd

Typeset in Australia
Printed and bound in Hong Kong through Bookbuilders Ltd

National Library of Australia
Cataloguing-in-Publication data

Pownall, Eve.
   Australian pioneer women.

   Bibliography.
   ISBN 0 670 90075 3.

   1. Women pioneers — Australia. 2. Women — Australia
   — History. 3. Frontier and pioneer life — Australia.
   I. Title.

994

Preface

This book is a record of the part played in the making of Australia by some of the women who stood with their menfolk on the threshold of districts and eras.

Gathering the material has been at once exciting and frustrating. It was a journey back through time, peering through the tide of the years to life beneath the surface.

Sometimes everything showed clear and sharp, and life darted by in sunny stretches. Sometimes it was clouded over and figures could be seen only dimly through the murk. At others there were depths that could not be penetrated, spaces where no life showed, although somewhere there in the past men had moved and women had lived and loved beside them.

History books gave very little assistance. Few of them recognized the presence of women in the country before about 1850 beyond a passing reference to Mary Reiby's success in business, and tributes to the drive and crusading force of Caroline Chisholm. One or two managed a bow in the direction of Government House: to Ellen Stirling in the West lending heart to settlers by her acceptance of discomfort and pioneering rigours, her tact and sympathy with those whose lot she shared; and to Jane Franklin in Tasmania, energetically forwarding the cause of education and science in a colony self-centredly concerned with problems of settling-in.

The rest of the women who went with their men along the pioneer trails are deemed to have been engaged almost solely in housekeeping, child-bearing and rearing. A visitor to the country interested to learn how early women had assisted the economy complained he was able to find little information. Yet there were women concerned in the growing and harvesting of the first crops, the establishment of the sheep industry, the setting-up of cattle stations. In the gold rush days they helped with the puddling, cradling, and storage of gold won from the dust. Clearing and grubbing, keeping station stores and accounts, milking and tending stock, were some of the many tasks carried out by women who stood on the threshold of the country.

Pioneer woman: an oil painting by M. H. Livingstone, 1875

There is no pretence that the picture given here is complete, for there is much that cannot be pinned down. Every time one ran into a 'first'—the first white women here or there, the first white child born somewhere else—sooner or later there turned up something that was less than a story, a hint, a few vague statements, a name or two, and a ghostly figure seemed to stand behind those others whose records and story could be vouched for.

Some of these figures could logically have existed. But no details were available and I am left wondering about Ann Small who *could* have been the first white woman across the Blue Mountains. Blaxland, Lawson and Wentworth, the legend runs, called on their homeward journey at the little farm where Ann lived with her husband and her six-weeks-old baby. The pathfinders told the story of the land they had discovered, and the Smalls allegedly packed up and went over the hills—hot on the tracks cut by Blaxland's party. Six weeks it took on pack-horse—the story was emphatic on that point, because the baby was three months old when they arrived on the other side of the barrier and began clearing a place to farm and live, somewhere in the Bathurst district. It is all so possible, so much like the pattern repeated again and again as settlement went north, south, east and west. Perhaps Ann Small did ride that trail with her baby on her arm to be the first woman on the other side of the Blue Mountains, but there is not the evidence to prove it.

I was luckier with another 'first'—the woman who preceded Mrs Aeneas Gunn at Elsey Station. This time there was no doubt, for her son, born out there where his mother travelled to Darwin by buckboard and determination to bear him, told me her story. He remembered in that northern isolation, her loneliness, and his lessons under her direction, given mostly out of her rich mind that had been tutored years before by her father, a Dublin University man, who was an early settler in Victoria.

Time may turn up other records and pin them in their proper place in the story of our country's unfolding. Although many have gone forever, lost in homestead fires or destroyed by the impatient hands of later generations, there still, I am sure, exists a reservoir of stories that will feed our knowledge of our own beginnings as the artesian water has been brought up to feed our soil.

Many of the names which appear in these pages will be familiar. Others are known only inside their family circle. All of them saw some part of Australia in the making. They are pioneers not only by reason of the fact that they were the advance guard and endured early hardships and isolation, but because they were the torch-bearers of a better way of life. Harsh as the outlines of living stayed for many years, the fact that women were there did soften the grimness and lend comfort where otherwise there was none.

Where there were white women, the aboriginal woman was better treated. Where there were wives, comfort and ameliorating factors came faster. What the pioneer women brought with them, though they might never consciously recognize it, was the law by which we live. When they made their first candle, swept their first floor, set wildflowers in a tin pannikin on a bark table cut from a sapling, lined huts with the *Illustrated News*, they were not merely establishing Victorian housewifery: they were lighting the first beams of civilization in the wilderness.

They went into the bush and the sandhills, the rain forests, tropics and the frosty highlands, overlanding through the ferocity of summer, and the cool breath of winter when frost stood stiff on the blankets in the morning, and the water in the buckets was a block of ice; through the untracked wilderness where waggon wheels left a path for those who might come after, or following the ruts of the man ahead—weeks, months ahead. The herds and flocks set the pace—slow and steady. The clinking harness, the creak of leather added their rhythm to the orchestra of movement—the lowing of cattle, the bleating of sheep. Halts for the night's camp, and the fire lighting up a strange landscape, the trees still and sinister with perhaps a darker shape hidden in their own dark shadow, a shape which watched the coming of the white men and their horses. Night and the wide sky and the dingo's howl, a child's whimpering—was it sudden fear, or sudden illness? A mother lying with stilled breath until the sounds of quiet sleep returned.

Next morning the Biblical pattern reassembled. Stock and stockmen, horse and covered waggon, jolting cart or buggy faced into the long miles hiding the journey's end.

At last the chosen spot. 'This will do. Here is water and shade. This land will be ours.' The choice of the homing site. The clearing and cutting and log dragging. The erecting of slabs, the making of daub, the fashioning of bricks or pug. The homestead rising piece by piece, a tree to shelter it from the summer sun.

Often before the house was ready or the chosen spot was reached the babies came, a bush lean-to or hut for their only roof. Family records tell of them—the babies born on the way who lived to possess the land, and the others who did not live to see the home site.

As soon as the place was chosen, when home was a tent or a bed under the dray, household routine was established. Cooking out of doors in the Dutch oven, which should surely have a place in the Australian coat of arms, for it, more than the kangaroo and the emu, supported the pioneers. Water from the stream, wooden tubs for washing, the rationing of stores, the anxious eye on supplies, for the interval between loadings was always long.

As the homestead and the yards went up, the daily pattern grew more complicated: teaching the children their letters and numbers, candle-making, setting the slush lights; fever, flies and sandy blight. The men away at the cattle camps and the station work still to go on. Revolver or musket at the ready, for the inland blacks always knew when the men were away and appeared to demand food, or take out on the white Marys their sense of injustice. Sons and husbands away for long intervals exploring, scouting for new land. Families growing. Sons pressing on into the farther distance where pastures beckoned and fortune must surely lie.

Drought struck hard and often, floods swirled and carried away stock and hope, but when illness or accident happened the miles that walled in the homestead were the greatest enemy.

What we owe them, these women who faced those spirit-testing hardships, may never be fully assessed, but we can from time to time remind ourselves of our debt by calling them out of their past to live again the stories of their experiences, tell once more the tales of their pioneering as they stood on the threshold of the country and the riches that are our heritage.

Contents

	Preface	5
1	Stone Age Women	15
2	Enter the European Women	32
3	Women in Chains	35
4	Keeper of the Keys	48
5	Over the Hills to Goshen	63
6	Pioneers Farther South	69
7	Sarah of the South-west Plains	76
8	Swans on the River	81
9	Flowers in the South	87
10	Those Energetic Bussells	94
11	Women in the Fields	99
12	Home-makers Go Inland	105
13	The Pathfinders	110
14	Where the Red Cedar Grew	115
15	Pioneer on the Move	121

16	Home at World's End	138
17	Mary of Maranoa	149
18	Beyond the Nineteen Counties	160
19	Homes South of the Murray	164
20	Pastoral Partners	169
21	Observer in Blue Serge	174
22	Pioneer in Disguise	179
23	Advice for Migrants	182
24	The Northward March	187
25	Childhood of a Pioneer	191
26	No Medals for Mary	204
27	Matriarch of Cooper's Creek	207
28	Spinifex Pioneer	216
29	Reporter of the North	221
30	Paddles on the Murray	236
31	Along the Golden Miles	239
32	Nurses of the Inland	244
33	A Pepper Tree at Tarella	251
34	Past the Farthest Fence	257
35	Women in the Surgery	265
36	Sandhill Homestead	273
37	Pisé Homestead	278
38	The Frontiers of Misfortune	280
39	Pioneering for Tomorrow	288

O firmaments of time,
Where planets ages are,
Ye shall the past sublime,
And set each name a star.

For these were they who came—
A cockle shell for ship—
Daring the sun's red flame,
And the wind's wild whip.

The vast about them lay,
The unknown walled them round,
Like doors, that knew no way,
Loneliness was their bound.

Theirs but a grain of wheat,
Theirs but the small frail band,
But they gave the race to eat,
And they made the land.

        *   *   *

For they were women who at need took up
And plied the axe, or bent above the clodded spade,
Who herded sheep; who rode the hills, and brought
The half-wild cattle home—helpmates of men,
Whose children lay within their arms,
Or at the rider's saddle-pommel hung,
And at whose knees, by night, were said familiar prayers.

        *   *   *

If ever in the dark embrace
Of fear it is our lot to stand,
Vouchsafe, O God, to us this grace:
That we may be as those who stood,
Lone on the threshold of this land,
In their enduring womanhood.

MARY GILMORE
(From 'Ode To The Pioneer Women')

A family at Gulgong, New South Wales, about 1872

A Botany Bay family: an eighteenth-century engraving

I

Stone Age Women

Long before the butter churn and camp oven signalled the arrival of Western housewifery in Australia, and while Europe was still only guessing what lands lay below the Equator, the dark, thin-shanked aboriginal women lived and mated here, raised children, fed the fires, prepared food, performed family and tribal duties.

* * *

Where did she come from, this woman of the dark people? By what stepping stones did she arrive with her mate, her family and her tribe in the land where she was the first housekeeper? From India by way of Thailand, Malaya and the islands of Indonesia, say some. Possibly from Java, say others, where a species of Original Man evolved, the ancester of the people who eventually moved over the sea to our northern coastlands.

No one knows, and the years are piled high above the facts of her first coming. But old legends, sagas, and song cycles, shrouded in mystery and symbolism though they are, contain a small, hard seed of Truth from which grows a picture of dark people reaching Northern Australia in rafts and dugout canoes. They may even have swum part of the way for 'they are good long-distance swimmers and feel quite at home in the water'.[1]

As successive waves came up the shingle, the latest arrivals pressed the first-comers further inland. They fanned out through the continent along the line of rivers, drifting by waterhole and billabong into the heat and dry places of the inland, the regions of chancy rainfall and uncertain seasons, settling in hills and mountain districts, squatting on the plains, claiming forest lands or coastal sections. As the generations passed, tribal elders fixed the boundaries, which were only crossed on rare and special occasions. Violation of the frontier was a hostile act, likely to trigger-off inter-tribal war. But inside the borders lay the tribe's own 'country', its hunting grounds and living space. There the dark woman went about her foraging to fill the stomachs of her family. Man was the hunter of larger animals, but these were not always present, and it was Aboriginal Woman who brought home the greater part of the equivalent of the daily bread.

From her earliest years she was part of the daily excursions to collect the varied and sometimes hidden stores of her 'country'. At first she rode on her mother's back or straddled her hip; later she toddled by her side, with a little pitchi to carry as a white child carries a miniature shopping basket. And as soon as she became aware of her surroundings her training began. The track taken by the ants, where the bandicoot makes his nest, where the digging stick will turn up tubers and edible roots were elementary lessons that she absorbed, practised and added to endlessly.

A few short years and childhood was over. At puberty she was marriageable and mated with the man chosen for her. She may have been promised to him before she was born, or she might go to his fireside in payment of a debt, or to prevent hostility between groups.

Preparation for marriage varied from tribe to tribe. In north-west New South Wales[2] the bride-to-be was taken off to camp in the bush by her mother's mother. She returned by progressive stages to the main camp, which she entered wearing flowers in her hair and in her armbands, while the women of the tribe greeted her with songs as she passed to place feathers or flowers on the head of her future husband. At the last campfire her grandmother told her to go and sleep by the side of the man who was now her husband and be true to him all the days of her life.

After marriage the dark woman played an important part in the tribe's economic framework, and her foraging was the main food supply for her mate and family. What she brought back in her dilly bag depended largely on the season, and the 'country' where the tribe wandered.

> They collect wild fruits—black or green plums, wild apples or peaches, long sweet yams or bitter roots that need special treatment; stems and roots of the blue or red water lily or seed to be crushed for damper; possums and bandicoots, witchetty grubs, honey mats and various nuts. Or they go down to the sea and

get shell fish, oysters and mussels, or big mangrove crabs to be cooked on the coals.[3]

For her foraging and cooking she had the coolamon (a hollowed-out wooden dish which carried water or cradled a baby), grinding stones to crush grass seeds into durri (flour) for little cakes, dilly bag of woven reeds, digging or yam sticks, and a fire stick which must always be kept burning.

When she knew she was pregnant, the aboriginal woman believed this was due not to sexual relationship, but because the child had been 'dreamed' (usually by her husband), and had entered her body from one of the traditional places where unborn children existed. Or did she really believe this? Present-day theories doubt whether the tradition had anything more than lip service. Tribal elders, they say, certainly knew the cause of pregnancy, and declare that women only pretended to be ignorant of the facts. But Daisy Bates maintained that belief in 'dreaming' a child was firmly established, and tells of Fanny Bulbuk, one of the last aboriginal women of Perth, who 'even when she was a fat old woman, and her seven husbands and numerous lovers had long preceded her to the Bibbulmum heaven . . . assiduously avoided every "baby stone" from which a babe might come to her'.[4]

The mother in labour was supported by the presence of women of her group who sang ritual songs to prevent haemorrhage, to make birth easy, or to welcome the child.

> One calls: 'Come now, here's your auntie waiting to see you.' Then: 'Here's your sister.' Then: 'Here's your father's sister.' and so on through the whole list. When the child seems in no hurry to accept the invitation, she goes on: 'Make haste, the bumble fruit is ripe. The flowers are blooming. The grass is waving high. The birds are all talking. And it's a beautiful place, hurry up and see for yourself.' But it generally happens that the baby is too cute to be tempted, and the old woman has to produce what she calls a wimouyan—a clever stick—which she waves over the expectant mother, crooning a charm which brings forth the baby.[5]

Motherhood brought more duties dictated by tribal customs. Powdered pollen from the needlebrush tree for the baby who slept fitfully. A fire of buatha twigs to smoke out the devil from one who cried too much. When a mother woke at night, she warmed her hands and massaged her baby so that its limbs would grow supple and well-shaped. If the baby slept with his mouth open, she closed it promptly. Good mothercraft, this, although tribal tradition said it prevented the entrance of a disease or an evil-working spirit.[6]

When the baby began to crawl, there was another routine.

> The mother finds a centipede, cooks it, takes it from the fire, and catching hold of her child's hands, beats them with it, crooning as she does so . . . 'Kind be, Do not steal, Do not touch what to another belongs. Leave all such alone, Kind be.' And when the child is four years old, it must be beaten over the shoulders and under the arms with a bustard's wing, while the mother makes a clicking noise with her tongue and croons: 'A swimmer be, Flood to swim against, No water Strong to stop you.'[7]

Child training was the mother's job. Through her the generations were linked on the chain of tradition: 'first' songs and rhythm, foraging lore, the distribution of food within the group, the group totem, tabus, and early lessons in personal relations: who were relatives and what was the structure of group relationships, a most important part of tribal life not understood by early European observers.

Within the tribe there were duties, company, gossip, drama, excitement, and entertainment for the dark woman as for her husband. In spite of comments by early European observers, her life had undertones and overtones, her role was more than that of extra at ceremonial occasions charged to beat 'rolled up opossum-skin rugs, and sing the corroboree songs in voices shrill to sweet'.[8]

What if men played the major part in the great corroborees? Women had their place, and for that matter their own corroborees when they went apart and enacted certain rites, usually designed to entice a lover.

> It took place in the brilliant sunlight, against a background of red sandstone, the long yellow grasses and bauhinea trees with their crimson seed pods. The women themselves were greased with fat till their skins glistened; bold designs in charcoal, red ochre, and clay were drawn on their bodies, so that they seemed the living incarnation of the landscape itself; almost as though they had been impregnated with its harsh and vital colouring.[9]

Mistress of ceremonies on these occasions was a middle-aged woman, an authority on mythology and experienced in ritual. When the women returned to camp after their performance it was their turn to look secretive and toss their heads at questions and comments made by half-amused, half-frustrated males.

Although boys and girls stayed with their mother for the first ten or eleven years of life, a mother's part in her son's training ended with the corroboree which was his farewell to camp before his initiation into man's affairs.

This night, when the Bora corroboree began, all the women relations of the boys who were to be made young men corroboreed all night. Towards the end of the night all the young women were ordered into bough humpies, which had been made previously all round the edge of the embankment surrounding the ring. The old women stayed on ... When every man had, at a signal, taken his charge on his shoulder, they all started dancing round the ring. Then the old women were told to come and say goodbye to the boys; after which they were ordered to join the young women in the humpies.

About five men watched them pass into the humpies, then pulled the boughs down on top of them so that they might see nothing further. When the women were safely imprisoned beneath the boughs the men, carrying the boys, swiftly disappeared down the track into the scrub.

When they were out of sight the five blackfellows went and pulled the boughs away and released the women, who went to their camps. But however curious the women were as to what rites attended the boys' initiation into manhood, they knew no questions would gain any information. In some months' time they might see their boys return home minus, perhaps, a front tooth, and with some extra scarifications or weals on their bodies, but beyond that, and a knowledge of the fact that the boys had not been allowed to look on the face of a woman since their disappearance into the scrub, the women were never told anything.[10]

In spite of the seeming finality of this separation, Phyllis Kaberry, who studied tribal life in close contact with its actors, found 'A son, though he is separated from his mother during periods of initiation, cherishes a strong affection for her during his lifetime. He gives her food and cares for her in old age'.[11]

As children married and departed to live in other groups, the mother visited their camps, and watched carefully to see they kept the tribal law. She did her best to break up illicit attachments, but if this were not possible, shrugged and accepted the accomplished fact. That was that, and nagging and reproaches stopped.

The peace of the tribe, the continuance of its pattern—these in her later years were her main concern. If her husband brought a younger wife into camp, the older woman usually accepted the arrangement without rancour. Food gathering demanded activity; youth could fill the dilly bag better. The same philosophy held for the young girl married to an elderly man. Someone had to look after him and see he did not starve, was the accepted attitude.

If she had character, age gave the dark woman a certain status. But querulous, uncertain temperaments could not depend on their years alone to earn them respect. That went then, as now, to personality, to the woman who could use a lifetime's experience with tolerance and wisdom. The outstanding aboriginal woman has been sympathetically described by Phyllis Kaberry.

> She has a profounder knowledge and interest in mythology than the average person; she possesses a fund of experience drawn from her journeys over wide regions, her attendance at intertribal meetings and the quarrels she has witnessed over marriage, wife-stealing, sorcery and death. She and other women of her age enjoy a great measure of authority, though this will vary according to assertiveness and temperament.[12]

Miss Kaberry produces witnesses to back her statement: everyone's favourite, Laidbis, 'gentle-voiced and kindly', whose occasional judgments were always carefully listened to; Amel, reserved and dignified, a tactful, competent settler of camp disputes; Yudubein, an authority on mythology, respected for her refusal to tolerate marital infidelity; and Bangudenangga, an independent character, whose wit could puncture the balloon of a boaster's conceit on the points of women's laughter roused by her sally: 'That man got 'em big throat.'

As the arc of the years swung round, the dark woman lost firmness of muscle and flesh, and her breasts shrank into flabbiness. Her physical powers decreased, but her group gave her social security. Someone saw to her needs, set food within her reach, led her away from danger from either Man or Nature. At last she entered the Dreaming, and the pattern she inherited and handed on in her turn was rounded out and completed.

A dull, drab existence? She had known joy and sorrow, had place and position, worked, was entertained, walked sometimes close to Mystery and forces greater than nature, had beliefs, traditions and a way of life that served her physically and satisfied her mentally. It could be that some present-day societies uphold their members less firmly than those we sweepingly call 'primitive'.

*   *   *

No one knows how long the dark woman went about her housekeeping unknown by other races. On European maps, Australia was

Aboriginals sketched by a First Fleet artist outside their shelter

still only a vague shape labelled 'Great South Land' when the first visitors arrived. These were Malay fishermen sailing their moon-shaped praus along the north coast in search of trepang, or bêche-de-mer, and the great tortoise whose shell was prized throughout the East wherever shrewd-eyed traders gathered.

Some Malays brought women on their boats, the yellow-skinned women of their own race mentioned in songs recorded by Catherine and Roland Berndt in their field work among the tribes of Arnhem Land. Occasionally these alien women lived on shore in houses built Malay-wise, on wooden stilts, with gardens where they grew and harvested Australia's first rice crops. Other Malays had aboriginal women supplied by tribesmen whom they co-opted into a working partnership to help with the fishing and trepang smoking. In the latter period of the Malay visits, the season ended with feasting and drinking dreaded by the dark women because of the violence they suffered in such orgies. Then the Malays departed till the following year, and native life went back to its accustomed pattern.

But the centuries were passing, and sailors of Europe were coming ever closer to the shores of the Fifth Continent. When they reached it, and in fact for long afterwards, they thought the Australian native, whether man or woman, an oddity like the kangaroo and emu—something strange and different, and not to be taken seriously. They regarded the dark woman as passive and subservient, a chattel or patient slave to fetch and carry, endure and tend; a being without authority, place or prestige, and with little but patience and devotion to sustain her. They found no Boadicea, Elizabeth or Joan of Arc with a sense of politics, and deduced that the tribal woman was a poor creature, leading a drab, colourless existence.

Was it true? Katherine Langloh Parker, who lived a good deal of her life close to the dark people, once remarked drily on the subject of the native woman's bullying by her menfolk: 'I have seen henpecked black husbands.'

The first Englishman who saw anything of the original Australians was William Dampier, roving reporter of the seventeenth century, who reached the north-west coast in the *Cygnet*, pirate ship, second class. Mr Dampier was unimpressed by the aboriginal people; in his much-quoted phrase, they were 'the miserablest people in the world'. He did not like their appearance, he thought their diet poor and unsatisfying, and he marvelled that they had 'no sort of cloaths', no herds or houses, 'the Earth being their bed and the Heaven their canopy'.[13]

Actually, Dampier did not see the native people at close quarters.

Two eighteenth-century views of Aboriginal women

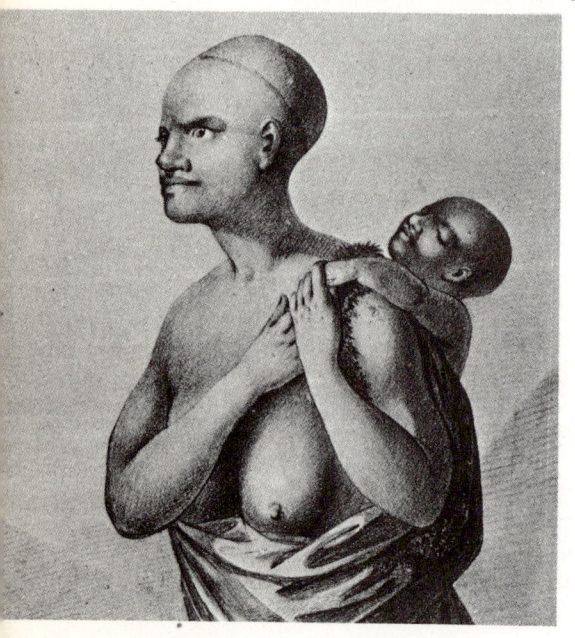

They were apt to make off quickly at the sight of the Englishmen, as on the occasion Dampier recorded:

> The lustiest of the women, snatching up their infants, ran away howling, and the little children ran after, squeaking and bawling. Some of the women and such people as could not go from us, lay still by a Fire, making a doleful noise, as if we had been coming to devour them.[14]

Their tendency to run from the stranger gave the indefatigable note-taker no opportunity to answer his own question. Did the women he saw in groups have one mate, or cohabit promiscuously?

Almost a hundred years later, Cook and Banks ran their keenly-observant eyes over the native people of the East Coast, noted their weapons and utensils, including 'bags in which they carried their furniture [sic] ... something between netting and knitting',[15] their methods of cooking under hot stones and so on. They came no closer than Dampier to understanding the pattern of aboriginal life in general and that of the aboriginal woman in particular.

Eighteen years after Cook, the First Fleet brought white settlement to Australia, and a host of diary-keepers and 'Account' writers, who gave their considered opinions of the land and its original people in stilted eighteenth-century English.

Surgeon-General White said 'many of the women were strait, well-formed and lively.'[16]

But Captain Watkin Tench of the Marines, a fastidious young man, would have none of that. He found the dark women's voices soft and attractive, their manner timid and bashful; but he shook his head over their general appearance. 'Of the other charms of the ladies I shall be silent', he wrote. Only one Port Jackson belle stirred him to eloquence—Gooreedeeana, an outstandingly good-looking young woman of eighteen, who, to judge from Captain Tench's account, was much discussed in the officers' mess.

Tench says the men of the tribe had two attitudes to the relation of their women and the white strangers: 'The women were sometimes kept back with every symptom of jealous sensibility; and sometimes offered with every appearance of courteous familiarity.'[17]

First Fleet officers trod carefully, not wishing to offend

> the feelings of the men on so tender a point, we have constantly made a rule of treating the females with that distance and reserve which we judged most likely to remove any impression they might have received of our intending aught which could give offence on so delicate a subject.[18]

There are accounts by other diarists of fish hooks given to native women—a gift of importance to a people dependent on seafoods for much of their diet; of buttons strung on cord to adorn them, and handkerchiefs torn into strips to tie around dark arms—all done in kindly patronage as one might amuse a group of children, soothe their fears, or coax them to be friends.

Deeper compassion was shown to the ill or handicapped. Captain John Hunter[19] recorded the story of a native girl encountered at Broken Bay where Phillip had taken an exploring party. A group of native women left their fishing and ran off as the white men approached—except one who went to ground. A soldier fired at a hawk; the shot brought a cry of terror, and a search revealed a frightened girl crouching in the long grass. Against the background of the great bay's timbered coves and headlands, uniformed soldiers of His Majesty's forces grouped round the panic-stricken girl crying and cowering at their feet. She was obviously a victim of smallpox and still weak, or she would have run with the others to escape the strange beings so suddenly arrived in her 'country'.

The Englishmen tried to soothe her, and as practical proof of their friendliness gathered grass, dried and spread it round her for warmth. Then they 'shot some birds . . . hawks, crows and gulls, skinned them and laid them on the fire to broil, together with some fish, which she ate; then we gave her water of which she seemed much in want.'[20] Before they slept, they took her more firewood, covered her with more dry grass, and 'left her to her repose'.

She seemed less frightened in the morning, when they again gave her food and water before leaving to explore the bay. When they returned at evening she had moved into a native shelter on the beach, and now had a companion—a child of about two, 'as fine a little infant of that age as I ever saw', declared Hunter. 'The girl, who could have been its mother, flung herself across the child to protect it.'

> The Governor's party lifted her up and tried to reassure her, but she sat on the ground with her knees up to her chin, and her heels under her, and was at the moment, I think the most miserable spectacle in the human shape I ever beheld. The little infant . . . lay with its face upon the ground, and one hand covering its eyes.[21]

Gradually the white men won the child's confidence, and were allowed to take her hand. Again they supplied birds, fish and fuel, pulled grass for a bed, and covered the little hut to keep out the weather. Before they left next morning they gave the native girl all the fish left from their catch, cut firewood, and set water within reach.

One wonders how the dark girl interpreted their appearance and behaviour, and whether she ever again came into contact with the people who had invaded her country.

There was a reverse side to the picture of kindness on the official level. In 1832 James Backhouse of the Society of Friends found something quite different: exploitation of the aboriginal women by sealers working round the Tasmanian coast, and fear which stemmed from their experience of what white men could do and had done. The women, dressed in frocks of wallaby skins, worked the sealing boats under compulsion, snared mutton birds and acted as jills-of-all-trades for their kidnappers. Government officials tried to rescue them, but the women were often too terrified of the sealers to admit their plight. It took much patient coaxing to persuade them the officers were their protectors, but once convinced they became different beings, talked and laughed, and happily turned their backs on their captivity. Backhouse mentions one woman 'on the jetty "growling", as they term expressing displeasure, towards the cutter; but this also proved to be assumed by the direction of the sealers; and she likewise with her baby was rescued'.[22]

One elderly woman had been lured away by the sealers when a young girl. Once she had managed to escape by swimming some miles from an island, but had been recaptured by the men and taken back to her life of enslavement. Backhouse was deeply moved by her miming of the way

> these men flogged the women who did not pluck the mutton birds or do other work to their satisfaction. She spread her hands to the wall to show the manner in which they were tied up, said a rope was used to flog them with and cried out in a failing voice till she sank upon the ground, as if exhausted.[23]

By the time Backhouse was viewing these dark, patient women with compassion, sea changes had occurred in the lives of their sisters in other places. White settlement spread over the country slowly but surely, and the native people either went down before it, or moved farther and farther out.

The first white women who wrote of early Australia are inclined to draw aside their petticoats and express a feeling of revulsion towards the aboriginal women. There was little understanding of tribal patterns even from an Australian-born like Sarah Musgrove. Sarah grew up near Young (New South Wales) and was accustomed to aborigines from her earliest years, but she thought dark women wounding themselves at the death of a group member were merely exhibiting hysteria, and evidently made no effort to discover the tradition behind the act.

But if nineteenth-century housewives did not understand the background of the native women, those who followed their men to the farthest-out places where lines of communication were long and frail came to appreciate many qualities of the dusky Eves who helped them in their isolated home-making. Cheerful humour that lightened the burden of loneliness in many far-off homes offset the exasperation which a too-casual approach to white women's domestic habits often caused.

'Little fella gunty', exclaimed Kitty, a lubra on the Costellos' station, Valley of Springs, on the Limm River, when she saw her mistress and daughters open parasols under the Gulf Country sky in the 'eighties. Years later they recalled her astonishment at the swiftness with which the little 'gunty' (house) was erected, and her delight as she ran in and out of the parasol's shade.

As the herds and flocks moved farther west and north, aboriginal women played an important part in establishing pastoral Australia. Catherine Berndt declares that the dark women were preferred as station workers because they were 'more obliging and adaptable'.[24] Most of the settlers were unmarried, or did not bring their wives to the inland loneliness. For these men the aboriginal women performed 'domestic and sexual duties' and acted as a link between the settlers and the tribe, while 'the young and able-bodied rode with the stock camp, mustering and yarding, droving and branding, or went out to help the fencemakers and well sinkers'.[25]

The dark woman's loyalty was not alway returned in kind, and from time to time a grim note is struck in the concerto of black-white association. Tasmania's early history contains the story of Black Mary and her relation to bushranger Michael Howe (who sent the notorious message to Lieutenant-Governor Sorrell headed: 'From the Governor of the Bush to the Governor of the Town').

For years Black Mary was Howe's faithful companion, sharing his wild life, running when he ran, helping with her native lore to ease his existence in the bush. But there came a time when Howe's exploits brought determined official action against him, and he was constantly on the run. Howe decided Mary was a drag and a hindrance. Without her he could travel faster, so he drew his gun and shot her.

Then and there he exchanged devotion for retribution. The

Truganini, one of the last of the Tasmanian Aboriginals, in her youth

Truggernana, Native of Recherche Bay.

wounded woman allied herself with the soldiers as they closed on the outlaw. Knowing where he made his camps, she led the troops from hideout to hideout, until the chase grew too hot and Howe surrendered. To save his own neck he betrayed the rest of his gang, but it gained him only a short respite. He died violently in 1818, two years after the dark finger of Black Mary had pointed out the place where the soldiers took his surrender.

* * *

The native women's knowledge of simple remedies helped many white wives and mothers raising families on the outer edges of settlement—days, often weeks, away from any form of medical assistance.

Muggaree, a crippled house gin at Mooraberrie Station in Western Queensland, came to the aid of Kate Bancroft Miller's youngest child, badly afflicted with sandy blight. Muggaree, dragging herself along on two sticks, took herself off for a few days, and returned with a handful of leaves picked from a native plant. She bruised these in water and applied the lotion to the child's eyes. Within a week the cure was complete.

Mrs Langloh Parker has left the story of Old Bootha[26] and her powers of diagnosis. When she was over sixty, her favourite granddaughter died, and grief-stricken Bootha cut herself mercilessly, threw away her 'white-fella' clothes, and retired to an underground cave with only her dogs as companions, speaking to no one, and withdrawing from all human contact. Mrs Parker saw she was supplied with food, and gradually Bootha resumed her life (and clothes) about the station. It was then her reputation as a healer began to grow.

> We heard of wonderful cures she had made, how she always consulted the spirits about any illness; and how there were said to be spirits in some of her dogs; how she was a rain-maker and, in fact, a fully-fledged witch.[27]

Mrs Parker had first-hand evidence of Bootha's ability when her own husband developed a pain in the knee which set him limping. Bootha came to see him, summoned her familiars by singing, and declared: 'Too muchee water there; you steam him, put him on hot rag; you drink plenty cold water; all lite, dat go.'

A few days later a doctor passing through the district gave his diagnosis. He prescribed 'hot fomentations to the place affected, poultices, a cooling draught' to disperse fluid at the knee joint. Says Mrs Parker: 'I thought Bootha ought to have been called in in consultation.' Diagnosis differed only in idiom.

The old medicine woman had a more difficult case when a girl visitor to the station fell ill. Bootha entered the sick room, hanging her head and muttering in a dialect Mrs Parker had never heard. 'A most peculiar whistling sort of voice' replied. This, Bootha said, was the spirit of Big Joe; but when he could not help she spoke again to summon the spirit of her grand-daughter.

Again no help was forthcoming, so Bootha called on another dead girl of the tribe and this time made a pronouncement; the patient was ill because she had bathed in the shade of a tree that was tabu, and the bees dwelling there had resented the breaking of the law. Mrs Parker dismissed this as so much nonsense. No members of the household ever swam in that area. But the patient said yes, she had bathed under the forbidden tree one morning. Closer inspection revealed that the irritation pimples across her back were bee stings, and her fever and discomfort caused by their poison.

Bootha prescribed cold water as treatment, rubbed the patient's wrist several times, muttered an incantation and went off, taking away the bad spirits inside her, she said. Whatever the facts, the girl slept well that night—the first time since her illness, and quickly recovered.

*   *   *

Aboriginal women brought warning, often at great danger to themselves, of mischief planned in the native camp against the whites, and some day no doubt their devotion will be dramatized as the history of our settlement is staged or screened.

In a different key is their good temper and kindliness as nursemaids to white children, and their support of white mistresses in time of need. Stories of native women who acted as emergency midwives appear in every district. Mrs A. M. Duncan-Kemp has recounted the help and support given to Kate Bancroft Miller, first white woman at Mooraberrie, in the Charters Towers country.[28] Kate's husband was away with the cattle, thirty miles off, when her third child arrived. Minnie, one of the house gins, helped her through a long and difficult birth, carrying out the instructions Kate managed to give her. When Miller arrived home in answer to smoke signals sent up by the station natives, his new-born child was safely delivered and eight hours old. At her fourth confinement Kate was again alone. This time the house gin, Muggaree, had been crippled by a kick from a cow and could not help. But somehow she managed to crawl from the homestead to the native camp, and brought back one of the bush women. Then she remained to translate Kate's instructions to the wild gin, who acted as midwife and saved the mother and child.

But a story of really heroic proportions comes from the same Mooraberrie. On this occasion one of Kate's children was ill of pneumonia. Household remedies failed, and the child was sinking rapidly. A gin mounted a horse and rode two hundred and forty miles in a day and a night to bring medicine and help. The fact that they came too late to save the child does not detract from the amazing exploit of the dark woman, nor the spirit which prompted it.

* * *

Today, as then, the wild bee builds the prized honey bag, the witchetty grub wriggles blindly when disturbed, the seasons which brought their special offerings for the dark woman's dilly bag come and go, and the lagoons where she submerged herself in the reeds to gather the wild duck from his dabbling—these, all these, are still there. But the years have brought changes in the life of the women who used them. The coming of the white man, the opening of the north, and the establishment of station life have altered the texture, the essence of her 'country'. Even its skies, that once belonged only to her tribal spirits, have been taken by the white man's planes, and year by year our living patterns press and narrow the circle of old tribal ways.

For a time it seemed that the dark woman and her people would vanish before the tide of white settlement, but now their numbers are holding, consolidated mainly in the north. There has even been an increase among groups whose birthrate had fallen away markedly. But still their place in a white man's land is not defined, though we feel the truth of Mary Durack's declaration in *Keep Him, My Country*—'We're driven along on the tide of our time and the blacks are coming too.'[29]

On the threshold of the atomic age no one can predict where that tide will take us or the descendant of Australia's first housekeepers. But if she needs support and advocates at the bar of public opinion those who knew her first should be heard. Mary McManus, who came to central Queensland over a hundred years ago, lived to write: 'We could never have managed without the blacks.' And Kate Bancroft Miller acknowledged with gratitude the devoted help the aboriginal woman gave to many a white woman on the farthest-out stations.

A Port Jackson Beauty

Gooreedeeana . . . excelled in beauty all their females I ever saw: her age about eighteen; the firmness, the symmetry and the luxuriancy of her bosom, might have tempted painting to copy its charms: her mouth was small; and her teeth though exposed to all the destructive purposes to which they apply them, were white, sound and unbroken. Her countenance, though marked by some of the characteristics of her native land, was distinguished by a softness and sensibility unequalled in the rest of her countrywomen: and I was willing to believe that these traits indicated the disposition of her mind. I have never before seen this elegant and timid female of whom I had often heard: but the interest I took in her led me to question her about her husband and family. She answered by repeating a name, which I have now forgotten: and told me she had no children. I was seized with a strong propensity to learn whether the attractions of Gooreedeeana were sufficiently powerful to secure her from the brutal violence with which women are treated; and as I found my question either ill understood or reluctantly answered, I proceeded to examine her head, the part on which the husband's vengeance generally alights. With grief I found it covered with contusions and mangled scars. The poor creature, grown by this time more confident, from perceiving that I pitied her, pointed out a wound just above her left knee, which she told me was received from a spear, thrown at her by a man who had lately dragged her by force from her home, to gratify his lust. I afterwards observed that this wound caused a slight lameness and that she limped in walking. I could only compassionate her wrongs and sympathise in her misfortune: to alleviate her present sense of them, when she took her leave, I gave her, however, all the bread and salt pork which my little stock afforded.

W. Tench, *A Narrative of the Expedition to Botany Bay.*

2

Enter the European Women

Almost any Australian child can tell you the story of Dirk Hartog's pewter plate, practically the symbol of the white man's coming to Australia.

But Hartog nailed up his famous plate on an island in Shark Bay in 1616,[1] and did not set foot on the mainland. Neither did the first European women reported in Australian waters. They were put ashore on a group of islands that spatter the map about two hundred miles north of Perth. Their coming was unplanned, their landing was perilous, and their stay marked with murder and mayhem.

The story belongs to the days when the Dutch had found their way into the Indian Ocean, seized a share of the coveted Eastern market from the Portuguese, established themselves at Djakarta (which they renamed Batavia) and shipped home to Europe the fabulous goods of the Orient. Cargoes with names that shimmered and glowed—musk, ebony, ivory, brocade, pearls, porcelain and many pungent spices so necessary to disguise the flavour of food in the days before refrigeration—were loaded into the holds of sturdy East Indiamen plying to and fro between Indonesia and the Hague.

Inevitably, some ships on their way out were blown off course to the shores of Western Australia. Some piled up on the reefs and cliffs of the coast; others dropped anchor and stayed while their shrewd and able captains charted the shore and looked over the scene. They found nothing to interest their trading masters, but the winds of the South Indian Ocean continued to bring the small ships to the land they called New Holland until they knew most of its coast from the Bight to the Kimberleys and into the Gulf.

But that coast could still surprise them, as the crew and passengers of *Batavia* discovered.

Enter the European Women

Sailing quietly on a still night in 1629, a sleeping ship with only the officer of the watch and the helmsman on deck, *Batavia* was northward bound on the last leg of the voyage to Djakarta. Even a white patch on the sea ahead pointed out by the helmsman aroused no alarm. Only moonlight, said the officer, and the ship sped on.

Suddenly with a bump and a lurch it pulled up short. The white patch was no glimmering moonlight, but water snarling above an unmarked reef, and *Batavia* had struck it full on.

Morning arrived with rain and wind. The vessel was past saving, the sick groaned, women and children sobbed, and Captain Pelsart decided to abandon ship. The nearest land was nothing but a cluster of little islands, flat as plates and almost as bare. Not a tree broke their outline, or raised the eye above ground level; they had no cave or shelter of any kind, and the only vegetation was a sort of tussocky grass where seabirds nested.

The ship's boats were launched and landing effected with difficulty in the rolling sea. Passengers and crew, food, bread, wine and chests of clothes were brought ashore. Tents were pitched as some small protection from wind and weather, and sheltered the first attempts at European housewifery on the Australian continent.

But whether pans and kettles were also landed, who cooked and what provided fuel for fires, how the sick fared, how clothes were washed (if they were washed) or mended, was not deemed interesting enough to report to the Governors of the East India Company. Instead, what was set down amounted to a tale of gangsterism in which women were raped, murdered, and drowned.

The main camp was made on one island, and groups scouted for water among the rest. Captain Pelsart and some of the crew set out in a ship's boat and even inspected part of the mainland. When his search, too, proved unsuccessful, he decided to steer for Djakarta and bring back a rescue ship to take off the survivors of the wreck.

He was scarcely out of sight when there drifted ashore on a spar one Cornelius, until then busy on board helping himself to the ship's liquor. As supercargo, that is, company's agent in charge of the sale of merchandise, Cornelius was entitled to assume command in the captain's absence, and this he did.

It was said later, he had plotted during the voyage to seize the ship and turn pirate. If this is true, there is a certain logic in his later behaviour. He gathered round him some pretty villains among the crew and signed them up as his executive officers in a kind of brotherhood of blood, all swearing to stick together to gain their ends, which were to capture the rescue ship and sail off under the black flag with the money chests and the women.

Cornelius gave himself the flamboyant title of Captain-General, ordered the chests to be broached, and decked himself and his followers in lace- and gold-trimmed coats, plumed hats and silk stockings. Then he looked over the women and divided them among the members of his gang, choosing for himself the widow of one of the crew drowned in the wreck. She and some others were willing to enter into the plot Cornelius and his lads were hatching. But some women resisted the attentions of the Captain-General's company, and were seized forcibly. Others, led by the pastor's daughter, Anna, managed to escape to another island, where a minor camp was located.

Cornelius led an attack on the island, but was taken prisoner in the struggle and his men driven off.

Their next move, dictated, they said, by the need to conserve food supplies, entailed the slaughter of all not in their immediate company. With swords, axes and knives, they advanced on their victims—men, women and children—till the seabirds took off in panic at the shrieks of the murdered, and the floundering of those driven into the water and left to drown.

Another attack would certainly have been made on the group holding Cornelius prisoner, but time forestalled it. Pelsart's rescue ship came in sight, and the group with whom Anna had taken refuge sent a boat to meet it.

When the Captain-General's men rowed out to greet Pelsart, smiling and bowing, but with weapons concealed in the floor of their boat, they were received sternly and clapped into irons. The rack extracted confessions from any who held back, and the gibbet claimed the rest—except two men who were left on shore to survive if they could and were never seen again.

Then the rescue ship raised sail and steered over the horizon towards Java, while the waves washed in and out above the lonely reef where the dead men and women and the dead ship lay. The wind's moan and the harsh cry of the gulls farewelled the first European women to land on Australian soil.

3

Women in Chains

THE EIGHTEENTH CENTURY gave shape and reality to maps of the world. New names appeared, old tales died out. But the myth of the Great South Land faded slowly, although unknowingly the Dutch had dealt its death blow by their discoveries of New Holland. Then in 1771 Cook came home with his report of the South Seas—Captain James, commissioned to watch the stars move above Otaheite (Tahiti), had gone on to haul the islands of New Zealand from the mists of legend, and draw the east coast of Terra Australis out of fancy into fact.

There they were, claimed in the name of England's King, and set down with seamanlike precision on the maps of the world and in the records of His Majesty's government.

But who wanted an unknown country at the other end of the globe, a place without obvious resources or attractions, which a few primitive savages occupied but did not mine, farm or otherwise develop? Not the British government, that already found itself with trouble on its hands in the American colonies.

When that trouble developed into war, the American colonists cut themselves off with victories on the field and high-sounding phrases relating to love, life and the pursuit of happiness. The disgruntled British were convinced that founding an overseas empire was a pesky business and best left alone.

But for better or worse, the islands of New Zealand and the land called New South Wales had been added to His Majesty's possessions. They could be and were ignored for a time, but history, destiny, or the law of expediency called them out of their pigeonhole and set them fair and square on the agenda of world affairs. Managing without colonies was one thing, but coping with unwanteds at home was quite another. The business papers of Cabinet were soon bristling with questions about the disposal of convicts, once transported to the American settlements, but now overcrowding the prisons and likely to spread jail fever and infection through the country. Evidence piled up that England did not possess enough dank, grimy walls, dripping ceilings and damp floors to confine the men and women, victims of character or society, who passed through the courts.

Flotsam and jetsam of fate, it was the need to remove them from Britain which chiefly drove an unwilling government to consider the possibilities of the land Cook had discovered.

Cook, dead of a spear thrust in Hawaii, could give no advice, but his reports and charts were spread before committees, and the opinions of the esteemed Sir Joseph Banks, who had sailed with him in *Endeavour*, were sought and listened to with flattering attention.

Months went by while officialdom considered and recommended, dallied and delayed, but the prisons, with their tattered, battered inmates, their fevers and plagues remained to goad the government. It moved at last and decision was made. A batch of convicts and supplies (unsuitable and inadequate on many counts) would be transferred across the globe, a gaggle of humanity destined to become the first settlers of the Australian nation.

The charge of getting them there was given to a retired naval officer on half pay, Captain Arthur Phillip, first Governor of the colony of New South Wales, who took the ships (historically they became the First Fleet) with outstanding competence across the world. He sailed from Portsmouth in May 1787, heading south into the unknown.

* * *

There were eleven ships in the convoy, none of them in first-class condition. They carried officers, marines, a few (twenty-eight) devoted wives, some children, doctors, a chaplain and 778 convicts, of whom 192 were women.[1]

Like the men, the women were herded below decks at night and during storms; the hatches fastened so that they should not associate with the sailors or male convicts. But this latter order was overcome 'in a way so expected', writes M. Barnard Eldershaw in *Phillip of Australia* as 'hardly to deserve comment': the bulkhead was broken down and the women visited the sailors. Lieutenant Ralph Clark was completely shocked.

I never could have thought there were so many abandoned

Convicts on their way to Botany Bay: an eighteenth-century caricature

wenches in England, they are ten thousand times worse than the men convicts, and I am afraid that we will have a great deal more trouble with them.

Clark seemed to have no sympathy with them. He resented Phillip's order that, for their health's sake, convicts should spend part of each day on deck out of irons, and he derived pious satisfaction from their punishment. When some of the women were moved to other ships to make room for sheep bought at Cape Town, he was sure 'we will find them (the sheep) more agreeable ship mates than they (the women) were'.

None of the women kept a journal that has yet been discovered, but several officers of the First Fleet were busy diarists and travel-book makers. Through these, and through official records, one glimpses a rabble shipped without any attempt to select those who might best stand the moral and physical strain of the voyage and what would come after. (One woman was 87; she died on the way out.)

The women were embarked with only such clothing as they wore. (Phillip had protested about this in vain. He had to sail before he could stir the government—was it callous or inefficient?—to supply what was needed.) At various ports sailors bought garments for women with whom they had formed attachments; the rest made the voyage to Terra Australis in clothes that were little more than rags.

The women fainted in their cramped, overcrowded quarters as the ships ploughed through the tropics. Most of them suffered from seasickness and several times they were washed out of their bunks by high seas. One gale was so violent that the terrified women prayed loudly (although Surgeon Bowes acidly noted that when the storm abated their language was as full of oaths as ever). Several were delivered of children on the voyage.

The defiant ones ('saucy', the diarists called them) were flogged.

Captain Meredith ordered one of the corporals to flog with rope Elizabeth Dugeon for being impertinent . . . the corporal did not play with her, but laid it home, which I was very glad to see, then ordered her to be tied to the pump, she has been long fishing for it, which she has at last got.[2]

Occasionally the punishment varied.

Upon any very extraordinary occasion, such as thieving, fighting with each other or making use of abusive language to the officers, they have thumb-screws put on them or iron fetters on their

Women convicts exercising in a London prison

wrists, ... and sometimes their hair has been cut off and their head shaved, which they seem to dislike more than any other punishment they underwent. At first one or two were flog'd with a Cat of 9 tails on the naked breech, but as there are certain occasions when such mode of punishment c'd not be inflicted with that attention to decency everyone whose province it was to punish them, wished to adhere to, it was totally laid aside. They were also whilst under punishment so very abusive that there was a necessity for gaging them.[3]

Fever broke out from time to time, but on the whole the Fleet showed a bill of health quite remarkable in view of the length of the voyage and the sub-standard ships. Male and female convicts were looked after with professional detachment and efficiency by Surgeon-General White. Assistant Surgeon Bowes thought they were pampered: he did not approve of special diet for sick prisoners.

Sick or well, there was scarcely anything to keep the women occupied, apart from a little sewing and laundering for the officers (When one woman reported she had lost overboard seven pairs of stockings belonging to the doctor, Lieutenant Clark declared viciously: 'If they were to lose anything of mine that I gave them to wash I would cut them to pieces.'[4])

But for the majority, the long trip of eight months one week was an aimless sitting-out of empty hours while the seas rose and fell around the ships, the sails filled and emptied at the wind's whim under skies which changed from stormy to fair or were blotted out by fog. Through northern waters to tropic zones, through days of heat or cold, and nights when the ocean slithered by under the ship's keels in a flurry of phosphorescence, the women gossiped and fought, thieved from each other, carried on intercourse with the seamen, were flogged or 'ironed' for impertinence to officers or other misconduct, and endured in some way the voyage from a land where their plight was almost hopeless to a new country which they viewed without hope.

*　　　*　　　*

Their arrival in the colony was lit with violence and shot with tempest: a stormy overture to settlement.

The women convicts were disembarked on February 6, and immediately a saturnalia began. The sailors joined in, bringing grog. A violent thunderstorm broke over 'the scenes of Debauchery and Riot that ensued during the night'.[5]

Until trees were felled and some kind of rough huts put up, the convicts slept in the open at Sydney Cove under pieces of old canvas issued from the ships' stores, and those who found hollow trees to bunk in were lucky. Food was scarce, the ground infertile, and supply ships long in coming. For years the grey shape of Famine hovered over the colony and its inhabitants.

When more settlements were made, a proportion of convict women was moved to each new centre. Reluctant pioneers, they saw the *Sirius* sink in the surf at Norfolk Island; they fought and squabbled at Hobarton, and were midwives at the birth of Newcastle, Port Macquarie and the Moreton Bay settlement which grew into Brisbane.

Usually the women belonged to one of three classes: the hardened criminal of many convictions, the first offenders whose crime might have been some piece of petty pilfering, and the wife or mother driven desperate by sickness of her husband who 'may pawn the sheets of her lodgings or articles which she was trusted to wash or make up'.[6] There were also a percentage of political prisoners: one women was transported for assisting a French officer to escape.

The usual term of sentence was seven years, and for the first thirty years or so of colonizing this meant separation from husband, children and family—usually forever. Men could work their passage home on ships after their sentence had expired, but not women; and not many could pay the fare.

Phillip promised leniency and official consideration to those who kept the law, but some were beyond reclaiming, like Ann Davis, who, caught housebreaking, was condemned to death. No one mourned, apparently. 'She died generally reviled and unpitied by the people of her own description', reported Captain John Collins. And Ann Fowles offended even eighteenth-century standards for female transportees. She was considered an unfit guardian of her own child who was taken from her and made a ward of the state. These and others who came to holts with authority defied any efforts to rehabilitate them and achieved a notoriety from which all the rest suffered.

Admittedly it was harder for women than for men convicts to find a foothold in the soft clay of the newly-found colony. To begin with, conditions on the ships which brought them were little short of prostitution, as Governor Macquarie pointed out:

> the unfortunate Creatures (several of Whom are Young and when Embarked it is to be hoped Not Altogether abandoned) are but too frequently Exposed to such Scenes of Debauchery during the Passage, as To Leave but little Hope of their being speedily reclaimed after their arrival here ... and I cannot but

Attribute this Melancholy Fact to the glaring and gross Practices to Which they are Exposed . . . on the Passage hither.[7]

Occasionally there were complaints and enquiries. One flagrant instance, that of the ship *Janus*, received a public airing through a convict woman's letter asking for a pass to meet the man who had caused her pregnancy on the transport. The desperate earnestness of the request still throbs through the print of the *Historical Records of Australia*, but the fate of its writer is unknown. Conditions on *Janus* grew out of the system of sending women convicts straight from the grisly prison of Newgate to the transports, usually without change of clothing, seldom with training or a craft of any kind, and with no occupation or proper supervision for the voyage. No one thought of separating the hardened cases from the less venal, and after months of associating with the depraved and ineducable on the long voyage out, when they fell victims of the crew's lust either by force or consent, it was almost inevitable they should follow the same path when they arrived in the colony. There was little work for them other than domestic service, and until free settlers were more numerous even opportunities for this were limited.

The Female Factory at Parramatta, theoretically the home of those not assigned to private employers, actually had room for very few.

> The number of women employed at the factory . . . is about one hundred and fifty; they have seventy children. There are only two rooms and those are occupied as work shops. In these rooms there are 46 women daily employed. Many of these women have little, and some no bedding; they all sleep on the floor; there is not a cradle or bedstead belonging to the factory.[8]

Accommodation of a kind for less than fifty women—but it was conceded that there were often as many as two hundred in the district. These were given part-time work in the Factory, and allowed half a day to work for themselves and find lodgings. Most of them drifted into prostitution and came continually into conflict with the law. 'Worse than the men—they're worse than the men'—it became the chant of harassed officials, pious respectables, and shuddering matrons. The bold, brawling, drunken, tattered hussies ('all the women look like gypsies', wrote a male convict in 1790) were the symbols of women transported to Botany Bay, though behind the ranks of the brazen and broken there were other figures who, through some spirit of enterprise, or with help at the right time, achieved rehabilitation, and lifted themselves by the bootstraps of their own character. 'If a

The penitentiary for female convicts at Parramatta

convict woman gets a good mistress she turns out well—if a bad one, she quickly becomes degraded', was given as late as 1850 as the opinion of one who was 'well acquainted with Colonial matters'.

In the new land there were opportunities and rewards. James Ruse brought in the colony's first successful wheat crop. Behind James in sunbonnet and slop clothing is Elizabeth Perry, convict woman who became his wife, helped him clear the land and bring home the first harvest of Australia.

Where the Hawkesbury winds richly past the flats it has so often submerged, you may still catch echoes of Margaret Catchpole's name. Margaret, the dark-eyed lass who loved a smuggler devotedly for many years, stole a horse and made a Dick Turpin ride to London for his sake. Arrested and imprisoned, she broke out of jail—only to taste the bitter draught of recapture. Her death sentence commuted to transportation, Margaret entered domestic service in the colony, and eventually owned a small farm at Richmond below the blue heights of the Kurrajongs. Farming, nursing, helping settlers' wives bring their babies into the light of the colonial sun, selling tapes and bodkins, calico and thread as a sideline, Margaret found a niche in the district little different from that of the other settlers, free or emancipated, who farmed the Hawkesbury flats. Legend says she saved a family from drowning in one of the floods which so regularly covered the farms, and her death was caused by an illness she contracted when nursing a neighbour back to health.

The best-known success story among the convict women is that of Mary Reiby, also transported for stealing a horse, though this time the act was little more than an adolescent prank.

Mary married Thomas Reiby, an officer on the transport which brought her to the colony. Together they built up and ran a general store close by the place of the First Landing. Mary bore seven children to her Thomas—three sons and four daughters. She encouraged and helped his shipping and sailing enterprises and his boatbuilding yard on the hill above Farm Cove. Flourishing store and subsidiary interests to keep her mind busy and alert, a growing family to round out her emotional experience, a niche in the marble of the young colony—if Mary Reiby knew homesickness it could only have been a small eddy in the hurrying current of her life.

When Thomas died, Mary was a long way from the prankish adolescent transported for behaviour that scandalized the society of her youth. A woman of character, she took firm hold of Thomas' affairs and controlled them with efficiency and shrewdness, increasing the family standing in wealth and importance. In middle age she brought the orchestra of her life to full crescendo by making the voyage back to England and revisiting the scenes of her girlhood. Wealthy widow, respectable matron, and successful careerist—what an entrance she must have made returning in triumph to the place she had left in disgrace.

Back in the colony, she saw her children settled in life, in 'good' marriages, fine homes and respected positions. Entally, established by her eldest son, Thomas Haydock Reiby, near Launceston, is now a National House, a memorial to all Tasmanian pioneers, and especially the family Mary bore in the first years of Australian settlement.

There were, of course, few Mary Reibys, and though many 'Government women' obtained security and opportunity for a wider life than they could ever have dreamed, for years the sum total of misery carried over the ocean to the wide waters of Port Jackson or the Derwent must have made the angels withdraw behind their wings and weep.

It was not until the work of Elizabeth Fry took effect in English prisons that conditions changed. Women transportees were trained in domesticity before sailing, taught sewing, given help in character building, and a matron or supervisor was placed in charge of their quarters on the voyage out. Mothers were allowed to bring their children, and convicts' wives, themselves free women, could immigrate on the same ship as their husbands, in special quarters where they were not subject to insults from the crew. What these women did in rehabilitating themselves and their partners cannot be assessed, but their courage and devotion went into the weft and weave that created the pattern of Australia's early days.

The land offered them a second chance. To those with even a modicum of character, initiative or luck, it was a chance to shed the shackles and leave behind the clanking chains. For those who failed to take it there can be nothing less than pity. But to those whose work raised them from despair there should be praise for the part they played. In the land that was their assigned prison they found purposeful lives as they helped turn the slow-moving wheels of colonialization.

Voyage of the Lady Juliana

Sydney Cove,
Port Jackson,
24th July, 1790.

We arrived here safe after a long voyage, in very good health ... as we had everything that we could expect ... and all our provisions were good. We landed here 223 women and twelve children; only three women died, and one child. Five or six were born on board the ship; they had great care taken of them, and baby linen and every necessary for them were ready made to be put on. The greatest part of the women were immediately sent to Norfolk Island, a place about 100 miles from here. ... This place was in a very starving condition before we arrived, and on allowance of only 2lb. of flour and 2lb. of pork for each man for a week, and these were almost starved, and could not work but three hours in the day; they had no heart, and the ground won't grow anything, only in spots here and there. There is a place called Rose Hill, about twenty miles from this, where they say there are four cornfields, but it does not grow much wheat; we are now much in want of everything; we have hardly any cloaths; but since the Scarborough, Neptune, and Surprize arrived we have had a blanket and a rug given us, and we hope to have some cloaths, as the Justinian, a ship that came from London with provisions, (is) bringing some cloth and linen and we are to make the cloaths. Oh! if you had but seen the shocking sight of the poor creatures that came out in the three ships it would make your heart bleed; they were almost dead, very few could stand, and they were obliged to sling them as you would goods, and hoist them out of the ships, they were so feeble; and they died ten or twelve a day when they first landed; but some of them are getting better ... They were not so long as we were in coming here, but they were confined, and had bad victuals and stinking water. The Governor was very angry, and scolded the captains a great deal and, I heard, intended to write to London about it, for I heard him say it was murdering them. It to be sure was a melancholy sight. ... I don't think I ever shall get away from this place to come again to see you without an order from England, for some of the men's times were out, and they went and spoke to the Governor ... He told them he could not send them home without orders from London ... I hope you will try to get an order for me, that I may once more see you all.

From a letter by a female convict.
Historical Records of New South Wales, vol. 2 (1893), p. 767.

Letter from a Female Convict

Reprinted from the *True Briton* of 10 November 1798. Prefixed 'Letter of a woman lately transported to Botany Bay to her father.'

I take the first opportunity of informing you of my safe arrival in this remote quarter of the world after a pretty good passage of six months. Since my arrival I have purchased a house, for wh. I gave £20, and the following articles, wh. are three turkies, at 15s. each; three sucking pigs, at 10s.; a pair of pigeons, at 8s.; a yard-dog, £2; two muscovy ducks, at 10s. each; three English ducks, at 5s. each; and a goat, five guineas; six geese, at 15s. each. I have got a large garden to the house, and a licence. The sign is the 'Three Jolly Settlers'. I have met with tolerable good success in the public line. I did a little trade in the passage here in a number of small articles, such as sugar, tea, tobacco, thread, snuff, needles, and everything that I could get anything by. The needles are a shilling a paper here, and fine thread is sixpence a skain. I have sold my petticoats at two guineas each, and my long black cloak at ten guineas, which shews that black silk sells well here; the edging that I gave 1s. 8d. per yard for in England, I got 5s. for it here. I have sold all the worst of my cloaths, as wearing apparel brings a good price. I bought a roll of tobacco at Rio Janeiro, of 54lb. weight, which cost me 20s., which I was cheated out of; I could have got 12s. a pound for it here. I likewise bought a cwt. of sugar there, and also many other articles. Rum sells for 7s. 6d. per gallon there, and here at times £2. Any person coming from England with a few hundred pounds laid out at any of the ports that shipping touch at coming here are liable to make a fortune. Shoes that cost 4s. or 5s. a pair in England will bring from 10s. to 15s. here.

On our passage here we buried only two women and two children. The climate is very healthful and likewise very fertile, as there are two crops a year of almost everything; and I really believe with the asistance of God, by the time that I have paid the forfeit, according to the laws of my country, I shall acquire a little money to return home with, which I have not the smallest doubt of and to be a comfort to you at the latter end of your days. Any person that should have a mind to come out here as a settler, by applying at the Secretary of State's Office, may have a free passage, and likewise two men and a farm here, which is great encouragement. I should be very glad to hear from you the first opportunity. I live by myself, and did not do as the rest of the women did on the passage . . . Your affectionate daughter till death, S.B.

Historical Records of New South Wales, vol. 3 (1895).

4
Keeper of the Keys

AFTER THE HUBBUB of disembarking, came the real work of settling-in. Eucalypts fell to the axe, became slabs for the first huts, fuel for the first fires. Food stocks were low, and the land added little to the larder but a kind of wild spinach and a native plant whose leaves were used for tea. Phillip put everyone on rations, himself included, and twice the ration was reduced before the position eased. Convicts worked unwillingly; soldiers thought their only duties should be marching and mounting guard. But that fed no one, nor did the first sown seed, which did not germinate in the sandy soil marked off as crop land above Farm Cove.

But there was fertile land on the nearby rivers, and there the first farms were set. With a continent to conquer, a wilderness to subdue, there was work, literally, for all hands and the cook. So on the Hawkesbury and Nepean flats women helped build a granary and market garden for the settlement. Bearing and rearing their children where the flood waters often swirled twice a year, they took their turn in the fields, wielding a spade or hoe when the ground must be tilled, a sickle when the harvest must be gathered, stooking sheaves, threshing, winnowing. Hard-working, inarticulate Marthas, their hands helped feed the early settlement, though they had little praise or notice for their labour.

A few women were landowners in their own right. Their names are sprinkled through the early pages of the *Historical Records of Australia*, but usually without details or comment to add flesh to the bare bones of official statement.

Hannah Laycock, a quartermaster's wife, was granted 500 acres of Botany Bay Crown Lands in 1804. What was she like, this Hannah who lived on the fringe of settlement? Was she childless or a mother? Was she widowed or did she share the farm (called King's Grove) with her husband? We can only imagine her in the district where she was the first settler, in a small house (almost certainly bark and slab or daub, with a thatched roof), visited occasionally by the natives, raising cattle and horses, and going when necessary to Sydney Cove around the head of Cook's River.

As intriguing but almost as sketchy is the story of Eliza Walsh's farm which she acquired by persistence and correspondence. Miss Walsh arrived in the colony in 1819 with her sister and brother-in-law, Deputy Commissary General Drennan. About a year later she wrote Governor Macquarie[1] that she had spent £1,000 on horned cattle and a small property and was prepared to spend another £1,000 on improvements if Macquarie would grant her more land.

Governor Macquarie refused on the grounds that it was 'contrary to regulations to give grants of Land to Ladies', presumably a generic name for spinsters, for grants had already been made to married women, including Mrs Governor King. The fact that Macquarie was at odds with Drennan, Miss Walsh's brother-in-law, may have been a factor in the Governor's ruling, but that was not mentioned in the official correspondence.

Eliza would not accept the decision. Commissioner Bigge was in the colony to investigate complaints about Macquarie's regime and Miss Walsh presented her case. Bigge wrote to the Governor on her behalf and was told (this time without reference to regulations) that Macquarie believed it 'bad practice' to grant land to unmarried women. He was still Governor, and Bigge had no overriding authority, but he could and did advise Miss Walsh to carry the matter further.

So Eliza took up her quill and wrote to Earl Bathurst. She informed his lordship that her sister and brother-in-law had left the colony and she wished to provide for her own future by adding to her holding. Her 'increasing Herd of Horned Cattle, upwards 1080 Head', would overstock her existing allotment, and she could no longer use the local common because it was being parcelled out in grants. If his lordship were favourably disposed to her request for more land, Miss Walsh undertook not to sell any part of it for at least two years. Furthermore, she would build a house on the land and live there at least some of the time. And with the hope 'that the mere circumstance of Sex' would not operate against her and her claim, she was his lordship's obedient servant.

By the time her letter reached the Earl, Macquarie had been recalled under a cloud, and Bathurst wrote Governor Darling:

> I am not aware of any reason why females, who are unmarried, should be excluded from holding Lands in the Colony, provided they possess sufficient funds for the purpose, intend ... to reside on their lands, and to fulfill any other stipulations which may be required of them in common with all other Grantees.

If the Governor had no other reasons for refusal, his lordship ruled Miss Walsh should have her land. She probably managed it and the horned cattle most successfully, but the *Records* do not round out the affair.

Where so much else is vague and frustrating, a clear, bright picture exists of Elizabeth Macarthur, one of the most successful estate managers of the early settlement.

It is doubtful whether Mrs Macarthur looked on herself in such a light, and highly probable she might have considered the term somewhat unseemly. But the fact remains that for nine years uninterruptedly and at other shorter periods she held in her hands the administrative reins of what has been called John Macarthur's 'princely estate'.

She was Elizabeth Veale when she met Macarthur, at that time a young officer on half pay toying with the idea of leaving the Army and studying law. Marriage with Elizabeth may have been behind his change of plans, for soon after Macarthur was a member of the newly-formed New South Wales Corps enlisted for service at Port Jackson, and Elizabeth was writing her mother in October 1789 of their imminent departure for the colony.

> I foresee how terrific and gloomy this will appear to you. To me at first it had the same appearance; while I suffered myself to be blinded by common and vulgar prejudices. I have not now, nor I trust shall ever have one scruple or regret but what relates to you.[2]

The Macarthurs, John, Elizabeth and their baby son Edward, sailed in the notorious Second Fleet, whose condition on arrival shocked the infant settlement and brought down Phillip's wrath upon the captains and contractors.

For Elizabeth it was a grim, exhausting initiation into pioneering which began before the ships sailed, when Macarthur and Gilbert, the master of the *Neptune*, quarrelled and fought a duel at Plymouth. Her emotions were not soothed by a visit to her mother from which she returned 'not much enlivened by the short interview I had with my friends, and considerably depressed with the Idea of parting with my sole surviving parent, perhaps for ever.'

The contentious Gilbert was replaced by Mr Trail, but that was no improvement. Trail allied himself with the captain, who was also on bad terms with John, and went out of his way to make matters uncomfortable for the Macarthurs. Elizabeth described him in a letter to her mother as 'a perfect sea-monster'.

The clash of temperaments was paralleled by the weather. Soon after sailing, the Fleet ran into a violent storm, and tossed on mountainous seas for days till Elizabeth was convinced the ship could not possibly survive.

The sea calmed down, but baby Edward became ill and remained weak and frail all the way to the Cape. The family's servant caught a fever raging among the women convicts, and Elizabeth lived in fear of infection.

The Macarthurs' quarters in *Neptune* were one half of the great cabin, divided by a partition from the women convicts in the other half. John hotly criticized the arrangement and the captain grudgingly allowed the family a private passageway, for which Elizabeth was thankful. The other access to the deck was dark and 'always filled with convicts and their constant attendants, filth and vermin'. Her relief was short-lived. Relations between Trail and Captain Nepean on one side, and Macarthur on the other, deteriorated rapidly. Within a few days the door to the private passageway was nailed fast, and Elizabeth became a voluntary prisoner

> within the narrow limits of the wretched cabin, for to add to the horrors of the common passage on the deck, Captain Nepean ordered it to be made a hospital for the sick, the consequence of which was that I never left my cabin until I finally quitted the ship.

The family wilted in the heat of the tropics, which aggravated the stench from the convicts' quarters. Even oil of tar used hourly could not disguise it. Through the thin partitions Elizabeth heard language and conversation that shocked her deeply. The quarters, the smells, the proximity of the convicts, a sick child, a fuming and frustrated husband—the whole situation must have had a nightmare quality; but that it could also have been a painful experience for the convict women does not seem to have occurred to Elizabeth.

Shut up in her cabin, she grew depressed and her health suffered. Breaking point came and Macarthur asked for an exchange to

Thatched cottages of settlers in New South Wales in the 1870s

another ship. The request was granted; the captain and Trail apparently were no more anxious to keep the family than they were to stay. On 19 February, a calm, hot day, the Macarthurs transferred to *Scarborough*, to happier relations with fellow officers and better living conditions for the rest of the voyage.

The Fleet reached Cape Town and Elizabeth wrote her mother of Edward's ill-health and their long struggle to keep him alive.

> Unless a very speedy change takes place I am well convinced he will shortly cease to be an inhabitant of this world . . . He is not near so large as children generally are at four months old, although he is now upwards of twelve. He is very sensible, very lively, and affords us much pleasure, but the trouble we have had with so delicate a little creature is indescribable.

The stay at Cape Town revived Elizabeth. She had all the linen 'washed and got up', and bought goods and provisions to take to Botany Bay. On her doctor's advice, she lived on shore. 'A genteel private family' gave her board for a dollar and a half a day, and Macarthur visited her when duty allowed.

Elizabeth thought Cape Town's citizens charged the ships' company outrageous prices. A cabbage, she said, cost 1s. 6d., bread was fermented, but grapes and autumn fruit were good, and wine 1s. a bottle. At Government House she sat politely but dumbly with the Governor's daughter as neither spoke the other's language. She was amazed by the height of the mountains backing the town, and found her walks 'very amusing'.

It was a relaxed, cheerful Elizabeth who prepared to embark for the run to Botany Bay, believing that the worst of the voyage was behind her. But three days before the ship sailed Macarthur went down with rheumatic fever, and it was several weeks before he recovered from the illness which he always blamed for 'the flying gout and nervous depression' he suffered periodically through the rest of his life. As nurse to a sickly child and a delirious husband, Elizabeth must have been near exhaustion when the Second Fleet reached Sydney on 28 June 1790, with its convicts in so deplorable a condition that most were carried ashore.

The settlement itself was in a state of near famine, which persisted until the following year, when ten vessels convoyed by H.M.S. *Gordon* arrived and relieved some of the pinch.

*   *   *

Elizabeth has not left a description of her first home in the colony, but it was probably a small slab cottage not far from the Governor's house. Here Elizabeth unpacked at least some of her belongings, hung up her bonnet and looked with curiosity at the scene she described as completely 'novel'.

She wrote little about the convicts for whom the settlement had been made, and whose presence had brought her husband and herself across the world. But neither did she complain of the lack of amenities, except to regret the lack of feminine company. Her only other social equal was Mrs Johnson, wife of the clergyman, and in her society Elizabeth found 'neither profit nor pleasure'.

Elizabeth's own position was unique in the little settlement. She was the only officer's wife present. She was young (twenty-one when *Neptune* cleared Plymouth), attractive and intelligent. She also possessed outstanding tact, a quality which served her well in after years when John was at odds with the government, but his wife was still welcomed at Government House.

To John's fellow-officers Elizabeth Macarthur was symbol of the life they had left, and they were only too happy to show her courtesies and attention. Even Phillip sent her grapes and little gifts, and at the austere dinners at Government House, to which everyone was expected to bring his own bread, he gallantly made it clear the rule did not apply to Mrs Macarthur.

Elizabeth tried to study astronomy with Lieutenant Dawes, but candidly admitted it was beyond her, and took up botany instead.

Macarthur's illness flared up again and Elizabeth was kept busy in the sick-room. Her second child was born soon after, and lived only one hour. Her experiences to date had been anything but ideal for easy maternity.

In January the family moved to a house Elizabeth found more convenient. Mr Worgan, surgeon to the *Sirius*, kept his piano there, and Elizabeth learnt to play. (Worgan made her a present of the instrument when he sailed for home.) She had no great opinion of herself as a musician: 'I am told, however, that I have done wonders in being able to play off "God Save The King", and Foot's minuet.'

Summer blistered the small settlement with several days over a hundred degrees and a peak reading of 112. Elizabeth found it very trying and not conducive to walking.

Her letters home praised the wide sweep of the recently discovered Hawkesbury and the spread of the harbour. But she regarded the country with the detached outlook of an interested onlooker who did not expect to remain long. She predicted the colony would never produce much corn. As for farming—the results achieved by other officers gave the Macarthurs no urge to copy them.

In June 1791 John was posted to duty at Rose Hill, and the family went with him. A few months later they returned thankfully to Sydney Cove, where Elizabeth found company more to her liking: 'There are so many ladies in the Regiment that I am not likely to feel the want of female society as I at first did.'

Phillip went home and the family pattern began to alter. Macarthur was promoted, granted 100 acres on the Parramatta ('some of the best ground that has been discovered'), and began building a house.

Elizabeth bore a daughter named after herself, and in May 1794 was 'happily brought to bed of a very fine Boy' called after his father. By then the family was living at Elizabeth Farm, and Mrs Macarthur wrote proudly of their 'very excellent brick building 68 feet in length and 18 feet in width, independent of kitchen and servants' apartments. I thank God we enjoy all the comfort we could desire.'

The family tree was sending roots into the colonial soil. Its farm lands totalled 250 acres, and although as yet less than half (100 acres) was cultivated, the year's sale of produce showed a net profit. Three acres of garden and vineyards made a bower round the house. There was corn in the granary; a horse, two mares, two cows, 130 goats, about 100 hogs and much poultry worked and fattened to feed the family; and a man servant with a pack of greyhounds kept the table supplied with wild duck and kangaroo. Each week, exulted John, 'the dogs kill not less than 300 lbs. weight'.

More children were born, and a happy, contented Elizabeth wrote her friend, Miss Kingdon, in England:

> It (the colony) seems the only part of the Globe where quiet is to be expected. We enjoy here one of the finest climates in the World. The necessaries of life are abundant, and a fruitful soil affords us many luxuries.

As the boys reached school age they were sent to England to be educated. Seven-year-old Edward left first, and the other sons followed. The same plan was tried for the girls, but proved unsuccessful, so Elizabeth's three daughters stayed with her and were educated at home. Their English governess, Miss Penelope Lucas, became Elizabeth's friend and confidant.

Macarthur increased his holdings, his cattle and horses, and ran about a hundred sheep. But there was no mutton for dinner, although, wrote Elizabeth:

> next year, Mr Macarthur tells me, we may begin. I have now a very good dairy and in general make a sufficiency of butter to supply the family, but it is at present so great an object to rear calves that we have to be careful not to rob them of very much milk ... We use our horses both for pleasure and profit; they alternately run in the chaise or cart.

When Elizabeth visited Sydney she drove in the chaise along what she called a good carriage road, but the track to the Hawkesbury was rougher, and there Elizabeth went on horseback.

Her letters by this time show how she was absorbing the details of farm and business management which she would apply in the period of her trusteeship.

Macarthur was now using the first plough in the country. He employed between thirty and forty labourers and servants, and Elizabeth complained of the high wages asked by ex-convicts. The government's method of meeting bills on the Commissary, how pigs were fattened and killed to feed the household, running the farm store for employess, and the system used by the Corps' officers buying goods from ships in port and reselling at profit were subjects for Elizabeth's pen and part of her unconscious training.

But while she subconsciously trained as a woman of affairs, Elizabeth described herself as a most contented wife.

> At this time I can truly say no two people on earth can be happier than we are. In Mr. Macarthur's society I experience the tenderest affections of a husband. He is instructive and cheerful as a companion. He is an indulgent Father, beloved as a master, universally respected for the integrity of his character. Judge then, my friend, if I ought not consider myself a happy woman.

By 1794 Macarthur was firmly convinced the country could became a producer of fine wool. In that year he added Bengal ewes to his flocks, and two years later imported from the Cape the famous Spanish merinos, part of a gift to the Dutch government by the King of Spain.

In the next five years John made two voyages to England. The first he took for the express purpose of interesting the government in colonial wool. The other he made under compulsion: he had wounded his superior officer, Captain Paterson, in a duel and was sent home by Governor King for censure. He took with him more samples of local wool, and used the opportunity to advance the cause of Australian wool-growing in the English market.

On each occasion Elizabeth managed the farm. Whatever decisions she made in Macarthur's absence must have been shrewd and capable, for the estate was returned to him in good running order.

On the second trip, Macarthur resigned his commission in the Army and returned to the colony with nine rams and a ewe from the King's flock. He also brought with him a document signed by Lord Camden, granting him 10,000 acres of fertile government land in the area known as the Cow Pastures (now Camden).

Elizabeth had not failed him. The farm on the Parramatta was prospering, Edward came back with him, and for the first time in years all the family but John the younger were together. Happy days for Elizabeth, devoted wife and mother.

The new grant was taken up at once, and when Governor King sailed home in 1807 Macarthur was the most influential resident in the young colony.

With the arrival of Bligh his life approached a crisis. The tale of the quarrels between these two strong men needs no retelling, and we pass to the point where Bligh has been arrested and John Macarthur has admitted his part in the affair. Governor Macquarie landed at Sydney Cove, disbanded the New South Wales Corps, and sent Captain Johnston home to England to the trial he had demanded. With him as witness went John Macarthur, destined to remain in political exile for nine years.

James and William, the younger sons, went with their father to be placed at school, and Elizabeth was left in full charge at the farm with her three daughters and Penelope Lucas, governess and friend.

John's ship was hardly outside Sydney Heads when the eldest daughter, Elizabeth, became seriously ill. Her recovery was only partial; her health afterwards was never sound. It was another anxiety Elizabeth bore alone in the nine years she carried the burden of Macarthur's many interests.

None of the letters she wrote him in that period have survived, but Elizabeth carefully treasured all of his, and through them one learns something of her occupations during those years.

> I am exceedingly pleased to learn that you had nearly got the kitchen finished and much gratified, as you may suppose, by your details of your improvements and your report of the prosperous state of all the stock.
>
> I am very glad that you proceed so smoothly with the Gov-

ernor and if you can negotiate an exchange of the Seven Hills Estate for Land at the Cow Pastures do, considering its contiguity you ought to have a larger quantity but I leave the arrangement entirely to you.

You have never informed me whether you got the Lease of the Sydney Cottage renewed. I am much pleased at the Grant of the Swamps, they make a desirable whole to the Farm to secure us from interruption.

Macarthur's plans for wool growing depended upon keeping the breed of his flock unimpaired. It now rested on Elizabeth to maintain the purity of the strain, and she did this scrupulously, scarcely needing Macarthur's admonition: 'Cherish the Spanish sheep.'

Whenever seasons permitted and ships were available she sent wool to John in London. Some was dirty on arrival and John protested. Elizabeth, who now had John's nephew, Hannibal Macarthur, to help her ('she proved the better business man', commented M. Barnard Eldershaw),[3] had the sheep scrubbed in the stream, as routine practice before shearing.

She built a new woolshed and received another grant from the Governor for her enterprise in stump grubbing when she had land cleared—a tidy habit not always followed in the colony.

Occasionally John's letters complained she did not give all the details he wanted, but there is no reason to believe that Elizabeth did not keep him fully posted about affairs at the Farm and in the colony.

The goods he sent out for trading, the farm, the stock, the crops, the household management, goods for the farm store, the children's health, coping with cold winters and 'a most astonishing Drought'—it is not difficult to imagine that Elizabeth never had an idle moment.

John himself was often lonely, sometimes sick and frequently depressed. In his affectionate, even yearning letters, he called her 'My dearest Elizabeth'; sometimes 'My Dearest, Dearest Elizabeth', or 'My Beloved Elizabeth'. Above his signature might appear: 'May God Almighty bless and preserve you all is the unceasing Prayer My Beloved Wife of Your affectionate Husband', or 'For the present, my dearest, best beloved Elizabeth, adieu'.

Homesick, he wrote: 'What would I give to know how you all do, particularly our poor Elizabeth, but it is vain to wish upon such a subject.' Or: 'What would I not sacrifice to be assured that you and *all* the dear Girls are well.'

Elizabeth disciplined her own loneliness as wife and mother to meet the moods of his letters. He fretted at the inactivity of his exile, and seriously thought of selling up his colonial enterprises and bringing his family to England, but left the decision to Elizabeth. Sturdily she came down on the side of the colony where the family had sunk its roots. She had now completely accepted the existence she praised in a letter as 'a mixture of town and country life; and yet in many respects unlike anything you can have experienced. Our climate is delightful,' she said, 'and the soil so fruitful that pigs are fed on Peaches, Apricots and Melons in the Season.'

As acting manager of the Macarthur estate, Elizabeth must have had many rewarding moments. But the harness of stewardship could have been irksome at times. It is possible she frequently re-read the letter where Macarthur feelingly acknowledged her quality as manager.

> I am perfectly aware, my beloved wife, of the difficulties you have to contend with, and fully convinced that not one woman in a thousand (no one that I know) would have the resolution and perseverance to contend with them at all, much more to surmount them in the manner that you have happily done. That I am grateful and delighted with your conduct I think it is needless for me to say, because the consciousness you must feel how impossible it is, that such exemplary goodness can have failed to produce that effect, must convince you I am so, more certainly than any assurance that can be given. May God Almighty reward you both in this world and the next, and may the remainder of your life be free from these cruel cares and sorrows that have chequered so many of the last ten years.

At last the exile ended. Macarthur was given permission to return to the colony, and in December 1817 he came home with his sons, James and William, to Elizabeth Farm. His wife wrote Miss Kingdon that it was the end of

> a cruel separation of 9 years. I am scarcely yet sensible of the extent of my happiness, and indeed I can hardly persuade myself that so many of the dear members of the family are united again under the same roof. Mr. Macarthur is occasionally afflicted with Gout—otherwise I perceive little change in him during this length of time.

Then Elizabeth handed back to her husband the keys of the kingdom she had managed so ably.

Her letters thereafter dealt almost exclusively with household affairs and social events. Her sons, James and William, were assisting their father on the farm, shooting wildfowl and riding for amusement. All the latest books came to hand from England. A daughter spent a few days in Sydney with her father. Son John in England was requested to be more careful when shopping for the family as 'the last cambric muslins we were greatly deceived in. Your sister made them up into dresses. They washed to pieces immediately—injured we suppose in bleaching.'

After the excitement of the captain's deck, the quietness of the linen cupboard. Perhaps the most remarkable quality of this truly remarkable woman is, not that she carried out her regency so ably, but that she laid it down so tactfully.

A new house was going up at Camden. A weatherboard cottage was built for the boys so they could clear the land ready for trees, plants and flowers imported from all over the world. Macarthur received awards for the quality of his wool, but his health was uncertain, and his gloom seldom lifted. He often walked on the high ground at Camden where the breeze came, and where he could see far and wide over his domain and the colony, now beginning to march inland.

But John Macarthur never saw the new family home. He died suddenly in 1834 at The Cottage, afterwards known as the Home Farm of Camden Park.

Elizabeth lived until 1850, the year before gold brought the country to the threshold of another age. Its prosperity and future were made more certain by the staple product, wool, which John Macarthur had pioneered, and which Elizabeth's careful stewardship had helped to establish.

The display of fruit in the grape season is very beautiful. Peaches also are most abundant, and very cheap; apples very dear, being chiefly imported from Van Diemen's Land, and frequently selling at sixpence each. The smaller English fruits, such as strawberries, etc., only succeed in a few situations in the colony, and are far from plentiful. Cucumbers and all descriptions of melon abound. The large green water-melon, rose coloured within, is a very favoured fruit, but I thought it insipid. One approved method of eating it is, after cutting a sufficiently large hole, to pour in a bottle of Madeira or sherry, and mix it with the cold watery pulp. These melons grow to an enormous size (an ordinary one is from twelve to eighteen inches in diameter), and may be seen piled up like huge cannonballs at all the fruit-shop doors, being universally admired in this hot, thirsty climate.

Louisa Anne Meredith, *Notes and Sketches of New South Wales* (London, 1844).

5
Over the Hills to Goshen

THE FIRST SETTLEMENT fanned out westward from Sydney Cove, passed through Parramatta, and by 1813 extended to the foothills of the mountain ranges. And there it stayed, backed by the blue mystery of the unscaled hills. Occasionally an enterprising party tried to conquer them, but the mountains remained aloof and uncrossed until Blaxland, Lawson and Wentworth in 1813 went up the slope from Emu Plains, and cut their way through the barrier of hills and gullies to reveal rolling country beyond.

On their trail, William Cox built the road over the mountains, and settlers moved out to take the inland.

For years the journey over those hills was no stroll in the garden, nor even a picnic in the bush, but an exhausting, anxious ordeal as Elizabeth Hawkins recorded in 1821.

Elizabeth was the wife of Purser Hawkins, R.N., who had found that England, economically fatigued after the wars against Napoleon, offered few opportunities for an ex-officer to bring up a family in comfort. Accounts of the young colony of New South Wales seemed to promise security, even wealth, so Hawkins uprooted his family (including his mother-in-law, Mrs Lilly) and sailed for Australia.

There is a portrait of Elizabeth Hawkins owned by her Australian descendants painted about the time of her departure for the colony—curls bunched at the ears, steady eyes, a full, firm mouth in a face of charm and character.

That character was soon put the test. Hawkins was appointed officer in charge of government stores in the village of Bathurst, a

Convicts building the road over Mt York towards Bathurst

house went with the job, and the family prepared for their journey to the first township of the inland.

How they crossed the mountains to their new home was told by Elizabeth in a letter to her sister, Anne, and told so vividly that one sits with her and the younger children in the cart covered with a tilt, and shares the many trials of the journeys as the wheels creaked and turned slowly behind the trudging bullocks, and the road unwound itself and climbed up from the ford across the Nepean.

As well as the cart there were two drays, one drawn by horses, the other by bullocks, carrying several months' food and supplies for the family and convict servants, the furniture (one table, twelve chairs), cooking utensils, bedding and a 'few agricultural implements'. Father and eldest son, Tom, rode on horseback.

The party left Sydney on Easter Saturday, April the fifth, rested at Government House (Rooty Hill) on Sunday, and reached the Nepean on Monday. The baggage was forded over, but the next day it rained and everything was brought back to be dried and repacked.

The Hawkins were invited to dine at Sir John Jamison's home near the river. They had 'mock turtle soup, boiled fowls, round of beef, delicious fish of three kinds, curried duck, goose and wildfowl, Madeira and Burgundy, various liqueurs and English ale.'

They walked in his garden, admired the largest apples and quinces Elizabeth had ever seen, vines, figs, peaches and apricots, English cherries, plums and filberts, oranges, lemons, limes, citrons, medlars, almonds, rock and water melons—in fact, 'all the common fruits of England' and most of its vegetables.

When the party set off again, Sir John presented them with a quarter of mutton, a couple of fowls, some butter, made his farewell and remarked that they were the first family of free settlers to make the journey over the mountains.

The difficulties of the trek were enormous. The cavalcade had hardly started when the bullock dray bogged in a sandy creek and took an hour to move.

There was little natural feed on the route, so corn was carried for the cattle and the bullocks were allowed free at night to graze. In the early stages these often returned to the starting place, and time was lost bringing them up again.

Progress was tedious. The cavalcade at its fastest covered eight or nine miles a day. One day they managed only a mile and a half. Sometimes the road was tilted high before Elizabeth's watching eyes. Sometimes it descended steeply into gullies. And always there were the endless trees.

Weary and stiff at each day's end, the women and children climbed down from the cart. Tents were put up and bedding unrolled, while the young ones whimpered and fretted with tiredness. Fires were lit and the evening meal prepared; cold salt meat, tea and damper. One of the men servants cooked food for the the next day—another piece of meat, a damper, or a cake baked in a Dutch oven.

Between breakfast in the morning and supper at night no stop was made for meals, but Elizabeth took a small basket of food in the cart 'to keep us from starving and provide some drink for the baby'.

Sometimes camp was made in the rain, and the party spent the night on wet ground. Even this they found preferable to the only two occasions when they slept under a roof. The first time was at Springwood in the cottage of a corporal in charge of the company guarding convict road menders. The corporal's wife stole spirits from the Hawkins' provisions and got tipsy with the soldiers. The children tried to sleep on mattresses on an earth floor which was cold and damp, with 'bugs crawling on them in hundreds', while the soldiers swore and wrangled all night, and sheep penned up in the yard bleated their unceasing protest.

The other time they stayed at a road mender's hut. It had no window, and a doorway but no door. Round the walls, a foot or so above floor level, was a broad shelf. Bedding spread on this was shared with the usual bugs and fleas.

But in spite of discomfort and weariness, Elizabeth was upheld by one of those moments which come occasionally and set life in clear perspective. It happened on the first night in the mountains.

> It was a lonely moonlight night, all was novelty and delight to the elder children. Immense fires were made in all directions. We gave them their supper, and after putting the young ones to bed, I came from the tent, in front of which was a large fire, our drays and carts close in view. The men—nine in number—were busily employed in cooking in one place, our own man roasting a couple of fowls for our next day's journey; at another the men, not the most preposessing in their appearance, with the glare of the fires and reflection of the moon shining on them, in the midst of a forest, formed altogether such a scene as I cannot describe. It resembled more a party of banditti, such as I have read of, than anything else. I turned from the view, took the arm of Hawkins, who was seated at the table with the storekeeper, and went to the back of the tent. Here we saw Tom and the three eldest girls trying who could make the best fire, as happy as it was possible for young hearts to be. There I seemed to pause. For the first time for many long months I

seemed capable of enjoying and feeling the present without dread of the future. 'Tis true we had bade adieu to our country and our friends, but in our country we could no longer provide for our children. I thought of my friends with regret, but the dawn of independence was opening on us. Hawkins was again an officer under the Government, we had a home to receive us, and the certainty under any circumstances of never wanting the common necessaries of life . . . These were moments of such inward rest that Hawkins took up a flute, calling Eliza to us, she danced in a place where perhaps no one of her age had ever trod before!

Elizabeth needed that moment of inward rest, for days of weary plodding and strenuous action lay ahead, and nights when Hawkins kept watch until dawn, snatched a little sleep in the cart with their belongings, and seldom removed his clothes.

Sometimes the bullocks were temperamental, lay down and refused to budge. Then whips cracked, dogs barked and snapped, and language flew. It usually ended with the horses from the dray being unharnessed and brought back to lend their extra strength for the pull. The whips cracked again, there was bellowing and urging, and slowly the wheels turned, and the party moved on.

Sometimes Elizabeth and her mother walked with the three eldest girls and gathered 'delicate nosegays from the flowering shrubs'. They saw kookaburras and Blue Mountains parrots. But the hills were 'almost perpendicular . . . and the precipices', wrote Elizabeth, 'enough to make you shudder'.

But everything dwindled before the hazards of the Big Hill. Twelve-year-old Tom rode ahead to investigate, and galloped back, exclaiming: 'Oh! Ma, you will never get up. I am sure you won't. I can't see much of the road, but I can see the valley you are to reach. It is dreadful.'

Everyone walked up the Big Hill (Mount York). For the descent, the men sat on fallen tree trunks chained behind the drays to act as brakes. The women carried the smaller children, their arms aching and their legs trembling as they braced themselves against the steep down slope. All were weary and hot when they reached the foot of the hill. Elizabeth handed round sugar candy from a tin, which made a cup for the cool mountain water they badly needed. Then they waited, not knowing that one of the drays had overturned and was only saved from hurtling into the gully with the bullocks and the entire load by a stump at the roadside. The convict driver went down on ropes to unload the goods, the beasts were unharnessed, and the cart hauled back, reloaded and made ready after many strenuous hours.

For Elizabeth, on the other side of the Big Hill without knowledge of what had happened, it was an anxious time. Darkness arrived before a cart reached them with shawls, greatcoats and a little food.

> I gave it to the poor children (said Elizabeth). To little Neddy I gave the arrowroot, and we hushed him off to sleep. Mother sat down with him in her lap before a fire. Ann and George wrapped up and laid on the ground outside. The four girls I laid in the cart with a greatcoat over them.

The next day they met 'a clergyman from Parramatta' (Reverend Samuel Marsden) returning from a trip to Bathurst. 'I congratulate you', he said. 'You are going to the Land of Goshen.'[1]

Never, one imagines, did a word of encouragement come at a better time to cheer the weary traveller.

When they crossed Cox's River a soldier's wife gave them a bucket of rich, creamy milk—the first they had tasted since leaving Emu Plains. At this spot the children all had 'a good washing and a change of clothes'.

For the last stretch of the journey the bullocks required more urging than ever. Up one steep hill, down the other side, then up the next. Waggon wheels creaking, bumping. The miles dropping behind slowly, endlessly. Over the Fish River, up the last long hill, then down into the beautiful rolling country beyond. They were nearing their journey's end and determined to finish it that night. Whips cracked more loudly, and the animals were urged forward so strongly that they almost trotted, while the cart swayed and jolted, and the women held the children tightly.

The way across the Macquarie River frightened Elizabeth more than anything they had gone through. The rocky bottom of the stream, the swift flowing river, water almost to the floor of the cart —she feared the bullocks would lose their footing and be swept away. But 'we reached the opposite side, and all at one moment exclaimed: "We are over!" A few minutes brought us to our house, where there was a blazing wood fire to warm and cheer us.'

So the Hawkins family came to anchor and the new land reached out and gathered them in. They had government rations for themselves and their servants, the use of two cows and two more of their own. Firewood was hauled to the door in government carts, they ate wild duck and turkey from the plains, and Eliza and Mary (the two eldest girls) were soon churning butter in the dairy.

As for Tom—within a few days he had visited the stock camps, slept on a sheepskin in front of a fire, and hunted his first kangaroo. Bathurst was occupied only by shepherds looking after the flocks of owners, who had taken up land but not residence in the first town of the west. This makes Elizabeth the spearhead of the army of women who went with their menfolk to conquer the inland. Alongside her should stand her mother, Mrs Lilly, the symbol of those grandmothers who also played their part in pioneering, tending the children, undoing buttons, hushing quarrels, midwife at their daughters' confinements, patiently enduring the discomfort and the strangeness of an alien land, surviving what must have been a violent uprooting so that their children's children might grow sturdily in another soil.

Blackdown, the house built for the Hawkins family, still stands at Kelso, Bathurst. It has been added to and altered over the years, but the bricks on the verandah floor are those made by the convict labourers whose quarters were separated from the house by a wall where the banksia today blooms like a small lemon rose. That building afterwards became the coach-house and stables, where the present owner, Mrs Una Brown, remembers climbing to the loft with her brothers and sisters to play childish pranks on the grooms ordered to prepare horses and carriage for the five-mile trip to Bathurst.

Bees busy themselves in the tall may tree near the bricked well with its thatched roofing which was the water supply for Elizabeth's household, and Blackdown bears its hundred and thirty years with serenity, facing across the flats to the modern city of the plains.

No convict servant maid comes now to draw a bucket from the well, and there is no sound of ghosty skirts trailing across the drive of the house where Elizabeth bore three more children and saw her family grow and link their lives with other settlers who pioneered the west. Their descendants tell of junketings, open-handed hospitality, and mighty feasts within the old walls. Perhaps Elizabeth, presiding over her house in sight of the blue hills she crossed with such discomfort, realized the truth of Samuel Marsden's prediction when he prophesied on the mountain road: 'You are going to the Land of Goshen.'

6

Pioneers Farther South

ABEL TASMAN discovered the island, which today bears his name, in 1642 while on a voyage of discovery in the south seas, ordered by Anthony Van Diemen, Governor of the Dutch East India Company. Tasman sailed into the southern waters below the Bight and made landfall on a hitherto unknown shore well to the east. He thought it part of the mainland and named it after Van Diemen, but later Australians re-christened it Tasmania after its discoverer.

As a white man's country, Tasmania is almost as old as New South Wales. It grew out of the second choice of Lieutenant Collins, sent in 1804 to make a settlement on Port Phillip Bay. Mosquitoes and (said he) lack of fresh water made that area unsuitable, and Collins voyaged on to the Derwent's broad mouth in south-eastern Van Diemen's Land. Where the whales came each year to bear their young, and Mount Wellington stood white-capped in winter, the first white settlement was made. Northward, at Launceston on the Tamar, the pattern was repeated a little later, and Van Diemen's Land became a familiar name on government reports.

Tasmania, perhaps more than any other part of Australia, is redolent of history. Old mills, old stone bridges, gracious old buildings that hold off the years and the rush towards modernization, draw the eye and tug at the mind. 'This is how it was in the days of your country's beginning', they seem mutely to say. 'Here children were begotten and borne, here women—some nurtured in soft circumstances in their home land, others more harshly treated in the land which cast them out—came untrained for pioneering, unprepared for life in a new, raw outpost, and made homes in the wilderness. Here are the mills which ground their wheat, here are stables which housed the horses which carried them and their babies over rough tracks to the nearest township. This stone bridge built by sullen convict labour under a bored guard knew the tread of those first feet, the rumble of cart and buggy wheels as the first-comers went about their business of carving homes in this little island.'

In time immigrant ships elbowed the whales out of the harbour, and settlers with sizable estates, convict servants and farm workers, lived rather in the manner of English squires.

A branch of the Reiby family is associated with Tasmania. Thomas Haydock Reiby, son of Mary and the first Thomas who won wealth and standing at Sydney Cove, established himself near Launceston and built Entally. His son, another Thomas, entered the Church, became Archdeacon and was one time Premier of Tasmania. He died without family to succeed him, and Entally is now preserved as a National House, with period furniture to show the background against which life was lived in early Tasmania.

> At the particular period during which 'Entally' was being settled, Van Diemen's Land was a very pleasant place for those with money. Land was granted free and labour was plentiful. Such settlers lived like English squires . . . A study of such places as 'Entally' and of other similar establishments in Tasmania shows that the settlers denied themselves nothing. There were the lovely houses often designed for colonial conditions by English architects. There were the quarters for the assigned servants. There were the stables for the hacks, carriage horses, and hunters. There were the walled gardens, the avenues of English trees, the rolling lawns, and the close-cropped hedges that were so familiar a part of the English scene. Inside the houses no expense was spared in completing the resemblance to the manorial homes of the old country. The furniture, wall hangings, silver, china, and glass were English and of the best quality . . . (Cedar) was imported in large quantities from New South Wales and was used as the modern builder uses hardwood—that is to say, for doors, jambs, architraves, and skirtings, etc. Practically all the furniture made in the colony was of cedar, although Huon pine was occasionally used. Cedar was used for furniture-making right into the latter half of Queen Victoria's reign. In spite of its softness, it was a highly satisfactory wood, and pieces made of it are highly prized. In a house such as 'Entally' cedar would not have been used as furniture in the main rooms. It seems quite certain, however that it would have been used in the less-important rooms.[1]

Money eased, but could not abolish all the jolts, as Mrs Michael Fenton discovered when the colony was twenty-five years old.

Mrs Fenton first sampled colonial life as the young wife of an army officer in India, where she led the cushioned existence of a memsahib, relieved of all household cares and worries by excellent Indian servants. When her first husband died from an unspecified fever a few months after their marriage, the young widow stayed in India. Eventually she married Captain Michael Fenton, and left the country with him late in 1828 to settle in the southern colony.

Captain Fenton pressed on to Van Diemen's Land, leaving his wife in Mauritius for her confinement. When her child was born she sailed to join her husband. After seven weeks of the most awful weather, with the decks under water and everything battened and fastened down so that no sunlight ever reached her cabin, Mrs Fenton arrived at Hobarton ('a small and irregularly-built town ... with an indefinable English air')[2] to learn that her husband had set out a day or two earlier to escort her home. A whaleboat commissioned to give chase fortunately overtook Fenton's ship, and brought him back to greet his wife and meet his daughter.

The reunited family lived for a year in town, in Macquarie Street, at the end close to the bush, which Mrs Fenton preferred to the dinner parties, races and regattas of colonial society.

After her well-trained Indian staff, she found convict servants completely exasperating.

> The perpetual encroachment of the servants on my time is indescribable. After our breakfast at eight o'clock, I order dinner and go with the cook to the store-room for anything requisite, for I need hardly remind you of the direful necessity of having to lock everything up yourself. Here my daily admonition is 'Take all you need *now*, for I will not come here again.' Then perhaps the cook departs to the markets for any small articles wanted; not an hour after, when perhaps I am nursing the baby or writing a letter, or arranging my clothes, a knock comes to the door: 'Please mum, will you give me some rice, or some sugar or spice, or something else out of the storeroom?' It is in vain to remind the offender that I said I would not go there again. His or her 'very well mam' will not supply the deficient article when dinner comes, and the only redress left me is sending him in, which will only give me another to pursue the selfsame plan of annoyance, which is repeated in every family of the colony. Well, if I cannot set aside the evil of returning to the store-room, I must lock all my trunks and drawers before I quit my room, and when I am again in the store-room my expert attendant puts his hand into the case or cask behind me while I am opening some box or canister, and abstracts a bottle of wine or porter or brandy and coolly departs with his prize under *his* coat or *her* apron.[3]

A bush homestead, New South Wales, in the 1870s

In July Captain Fenton bought a property at New Norfolk, and sent servants ahead with household goods and furniture to the cottage standing on the land. The family followed by buggy, crossed the Derwent, and jolted and swayed along rough, muddy tracks. They ran into a hailstorm, which turned to blinding snow, and were all wet to the skin when they sighted a light in a settler's house, and were soon comforted by a blazing fire and dry clothes.

Advised not to continue further along that side of the river, next day they went back across the stream and the buggy was ferried over by boat, wheels projecting at either side, while 'the horse swam the river gallantly'. But Mrs Fenton was terrified by the restiveness of the horse once it was again between shafts, and walked with her child in great discomfort.

> I wish . . . I could honestly keep back one fact, which was, that I had been so very *absurd* as to set out on this expedition in black satin boots; but the truth must be told, otherwise you could not understand why it was that ever and anon I sat down to ease the pain of my bruised feet for the boots were in fragments with the rough ground I had to walk through. Then . . . my strength quite failed. I put Flora, as the Indian women do, on my hips, on my back, tried to induce her to walk, all in vain . . . I lay down under a mimosa which spread bowerlike over the footpath, and some tears of weariness and pain were shed in spite of all my striving against them: and then again I pursued my way with the double toil of trying to amuse the child as well as carry.[4]

The next day they reached Fenton Forest and the 'long, shapeless brick cottage' which was to be home—to find their furniture and belongings piled about haphazardly, and the staff on a tremendous spree round a keg of rum.

There was no milk for the baby when Mrs Fenton called for it. The calves drank it all, said the cowhand. 'Then find me a cow about to calve,' ordered Mrs Fenton, 'that I may have her trained in the way she should go.'

Mrs Fenton soon had her chastened staff hard at work scrubbing, white-washing, hanging curtains, setting books on shelves and tidying up generally. With 'a good clean kitchen and neat little dairy', the first dwelling at Fenton Forest really became home.

Mrs Fenton proved adaptable to the demands of colonizing. Eventually sheep in the paddocks and wheat in the fields brought prosperity to the family, and a larger place was built. Did Mrs Fenton move, I wonder, without a backward glance, or did she remember with some wistfulness the first 'shapeless' cottage she turned into a home, where she served her apprenticeship in pioneering?

* * *

For the settler with less means than the Fentons, though many were as gently reared, initial stages of colonizing ranged from uncomfortable to grim. Women often slept under bullock drays while a small hut went up, helped clear the land, and sat up in bed 'immediately after confinement to sew sacks to contain wheat which must otherwise have remained loose on the floor.'

The bush crowded close to the huts, and the silence of isolation pressed hard on women left alone while their men tended the sheep. A woman pioneer of the north-west declared she often stood outside her house to hear the crack of a teamster's whip a mile or more away, or be reassured by the sound of an axe ringing in the forest that others lived somewhere in the quiet land.

Gradually the island developed a quality which cheered the heart of later migrants and visitors from the drier, more sun-scorched settlements of the mainland. It was something that raised nostalgic sighs and reminded them of the land at the other end of the world they still called 'Home'. It was a flavour made up of hawthorn hedges and old world trees which took so kindly to Tasmanian soil, a certain softness in the landscape, children's cheeks dyed bright scarlet in the crisp air, chilled by winds blowing from the mountain snow. To these, the island added its own specialties: forests full of sassafras and sweet native clematis, waterfalls in the gullies, whales moving majestically in the sea Tasman had sailed, waves rolling into a coast where mountains rose in tiers, guarding the regions of good pastures on their other side—that was Van Diemen's Land outside the dusty streets of the towns and the dark shadow of Port Arthur.

Many elements were synthesized to make the island-State. Homesickness, devotion, energy—the years took and fused them, evolving the snug farm with its oast house, hops in the fields, sheep on the hills, apples hanging in the orchards. Later generations harnessed the waterfalls, and machines processed timber felled on the mountains. But the special quality of the island remains.

7

Sarah of the South-west Plains

THE MOUNTAINS CROSSED, the explorers pushed into the west. Evans, Sturt, Oxley, Mitchell, Cunningham uncovered the rivers and left their tracks like arrows pointing to the slopes and plains of the inland for settlers coming after.

Soon flocks were on the move. Roaming through the hot summer days, yarded at night, thriving in the frosty winters, they and their masters pioneered the south-west. Those who came after planted almond and cherry trees whose blossom breaks over the plains in spring like songs arising out of the soil.

Young is the centre of the cherry district, and its high school is the ex-court-house where once the Riot Act was read to turbulent miners threatening violence on Lambing Flat. Today's bright-faced adolescents largely ignore the history of the past for that of the present, but in their library is a small pamphlet entitled 'The Wayback', written by Sarah Musgrave, the first white child born in the district.

* * *

Sarah was the daughter of John White, draper, of London, who sold up his business in 1828, and sailed with his wife to join brother James, already in Australia. James, bent on putting as much distance as possible between himself and the Hawkesbury whose flood-waters had washed him away on top of a haystack, followed the explorers' tracks west until he was 260 miles from Sydney. Local natives helped him choose a station site, Burrangong; he built a dairy, men's quarters and sheds, and had a pisé house ready for his brother and sister-in-law on their arrival.

In 1830 Sarah was born in the little pisé house without benefit of doctor or midwife. Her sister, Eliza, arrived fifteen months later at a neighbour's where the parents and Sarah turned in on their way back from Sydney—a trip made in bad weather which meant camping in the rain each night and frequent stops to dig the bullocks and dray out of the mud. Time of the whole journey was a mere twelve months.

Sarah was only four when her father lost his way in the bush and perished before he was found by a stockboy looking for cattle. James White took over the care of his brother's wife and family, and Sarah spent most of her life on or near Burrangong.

Her story is a plain, matter-of-fact account of life on a run during the squatting era, full of incident, but stated so calmly that at this distance the telling is almost dull. But look a little deeper and the warp and weft of the age are there: opening new territory, experimenting with stock, isolation, the wait for supplies, natives, tribal fights, and bushrangers. Sarah saw one native decapitated by a boomerang, two others killed with one spear. Bushrangers rode down from hideouts in the rugged Weddin Mountains to hold up homesteads. Two lined up Burrangong's household, one stayed on guard while the other looted the place. When the children cried the guard produced bull's eye peppermints to comfort them. The raid completed, the men of the station were forced at gunpoint to drink enough rum to make them insensible and enable the bushrangers to make their escape.

But things were quieter by '49, when news came of the gold strike in California's distant hills. The reverberations were felt on the south-west plains, where labour walked off the stations, leaving the teams without drivers, the stock without guard. For twelve months the wool clip stayed in barns and sheds, and women and children tried to harvest the wheat, but the task was beyond them.

Sarah acted as shepherd at Burrangong, following the sheep on horseback through the winter days, which were cold but fine. Summer came and so did the rains, the ground turned to mud where horses and cattle were bogged and Sarah could no longer ride, but followed the stock on foot. Surely, sometimes, she borrowed a male relative's trousers to do the job; but if she did, she does not mention it, and what the landgirl of the day wore to work goes unrecorded.

Flood with one turn of the wheeel, drought with another. Sarah says the worst drought occurred in 1849-52. Then the creeks, normally good for twelve months' supply, dried up. Grass withered, the Lachlan River, thirty miles away, was completely dry, and cattle trampled each other to death at the waterholes till creeks were filled with dead and rotting beasts. The hideous noise of crows feeding on dead bodies wore a groove in Sarah's memory, for she never forgot them. The crows feasted fat, but other birds 'dropped like berries from trees'.

As water gave out, squatters left their holdings and rode away. Burrangong, on the fringe of the drought area, suffered less, but even there water ran low and a chain of wells was sunk. Week after week, working well into the night, Sarah and a young visitor alternately manned the windlass, hauled up buckets and ran water into troughs. Their efforts helped keep the sheep alive till the drought broke.

Gold now on Victorian fields, and one day 'a yabber of unfamiliar voices' speaking neither English nor the local natives' dialect, drew Sarah to the window. Four men in loose shirts hanging over baggy trousers needed food, ate what she gave them, and established their identity by pointing from some bowls on the table to themselves. They were Chinese miners on their way to Ballarat.

In 1852 Sarah became Mrs Dennis Regan, riding to the church at Yass and back—seventy miles each way. She began her housekeeping with cooking lessons from her husband! Apparently competence with stock did not necessarily extend to skill in the kitchen for daughters of the south-west squatters.

Alone at mustering time and alone when her man went exploring the back country for likely runs, Sarah's lot was the same as other wives of the period. A trip to Victoria was also in the spirit of her times—a pilgrimage with her family to visit Sarah's mother, married and widowed for the second time, who carried on her late husband's station property near Rushworth, Victoria.

The Regans travelled in a large covered-in dray drawn by three horses with ten spares as relief, and drove 200 head of fat cattle. There was a nursemaid to help with the children, a man-cook, and a native boy to tend the stock.

The trip was comfortable, says Sarah. Her only complaint concerned a stretch where there was no wood for fuel, and the dry cow dung used to boil water tainted the tea. This she deplored more than the fact that at the Goulburn River the punt had sunk, and the dray was floated over on a pontoon of casks. The cattle swam and a bullock and seven horses were drowned.

The Regans returned to New South Wales to manage Burrangong for Sarah's ageing uncle. Horses, grown wild and untamed, had roamed as far away as Wagga, and Regan rounded them up into stockyards on Lambing Flats (named because the ewes went there

The Maids of the Mountains

In the wild Weddin Mountains
There live two young dames;
Kate O'Meally, Bet Mayhew
Are their pretty names.
These maids of the mountains
Are bonny bush belles;
They ride out on horseback
Togged out like young swells.

They dressed themselves up
In their brothers' best clothes
And looked very rakish
As you may suppose.
In the joy of their hearts
They chuckled with glee—
What fun if for robbers
They taken should be.

Just then the policemen,
By day and by night,
Were seeking Frank Gardiner,
The bushranger sprite.
Bold Constable Clark
Wore a terrible frown
As he thought how Sir Freddy
By Frank was done 'brown'.

They sought for the 'ranger
But of course found him not.
When suddenly Katy
And Betsy they spot.
'By Pott,' shouted Clark,
'That is Gardiner I see!
The wretch must be taken;
Come, boys, follow me!'

'Stand!' shouted the bobbies
In accents most dread,
'Or else you will taste
Our infallible lead!'
But the maids of the mountains
Just laughed at poor Clark,
And galloped away
To continue their lark.

The troopers pursued them,
And hot was the chase;
'Tis only at Randwick
They go such a pace.
Clark captured the pair,
Then, to show his vexation,
He lugged them both off
To the Young police station.

The maids of the mountains
The joke much enjoyed,
To see their brave captors
So sadly annoyed.
Next day they still smiled
As they stood in the dock;
Their awful position
Their nerves did not shock.

But Constable Clark
Did not look very jolly;
He had no excuse
For such absolute folly.
He admitted the girls
Were just out on a spree,
And hoped that his Worship
Would set them both free.

And so the farce ended
Of Belles versus Blues,
Which caused no great harm
And did much to amuse.
But the Burrangong bobbies
Will place in the cells
No more maids of the mountains–
The bonny bush belles.

      ANON.

to lamb). As their hooves broke up the ground glittering particles appeared, sending Regan and his men to prospect in the creek with shovel, pick and the lid of a billy as mining tools. They struck gold almost at once, and started the rush which brought 30,000 to Lambing Flats by the end of 1861, and began the town of Young.

Sarah states that the first death recorded on the diggings was of a woman camped with her husband in a dry creek. A thunderstorm higher up brought water rushing downstream, and the woman was swept to death trying to save her belongings.

None of Sarah's family turned miner; they continued pastoral occupations—mustering, shearing, lambing, dipping and the rest of the year-round activities.

In 1862 Regan was injured while rounding up brumbies and died nine months later, aged twenty-nine. Sarah, a widow with four children, married Thomas Musgrave two years later. She and her husband selected land across the creek from Burrangong and built a large home, Musgrave House.

Her story, 'The Wayback', is a picture of an era when the families of men who depastured their sheep on distant areas were shaping Australia. When she wrote it Sarah raised a hand in salute to the women pioneers of the district in their wood and bark homes, in the days when fires were lit with flint and steel, and housekeeping meant hard labour. 'Heroic', Sarah calls these early women, and seems unaware that she, too, might have some claim to the same title.

Captain Stirling's bivouac on the Swan River, 1827

8

Swans on the River

BLACK SWANS, majesty in ebony, on a river in New Holland so entranced a Dutch captain in the seventeenth century that he carried off specimens to his masters in Djakarta, gave their name to the river, and the river to the map. That was how the site of Western Australia's future capital first became known to the world.

* * *

Somewhere in Australia there should be a statue of Napoleon Bonaparte and a memorial of some kind to the French for the part they played in making us develop the country.

The first Englishman to see the Swan was Captain James Stirling after he convoyed a detachment of soldiers to Albany (south-west Australia) to forestall the French. Stirling's reports were so poetical that he roused the interest of people who move governments, and eventually a new colony was commissioned on the west coast of New Holland. In 1829 *Parmelia* sailed with the first batch of settlers, the Lieutenant-Governor, Captain Stirling, his wife, Ellen, and their young son to the new land of hope on the River of Swans.

It is a pity Ellen Stirling did not keep a diary of the journey out. Sixteen weeks on a tiny ship with a son aged three years and a baby (born evidently soon after England's coastline faded behind the stern) would have given a viewpoint on the enterprise rather different from the official records.

It would also have been interesting to know her opinion of the days after New Holland was reached, when *Parmelia* was almost wrecked negotiating the channel into the Swan, when its boats and those of the *Challenger*[1] worked hard to haul her offshore. The position improved when the ship was lightened by transferring some women and children to the *Challenger*, and twenty-eight others to Carnac Island. Mrs Stirling stayed with her husband until rising wind drove the vessel again into danger, when she and the remaining women were taken off to the battleship—how Captain Fremantle hated that feminine invasion!—and by daylight *Parmelia* rode at anchor near Garden Island.

So there were the Swan's first settlers, divided into two parties: those on the ships, and those on Carnac Island, the latter living 'entirely on salt beef and biscuits' with one only knife and one only drinking mug between them.

The new land now threw in a blustering welcome—a two-day gale which made matters, previously uncomfortable, almost intolerable.

As soon as the wind dropped, Fremantle rid himself of the women on the *Challenger* as fast as he could—with the exception of Mrs Stirling and Mrs Currie. On June 7 Stirling established headquarters on Garden Island, and there the first settlers endured rain and the cold wind of winter in makeshift shelters of brushwood. Even when the site of Fremantle was chosen, matters were not much better.

> When Fremantle was first occupied the beach was separated from Arthur's Head by a chain of pools, and the all-pervading sandiness to the long stretch of the low-lying coast reduced the ardour of the bravest of the pioneer band. They arrived in the very depth of winter; few or no tents had been provided for their accommodation and no sort of cover had been prepared on shore. The weather even for winter being unusually severe, the unfortunate women and children were exposed to the most harassing privations, and had frequently to sleep under umbrellas as the only covering from the deluge of driving rain that swept up from the Indian Ocean. Champagne cases, pianos and even carriages were later used in improvising temporary buildings. Only with the greatest of difficulty could these unfortunate people, unused as they were to rough colonial life, light fires for cooking purposes.[2]

(Lucifer matches had not then been invented.)

A good deal of limelight has been focused on the fine furniture and goods which arrived on the first ships and the fate they met in the sand and weather, for what could happen to pianos and delicate china in a country without roads, buildings, or a forseeable future? They were at first almost as useless as the half-ton of pins which Elizabeth Viner's husband, James Purkis, included in the 'refinements' he brought to mitigate the hardships of pioneering days. (Most of the pins he distributed among his fellow colonists.)

Many would-be settlers, daunted by early difficulties or discontented with the land available, packed up and left. Some went back to England, others to the east side settlements, New South Wales and Van Diemen's Land. But others remained and battled through with their wives beside them to become the founders of the State through their hard work, courage, and endurance.

The *Western Australian Historical Society Journal* has embalmed the reminiscences and experiences of some first white housekeepers of the colony. There was Anna Frances Isabella Hammersley,[3] seventeen years old, and called the 'Belle of Kent' at the time of her runaway marriage at Gretna Green with William Locke Brockman. The young couple arrived in the colony in 1829 with a prefabricated house. Anna sorted out its various sections like the parts of a puzzle, then turned to and helped erect it on their land at Herne Hill on the Middle Swan. She is described as a 'capable and intrepid pioneer', went exploring in a spring cart and brought up a family of six sons and three daughters.

Elizabeth Viner Purkis[4] lived for two years in a tent until her house was built. The tent was divided into three rooms, lined with blankets and carpeted with blackboy rushes covered with mats. Four smaller tents housed the staff, and another large tent was the 'living room'. Deep trenches surrounded them to keep away snakes and wild animals. Inside her canvas wall, Mrs Purkis maintained the customs of her homeland, and never failed to change into silk stockings and satin shoes for the evening meal.

Mrs Jan Dods of York wrote at the end of 1833 that she had been four months without oil or candles, three months without tea or sugar. She rejoiced, though, that the wheat crop was a success and there were 'bread and potatoes in plenty'.

Mrs Thomas Brown, also of York, wrote:

> We are almost without the common necessaries of life, although only 70 miles from Perth. We look forward to having them brought over the hills to our remote residence by degrees. The first object is to get ploughing and sowing done to provide us all with bread in the next years. It costs £25 per ton to convey goods from Fremantle to York (8 or 9 times the cost of bringing them 13,000 miles from England). Between Fremantle and Perth, and then to Guildford there is loose, deep sand and a horse cannot draw even an empty cart, so goods go by boat up the Swan to Guildford, although the river is very circuitous and there are

several shoals over which boats are dragged by the boatmen so there is no certainty of things being conveyed safely as the boats are often swamped. The boatmen are of bad character, seldom honest or sober.[5]

Even in its canvas tent period, Government House held receptions and dances that lasted all night. No one cared to cross the river in the dark because of quicksands and deep water, so quadrilles and gallopades went on until daybreak. Mary Shaw attended one of Lady Stirling's children's parties in the late thirties. She wore a net frock looped up with pearl ornaments, white silk stockings, blue kid shoes, and ankle trousers with frills. Lady Stirling did not approve the silver flower pinned in Mary's curls, and removed it.

Picnics and regattas were special occasions. The usual form of social gathering was to entertain friends at home with music and games. At ten o'clock everyone left, 'the house was locked up and the silver taken up to bed . . . It was thought dreadful to be out after ten o'clock.'[6] This was curfew hour, when the gaol bell rang to warn ticket-of-leave men lock-up time had come. If a girl found herself on the streets when the bell sounded, she picked up her skirts and ran.

By the late 'thirties and early 'forties there were many low, squat cottages of pug, thatched with rushes. In Guildford, third town of the colony, stores sold chests of tea at five to eight shillings a pound, barrels of pork, pipes of wine, rum by the gallon, 'a very superior musical box', hair oil, silk dresses, buff and dark nankeens, feather tippets, fancy waistcoats, figured black satin dittoes, and 'strong negro head tobacco'.

Roads and transport improved slowly. Even in the 'sixties settlers walked eighteen miles for stores. Mrs Phoebe Christie, née Smirke, remembers a woman trudging the distance, sustained by the thought of the well at the Ten Mile where she would rest and drink. But the well was minus a rope for the bucket and the water tantalisingly out of reach. Resourcefully she found a way to it. She retired into the scrub, removed her corset laces, tied them to her shoe strings and lowered the bucket into the well. Carefully she raised it, slaked her thirst, then into the bush again to lace herself once more.

The first years passed, the hard, strenuous years, and native-born children began growing up, to go out in their turn to land not yet taken.

Settlement fanned out and lonely women made homes far from their overseas birthplaces and far from the first Swan River landing —among the forests of jarrah in the south, or up north at Australind, coming only to Perth infrequently by bumping waggon. Small schooners took the more intrepid further north still, to the coast of mighty tides and the land of spinifex, and in the 'nineties, when men broke open the Golden Mile, women followed them to the dry land where wealth lay hidden.

The State stretched far and wide, and scattered through it were homes made by women pioneers. A visitor who saw them ten years after *Parmelia* avoided shipwreck at the river mouth praised their 'moral courage and unmurmuring perseverance . . . their great influence . . . on the community at large.' Give him the last word, for he saw them in action in the days when they were helping to found our largest State, begun in storm and stress when *Parmelia* reached the River of the Swans.

New settlers at Brunswick, Western Australia, about 1900

9
Flowers in the South

Pioneering was a challenge to some natures and brought its own reward in hard work and endurance. But to others it was a series of stresses which scarred and wounded, and finally killed. In the second group belongs Georgiana Molloy, sensitive and gentle, whose letters reveal the physical and mental loneliness which helped to crush her.[1]

* * *

There was considerable head-shaking among the friends of Captain John Molloy, veteran of Waterloo, when he announced he was off to the colonies and that fair-haired Georgiana Kennedy, eighteen, was prepared to marry and sail with him to the Swan River settlement.

Into the busy months before the ship sailed the young couple fitted their wedding, farewells to their families, and a journey to London to shop for livestock, furniture, provisions, clothes, tools and equipment for a colonial life. Servants were indentured and Georgiana ordered gowns ('very plain, without anything but hems and tucks') and 'cottage shape' bonnets.

A long wait at the port before departure, but at last *Warrior* was at sea. The Great Bear faded out of the northern skies, the Southern Cross hung above the mast in its place, and on 11 March 1830, five months after sailing, *Warrior* anchored off Rottnest Island. A ship's boat sailed the passengers up the river to Perth, and Georgiana stepped ashore in the country where she would spend the remaining years of her short life.

Settler's bark hut with verandah

The Molloys pitched their tents at Fremantle, attended the Governor's levee (present—eight ladies and fifty-eight gentlemen) and listened while Stirling explained that the best land along the Swan had gone. Enthusiastically he described the beauty of the south coast which he had recently visited, and urged them to consider settling there.

So, sight unseen, the Molloys chose Augusta on the Blackwood River, and sailed at the end of April in a government schooner to become, with the Bussell brothers, the first settlers of the district.

While some of the mighty jarrah trees were cleared, Georgiana's home was a leaky canvas tent. An umbrella was fixed above her bed when it rained. Here her first child was born—and died almost at once, an experience which scarred her so deeply that even three years later she wrote:

> language refuses to utter what I experienced when mine died in my arms in this dreary land, and no one but Molloy near me . . . I thought I might have had one little bright object left to solace all the hardships and privations I endured, and had still to go through. It was wicked, and I am not now thoroughly at peace.

When her second daughter, Sabina, was born, the family had a small house and garden in sight of the river. Felling was still in progress. Uprooting the giant jarrah trees was a long, tedious business which drove the first settlers to seek land elsewhere. The first wheat was affected by rust, but Georgiana soaked seed in salt water before the next sowing and that crop was more successful. In that isolated corner servants were hard to get and hard to keep. Georgiana had unending household duties and her child's prattle was often the only voice beside her husband's to hold off the surrounding silence.

Homesickness breaks through her letters again and again.

> I fancy myself arrived in the parlour (she wrote to friends in Scotland), and standing at the fire. Oh! my dear and lovely Roseneath! . . . I think of all the days I spent there; and all the violets and primroses are fresh in my memory. How does your garden get on? and did the Ayrshire roses entwine round the poles at the end of the garden?

Molloy was often away, sometimes in Perth on government business (he was commander of the local military detachment and police magistrate as well), sometimes out with the Bussell brothers on foot seeking land less difficult to clear and work than the jarrah country. They found what they wanted on the Vasse, and obtained grants on opposite sides of the river. The Molloys did not move for some years, but the Captain made frequent trips to supervise the building of a house. In his absence Georgiana faced daily routine and unexpected emergencies alone.

At sowing time Dawson, the manservant, must be set to work with the oxen and the plough. If natives appeared, they must be dealt with. Once Georgiana outfaced a group of twenty or thirty who came to thieve the potato crop. 'Ben-o-wai! (Begone!)' she ordered firmly, and they withdrew outside the house to shake their spears threateningly. 'I was afraid to show fear', she wrote later, although 'one cut the air so close to my head with his wallabee stick . . . and drew a piece of broken bottle close to my cheek.' Dawson managed to set a pistol and rifle where they could be seen. The band took the hint and gradually drifted away.

On another occasion a maid became ill, fell into several fits which alarmed and distressed Georgiana, and eventually died insane. She was buried at night in the presence of the servants, Georgiana's clear young voice solemnly reading the prayers for the dead, the torchlight casting strange shadows on the scene and accentuating the isolation of the little settlement and the silence of its vast forest background.

Not only physical loneliness but mental isolation fretted Georgiana's gentle spirit. Augusta was cut off even from the limited society of the south-west. There were seldom more than three or four visitors to the port in a year, and those who came were not brilliant conversationalists. 'Grubbing, hoes, beef, pork, potatoes, onions, anchors and anchorage, whaling, harpooning are the chief topics of conversation', complained Georgiana.

The ceaseless round of household duties cancelled out almost every other activity. If Georgiana took time off to write letters, she said her household sewing and mending suffered.

> I must either leave writing alone or some useful requisite needlework undone. There is not a person here to do any. I never open a book, and if I read a chapter on Sunday, it is quite a treat to have so much leisure.

When her next baby was coming she said the busy day left her no time to sew for its arrival. 'I have not a cap to put on the child's head,' she declared.

The child, another girl, arrived in June 1834. Georgiana was busier than ever.

> I have not only to nurse and carry her about, but all my former occupations to attend to, having only Mrs Dawson as a female servant. I do not hesitate to say I am overwhelmed with too much labour, and indeed my frame bears testimony to it, as I have every day expected to see some bone poking through its epidermis.

Sabina almost died of undulating fever, and Georgiana reproached herself. The hours and strength she gave to household chores left so little for her children. Frequent pregnancies sapped her strength, and she was often confined to bed through sheer exhaustion.

> This life is too much both for dear Molloy and myself . . . My head aches, I have all the clothes to put away from the wash; baby to put to bed; make tea and drink it without milk as they shot our cow for trespass; read prayers and go to bed besides sending off this tableful of letters . . . We have drunk the dregs since we embarked on this fatal Swan River expedition, fraught with continued care and deprivations.

But in all the stress and strain, Georgiana was sending down roots into the southland soil. There were moments when she relaxed and let the beauty of the place flow over her. Sometimes in the evenings she took Sabina on the beach. While the child rubbed cuttlefish on a nutmeg grater, Georgiana sat and dreamed while the waves of the Southern Ocean rounded Cape Leeuwin and ran over the sandbar.

She was enchanted by 'the beautiful little birds sporting round me' and the climate she described as heavenly:

> while you are burning the front breadth of your frock (she wrote) and the nibs of your shoes at an excellent fire of Newcastle coal, I am sitting on the verandah surrounded by my little flower garden of British, Cape and Australian flowers pouring forth their odour . . . Many of the shrubs are powerfully sweet, some like may, some like bergamot.

From the shrubs and flowers Georgiana drew strength and refreshment. Everything grew more brightly in Augusta, she believed, because of the powerful southern sun. She planted slips of fig trees which friends at home sent her packed in tanner's bark in a camp oven. She grew vines from seeds, and peach trees from stones brought from Cape Town. She loved them all, the natives and the exotics, but she was surprised when Captain Mangles, cousin of Lady Stirling, wrote to ask if she would collect and forward him seeds and specimens of Australian wild flowers and plants.

It was a challenge, a hobby, and a source of great delight for all the family. The next few years found Georgiana busy collecting, pressing and writing up plants and seeds. Her children helped, 'Their eyes being so much nearer the ground they have been able to detect many minute specimens . . . I cannot observe.' Her husband brought back samples when he visited Vasse; soldiers returned from duty marches with specimens in their packs, and the natives often brought contributions.

It gave Georgiana something to think about besides 'the odious drudgery of cheese and butter making' which must be fitted into the day, along with the children's lessons, the everlasting sewing, and 'innumerable other peremptory duties'.

The seeds she collected interested botanists in England and were propagated in several botanical gardens. Her knowledge of plant life increased, her interest grew and the collecting went on, interrupted by housekeeping, making and mending, pregnancy, birth, and by a great grief which again shook Georgiana's spirit and laid it low.

It came suddenly one fine morning after breakfast. The family finished romping with the youngest child, a boy of nineteen months, Georgiana went to the kitchen to bake and churn, and the others separated on various activities. A few minutes later the boy was missing. So short a time, but the little bell he wore at his waist in case he should wander could not be heard, and Georgiana's eyes went to the spot, about a stone's throw from the house, where a stand of vergillea and wattle screened the well. Her husband reassured her: 'Do not frighten yourself; he never goes there.' But he had, and all their efforts could not revive him.

It was months before Georgiana wrote again to Captain Mangles, excusing her dilatory pen on the grounds of her 'dangerous illness occasioned by the mournful event of my darling boy's death'. But gradually she took up the threads of the pioneer pattern, bore a fourth child (another daughter), and went back to gardening 'to the neglect of other concerns. Often had Molloy looked at a buttonless shirt and exclaimed with a woe-begone visage: "When will Captain Mangles' seeds be sown?"'

Her expeditions to the bush to gather specimens ('gypsy parties' she called them) were the delight of Georgiana's life, recreations for her mind and spirit. The company of her husband and children and the environment of the bush eased the tensions engendered by pioneer housekeeping.

Her garden that year was particularly gay and charming and often at night she would take

> a sort of piano-organ . . . out on the grass plot and play till late by moonlight, the beautiful broad water of the Blackwood gliding by, the roar of the bar ever and anon, the wild scream of a flight of swans going over to the fresh water lakes, the air perfectly redolent with the powerful scent of verginia stock . . . clove, pinks, and the never-fading mignonette.

Fairlawn, the house at the Vasse, was finished and the family prepared to move. Georgiana, who had found life at Augusta wearing and exhausting, was reluctant to leave. The transplanting made her feel like another Eve cast out of Eden. Her heart had twined round the house on the Blackwood as the roses embraced the pillars at far away Roseneath she had once recalled so longingly.

But the break had to come. The family made the first part of the journey by boat, then rode for three days, Georgiana on horseback carrying her baby, her other two daughters following on donkeys.

A new home and many new flowers helped Georgiana over the slow business of adjustment. The captain of an American whaler in Geographe Bay gave her an old log book to mount specimens for Captain Mangles, and sometimes she rode in the bush with her husband to gather flowers and seeds.

A fourth daughter, born early in 1840, left her weak and bedridden for some time. Her convalescent diet was kangaroo soup, pork and port wine.

Sabina, busy little nurse to her sick mother, had no time to botanize, so Dorothea, aged six, took over the search for specimens until Georgiana could go again into the bush on the expeditions she enjoyed so much.

> I should like nothing better than to kindle a fire and stay out all night . . . as I should be ready for my work early in the morning.

Winter found her at night by the hearth dressed in 'plaid of stuff', playing the piano-organ while her children danced. In summer she always wore 'dark cotton with a muslin kerchief, and a lighter print for Sundays'.

Flowers in the South

In January the family took a camping holiday at Cape Naturaliste. Georgiana was thrilled by the ocean views, and chose a site where she hoped they would one day build a house.

Back at Fairlawn she watched from her windows ('calico blinds stitched tight on square frames') while her husband laid out the garden. In June it was complete with shrubbery, flower and kitchen gardens, and Georgiana was expecting another child.

In December 1842 her fifth daughter and seventh child was born, and her garden-making was over. She died in April 1843.

But in the Vasse district and around Augusta there still bloom lilies, pinks and mignonette which have come from the seed sown by Georgiana Molloy, pioneer garden-maker with the gentle soul of a poet.

A garden in Kalgoorlie

10

Those Energetic Bussells

THE STORY of the Bussell women, who reached Australia when Perth was still small and new and the west taking its first, faltering steps in colonization, fairly crackles with energy and vitality.

These amazing women, prim but persistent, disciplined but adaptable, were made of different stuff from Georgiana Molloy. Children of the Reverend William Marchant Bussell, curate of St Mary's, Portsea, Hants. (dead some years before they went colonizing), pioneering did not dismay them; indeed, they throve on its variety, and accepted its challenge.

The first of the Bussell women arrived at the Swan in January 1833, with a fine flurry of pre-Victorian petticoats, in the wake of their four brothers who had sailed in the same ship as the Molloys. When the two girls, Frances (Fanny) and Elizabeth (Bessie) and a fifth brother Lenox joined them at the Blackwood, 'the dear boys' as they were frequently called in letters home to Mama, had a thatched cottage at Augusta, and a grant of some three thousand acres about fourteen miles upstream on a peninsula called 'The Adelphi'.

Charles, the second brother, was government storekeeper at Augusta, and the girls divided their time between the thatched cottage there and the farm and dwellings at The Adelphi. In November 1833 the main house so laboriously erected was burnt, and Bessie, who was there at the time, wrote a breathless report of the event to Frances at Augusta:

Off I went to tear down the books. Ally and Len pulled out the piano, tables and chairs. Emma got everything out of the kitchen. I ran to look after my dear crockery. Len cut down your cot. I was endowed with some unnatural strength, took your mattress, my own and your bedding, and rushed out of the room. I hope we saved the books and linen that were in the piano case under my bed. I ran off with all your chemises and etc., and our merino dresses, I think. Ally got into the loft through the ceiling and ... threw down the boxes helter skelter. All needles, tapes, bonnets, ribbons, pins are lost. All your shoes are safe. I have not a pair left, nor a bonnet. Poor Vernon has lost some shoes, Ally his pistols. Len saved Mr Mayo's medicine chest, but not in a perfect state, I fear. All the Bibles and the Byron are safe, but I dread to discover the loss of books. Ally tore out the windows and saved them, but could not the doors. Len ordered the gunpowder to be thrown into the bush. The piano got very hot after it was out. Music safe, desks, workbox. Your elegant extracts I saved with by own hands ... The cellarets were thrown out, not much breaking, I think. It was Emma who carried out your chest of drawers, Len mine. Phoebe active beyond compare. In fact, we have saved wonderfully, but lost immensely. I must have lost two or three frocks, and all my stays but one pair, all my frills and vanities till the last. Salt cellars and silver cruet stand are safe ... Looking-glasses safe. I wish it was daylight. It is the longest night I ever knew.

In April 1834 the boys moved to the Vasse River, where John, the eldest and leader, had discovered and obtained a grant of a fine piece of 'parkland'. Phoebe Bowker, an elderly woman servant who went with them, landed on the beach with the boys and the stores and slept in a tent until a store-room was built, when she turned in there, made doughboys and pancakes to relieve the monotony of the everlasting salt pork, and brewed coffee made from crushed wheat and drunk without milk.

There are only occasional glimpses of Phoebe as she moves about her duties, but there is no doubt she played a very real part in the Bussell ventures. She saw the clearing and building, well sinking and fencing at the new home on the Vasse. She was the first woman of the household to see Yulika, the cow which strayed from The Adelphi, but by a most happy coincidence found its way to the Vasse farm. Yulika staged her return the day before Mrs Bussell and daughter Mary called at the Vasse on their way to the girls at Augusta. The return of wandering stock at any time was an event, but when it occurred on such an occasion it had a special significance. So they commemorated Yulika's return in the name all had been seeking for the new property—'Cattle Chosen' they called it, and Cattle Chosen it remains to intrigue all who hear it for the first time.

The arrival of Mrs Bussell and Mary completed the family of the Western Australian Bussells. A closely-knit clan, young, unmarried and energetic, they pioneered with energy and gusto. Such a group was a bulwark for each of its members against the loneliness and isolation of colonizing, giving each other the physical and mental support which gentle Georgiana Molloy did not have and subconsciously yearned for in her solitude.

Each had a role to play, something to contribute to the common purpose, helping to establish the family's prosperity, adding to its comfort and sharing in the drudgery entailed.

Naturally the womenfolk took over the housekeeping, the making and mending and, later, the dairy and barnyard. They adjusted rapidly to the new world, and seemed to have had no regrets about their past life in England, for while they were still approaching the settlement, Fanny wrote: 'England already seems like the land of shadows, beautiful and beloved, but abandoned forever.' And a few weeks later: 'I do not at all join in the universal regret that we are soon to retire completely from the world and its gaieties.'

There is, indeed, very little fretting against their lot or conditions in the colony, except in a few early letters from Mary, the least enthusiastic pioneer of them all. (She is said to have left a romantic attachment behind in England, but even so did not take long to settle down to the pattern of the new life.) They regret the sight of the 'poor gentry' reduced to working on the roads while those who would have been their social inferiors in ordered England 'seem rolling in plenty'. They find the summer dust very trying, 'and the fleas!' almost eat them alive.

But they approved the maintenance of standards among the colonists, while admiring their adaptability. '... society (in Perth)', wrote Fanny, 'has not degenerated in the least. Instead ... I should say selectness and refinement are more prevalent than in England. Yet no one scruples to assist in the duties of the "ménage".'

The family faced misfortunes sturdily. Their silver and furniture were lost in a wreck, yet a few months later even Mrs Bussell could write philosophically:

> We shall appear the victims of misfortune and ill-luck, but it is not so. Are we not blessed with health, spirits and content? ...
> My dear, we have no servant. Think of our difficulties, but do not pity us. The wreck has been found ... but very little

property recovered, nothing valuable except my feather beds and a few blankets. You must not grieve for us. We have ceased to do so long since.

And she ends the letter: 'Do not be troubled about us, a more happy, cheerful group cannot be found.'

Bessie took part in several family adventures. After The Adelphi fire it was decided to abandon the ruin, and return to the thatched cottage at Augusta before the boys went to the Vasse. Two boats were loaded to capacity with personal belongings and live stock—pigs, poultry, cats, dogs, cockatoo and pigeons. The party was quite cheerful as they rowed downstream by moonlight, and 'the song, the laugh and the joke went round', said Bessie. No brooding over misfortunes for the Bussells. They breakfasted at daybreak on fish from the river, 'frizzling pork and pancakes' (Bessie ate hers from a saucepan lid), then rowed on to 'dear Fanny' at Augusta.

Bessie was also the first of the girls to see the Vasse. She rode there with her brothers in November 1835, through swamps she called 'fearful' and over creek banks ('very muddy and perpendicular'). She slept out of doors under a blanket, breakfasted on a biscuit, and dined at midday on food from the packs; then curled up like the boys and slept for an hour or so under a tree. The dogs started up kangaroos on the Vasse plains, and Prince, her mount, sensing himself near the journey's end, broke into his first voluntary gallop. Until then he had ambled most of the way except when pricked by blackboy tops hurled by the boys to urge him along.

Arrived at the house, Bessie, sunburnt and saddle-sore, bathed in a tub of water and went to bed. Next day Phoebe ('I be so glad to see 'ee, Miss Bessie, that can hardly wag') gave her 'delicious tea out of her little black teapot, after which I churned the butter, and then slept nearly the whole day.'

Recovered, she took over the management of the household, looked after the sewing and mending, helped Phoebe, put multi-coloured patches on the boys' clothes, and made new shirts for Alfred (the youngest) from good pieces of his brothers' discards.

In January 1836 Mrs Bussell and the other girls arrived at Cattle Chosen and the family was together again, the men in separate huts, the ladies in their own house whose sitting room gave them great satisfaction. Its wattle and daub walls were 'most beautifully plastered', its floor was clay; books stood on shelves down the length of the room, the piano was under the window, and the 'noble chimney' took up almost the whole of another wall. The single upstairs room formed a dormitory for 'all the females of the family'. It had a view of the river and the park-like country on one side; its other windows overlooked the outdoor cooking fire, the barnyard, the 'beautiful sleek cattle', the goats and horses.

Here the family quickly fell into a pattern, wakening to the sound of 'the great bell' at daylight, and spending the days in various duties. Bessie prepared vegetables for dinner, Mary cleared away and tidied the house, Fanny went to the boys' room 'to make their beds, look for their fleas, which we are gradually exterminating', and all helped Phoebe wash and fold the clothes, and churn the butter. After midday dinner they fed the poultry, 'the turkeys falling to Bessie's share, the ducks to mine (Fanny's) and the cocks and hens to Mary's'. Washing-up came next, then siesta-time, after which there were more chores until sunset when 'the cows are all milked, the horses praised and petted, and . . . we all sit down to our bread and milk supper.'

In a few months there were butter and potatoes for sale and later cheese. They marketed at the Swan River, and also traded with American whalers in Geographe Bay. Surplus stock was sold to other settlers, and as the district grew the family's prestige and income increased.

John went to England and brought home a wife; Mary married and moved away to King George Sound. Her first baby was born the day after she had given hospitality to some exhausted settlers who had lost their way in the bush. Mary climbed up and down the ladder to the upper story for bedding, cooked meals and tended them solicitously. 'The next day Missie came without any doctor', she wrote the family. The layette was unfinished, 'so the little grub made her appearance very ill-provided for . . . Patrick (Mary's husband) as he kissed her little cheek, thought she looked like a brandy-faced fish wife that had had too much grog tea.'

The family, most of whom were married, drew up a plan of operation to work the property as partners. Fanny, as superintendent of the dairy, received a percentage of its earnings. She and her mother also had the house which had first sheltered 'all the females of the family' at Cattle Chosen. Mrs Bussell died there in 1840, knowing her children had made a permanent home in the new colony. Busselton, the name given to the town which grew up around Cattle Chosen, is a memorial to the family whose womenfolk contributed so much energy to pioneering the parklands of the Vasse.

11

Women in the Fields

Take a river, sixteen hundred miles long, trail it through unmapped country, send out a man of vision to find and chart its course, and you have the extension of one State and the beginning of another.

* * *

Captain Charles Sturt, back from the perils and privations of his voyage down the Murray, was a fuse that fired certain minds in England to plan and press for more colonies.

Edward Gibbon Wakefield filled in the hours of his prison sentence (he had eloped with a ward in Chancery) drawing up a blueprint for colonizing, designed to avoid mistakes made in earlier settlements. It found many supporters. The government, reluctant as ever to make a beginning, gave way under pressure, a Governor was appointed (Captain Hindmarsh), with a surveyor (Captain Light) to lay out the settlement, shipping offices advertised accommodation in immigrant ships, and the first settlers for the new State set sail (1836).

True to form, the government made no advance surveys; Kangaroo Island, where the first shipload landed, was deemed unsuitable for permanent settlement, and discomfort and uncertainty depressed the would-be colonizers until Captain Light selected a site on the mainland a few miles inland from a beach on St Vincent's Gulf. Then the immigrant ships came up, the anchors went down, and if you peer into old engravings you will see how South Australia's first women pioneers went ashore—pick-a-backed the last few yards of the journey by water by sailors or relatives with trouser-legs rolled up.

A seven-mile trudge to the town site, carrying a child or laden with baggage, and several trips back and forth to the ships for goods and chattels, spades and axes. Tents were pitched and kindling cut for the fires. A scent of burning eucalypt on the air, flames curling and licking round quart pots, kettles and Dutch ovens, and the first meals were served on the banks of the Torrens to the founders of Adelaide and their families.

It was mid-summer, and the vista before these pioneers showed sandhills and lagoons in the foreground (the beach at Glenelg), with a bush covered plain stretching up to the thickly vegetated hills. Little did they know then, gazing at the hills, of the caves wherein bushrangers would lurk in years to come, ready to pounce on any unescorted bullock team, or unsuspecting traveller.

These women had lived on salt meat and hard tack on the long voyage out in the sailing vessel 'Buffalo,' and this still constituted their fare, except for a few edible fruits and roots shown them by kindly aborigines. Tents were hastily erected, followed gradually by huts of mud, reed and canvas. Later, 'wattle and daub', with a thatch roof proved the cheapest and most lasting house. Numbers of farms can still show portions of these in their old stables, and in deserted cottages by the creeks. Proximity to water was a primary need for all settlers in this particularly dry State. No roads or bridges confronted these early immigrants, and lucky were the women who scored a ride even in a bullock waggon on its jolting way up to the new capital of Adelaide, or down to the new Port Adelaide, set amongst swamps and known locally as Port Misery.[1]

There were the usual discomforts of settlement, taking—also as usual—a distinct local pattern. This time it was land speculation with each wave of immigrants selling out to the next and stirring up a merry brew of inflation. And because tilling the soil was a burdensome business compared with profit-making from land sales, there was little agriculture, and the settlement was on short rations of butter and eggs, fresh vegetables and meat.

The arrival of German settlers, refugees from religious persecution in their own land, introduced a saner atmosphere into the colony. It was not part of their policy or background to become land speculators. Sturdy farmer folk, they were only too glad to rig up their unusual ploughs and, in the country which had given them the right to worship as they wished, set about the job to making the new-old earth yield its harvests. Very shortly the German women were coming down from the hills wearing their native dress and carrying on their heads the farm produce grown with their help to feed the households of Adelaide.

> Up to the time of their arrival the inhabitants of Adelaide had been insufficiently supplied with vegetables and dairy produce, and these at an exorbitant price—butter at 2/6 a pound, and eggs 2/6 a dozen. The Germans very soon began to carry into the city for sale small supplies of butter, and, within a few months, vegetables, generally on the back of the females, and in the same manner taking back their supplies of rations. After a time a string of matrons and girls would be seen wending their way to the capital in their German costume.[2]

* * *

Their produce sold, they trudged back to the farms to work again by the side of their menfolk.

> For some time after their (the Germans') arrival we would see funny rings attached to one of their small ploughs or wooden harrows—say, a woman with a strap over her shoulder with a rope to the swingle-bar, a necessary advantage given to her in length, and at the other shorter end a small bullock, cow, or pony, the husband or father holding with one hand the one-handled plough and with the other a long pipe, which he was deliberately smoking.[3]

When sheep-raising began, the German settlers supplied the first shearers for the colony.

> The shearers were principally young women, who were waited on by men of the village, who, when called on, caught and carried the sheep to the shearer . . . The sheep was carefully laid down on its side; the young woman, without shoes and stockings, had a piece of thick soft string tied to one of her big toes, the other end was then tied to the hind foot of the sheep; her knee or left hand was pressed on the neck or shoulder of the animal, which was then left to her charge, and she commenced . . . clipping . . . most carefully avoiding any snips of the skin. The number shorn by one never exceeded thirty a day. At first I was inclined to laugh, but I was soon pleased to see how tenderly the sheep were handled. The wool was not taken off very close. The whole party worked with a will, and the amount they earned went towards the payment of their land.[4]

From another source comes further evidence of the work of the German women.

'The German females already in the colony,' remarks the Report of the South Australian Company of 1844, 'are very efficient labourers; a large proportion of our flocks this last season was shorn by them.'

The interesting . . . and instructive fact brought out by the extract given, is that the German women of the Lutheran congregation who went to South Australia . . . proved to be almost if not absolutely, the sole persons who could be relied upon to perform the shearing and make up the merino wool for market. Not only so, but in harvest time it is added these German women were employed in both reaping and threshing the corn.[5]

Gradually the colony stabilized, and the first wheat exported from Australia was grown between the hills and the sea.

South Australia's first wheat growers were John and Allan McLean of Strath. Allan's wife, Catherine, helped with the crop in the intervals of butter-, cheese- and candle-making, and the incidental occupations of rearing eleven children.

While hot winds blew from the north ('siroccos' the first settlers called them) wheat farmers' wives and families threshed grain with flails, and stood on stools to winnow, the wind taking the chaff away.

When rust struck the wheat, vines were planted as a trial crop, and soon clothed hills and slopes. The grapes not used for dried fruit were turned into wine. Processing was simple. Grapes were placed in a vat and tramped until bare feet were stained with juice. Casks were stored in cellars, and natives quickly learned the trick of thrusting straws into the barrels to get at the wine.

Not many of their descendants today see the crop which is such an important item in South Australia's economy.

* * *

Tucked into the folds of the hills about Mount Lofty (South Australia) are little villages which still offer proof of their German origin. Old mills and waterwheeels, sturdy churches where the Lutheran creed was preached far from its birthplace, and square-roofed buildings mark townships with Teutonic names. They are worth coming far to see, but are unforgettable in autumn, when the trees blaze red, bronze and golden like sacrificial fires lit to the changing season.

A visitor to Adelaide in 1839 has left this description of the German settlements:

Settlers in the Hills

The first village we passed was Klemzig, a settlement of Germans who had lately arrived in the Colony and who were busy erecting their houses and farming their little gardens. It was a beautiful sight in the Australian bush to see the neat and gabled houses with their small windows and large lofts arising after the fashion of the fatherland and to see the neat, quiet and respectable figures of the Teutonic occupants, the ancient frau seated at the door of the cottage knitting, the children in their costume with a handkerchief of many colours tied round the head of the girl, the men working with the everlasting pipe in their mouths, all ready with a kind and civil salutation so different from the rough, overbearing manners of our own countrymen. The S.A. Germans are strict Calvinists and each village has its pastor. They are gregarious people. They seldom set up as individuals in the far bush, living, working and acting for themselves, but they congregate in villages and the herds and flocks often belong to the people in common.

> James Coutts Crawford, Diaries and Notes from which he wrote *Recollections of Travel in New Zealand and Australia* (London, 1880). (Original in possession of Henry Crawford, Esq., Naughton Nome Farm, Fife. Microfilms at Australian National Library, Public Library, Adelaide.)

Glenelg in 1842 . . . contained a government cottage then called a custom house, an inn, Mr. W—'s residence, Mr A—'s, and a few fishermen's huts, but did not boast of even a butcher's shop. Yet the beach was smooth and delightful . . .(and) the bathing most enjoyable . . . To seclude the ladies entirely from observation during the unpleasant process of dressing and undressing in the open air, . . . Mr. C—had four light poles cut about seven feet in length, planed, and pointed at the ends. To these strips of canvas were nailed . . .

> Mrs Alfred Watts, *Memories of Early Days in South Australia* (Adelaide, 1882).

Dressed for riding, about 1870

12

Home-makers Go Inland

SETTLERS SOON FOUND their way over the hills behind Adelaide. Land was cleared, sheep grazed, little wattle and daub huts went up, and shepherds tended flocks where wattle and sheoaks grew, and blue herons fished in gully streams and along river banks.

The scene was exclusively pastoral until the green glow of copper brought miners to the scene—men of Cornwall who worked the ore found by a shepherd tending his flocks among the hills of Burra Burra. Housing was scarce, the creek was dry, and its banks offered a tempting solution to the problem of where to live.

> With the initiative of the pioneer, the houseless ones hollowed out shelters . . . in the banks of the creek, and turned them into veritable 'palaces'—even into six rooms. They found these 'residences' comfortable; cosy in winter and cool in summer.[1]

In the snug cliff houses, with boarded fronts and often a beer barrel atop as chimney, housekeeping and family-tending went along sedately for the mining families.

> The huts were whitewashed and properly furnished inside. Gutters were dug around the edges of the roofs so rain water would not soak through, and the roofs were also used for fowl pens.[2]

The greatest nuisance to such living was, not crowing roosters or busy hens, but small boys. They became very adept at hooking the kettle off the stove with wire pushed down the chimney, and delighted in the tutter that followed a stone dropped into a pan of frying bacon.

The cliff dwellers ignored the danger of flood, until a storm brought water racing down the dry stream bed. Several were drowned, and others escaped only by climbing up and out of their chimneys. Furniture and belongings were lost in the flood; so, too, were the snug little houses their occupants had literally hewn out of the soil of their new land using with initiative what lay closest to hand.

They built other homes and pioneered other towns, while the immigrant ships continued to set families ashore at Glenelg to find paths to a new life through uncleared bush and scrub and the loneliness of unmade country.

In 1850 Reverend Alexander Law left his work in the crowded slums of Glasgow for a wide Australian parish of scattered holdings around Stirling North. Most of his time was spent in the saddle, visiting the station people. For weeks at a time his young wife, the one white woman in the township, stayed in their small two-roomed house with only an aboriginal girl for company.

Heat, flies, duststorms and a child stillborn drove them to a parish further south, but in 1875 they threw in their lot with members of their congregation off to pioneer on the Murray Flats. Elizabeth Law, aged thirteen, stayed as housekeeper for her father until the affairs of the parish were settled. Mrs Law, with the five other children—Alexander, eleven, was the eldest, John, three, the youngest—travelled by waggon over forty miles of rough bush track to land on the Flats. Their home was a two-roomed wattle and daub cottage on the hillside looking over the plains and the land across the Murray.

Alexander and an elderly worker cleared the dense mallee scrub a few acres a year, and planted small areas with crops. He also added three small lean-to rooms to the house, using stones from the hillside held together with pug.

> Marion (aged nine) or Minnie, as she was called, helped to mix and carry the 'pug'. The roof of the house was shingled, so no rain-water could be saved, and all water for household use had to be carried from a small well about a quarter of a mile away. This well had to supply all their livestock also, and its supply was limited. It was very fresh and palatable to drink, but brown in colour, so was not suitable for washing clothes.

Laundry was done on the river bank:

> Mrs. Law and Minnie would pack all the soiled clothes, tubs, etc., in a cart, and drive six miles over a very sandy track through the mallee scrub to the River Murray. It was a community washing centre, with fireplaces for boiling the clothes, mostly in buckets. They took the clothes home wet to hang out.[3]

Three years passed before the family was reunited and Elizabeth, now sixteen, became school teacher for the district. Her class included her own brothers and sisters—with two exceptions: Alex and Minnie were too busy to go to school.

The family acreage was in two allotments, miles apart. On the farthest section a small hut was built, and when the girls were old enough they went there in pairs to shepherd the sheep by day and yard them at night. As they walked with the sheep or sat by the fire when the chores were finished, they knitted long stockings for themselves and the rest of the family from wool homespun from their own sheep.

There could have been few idle women in the days when South Australia was a State in the making.

* * *

Plodding bullocks on land, little schooners tacking along the coast and settlement moving further out. George Staples brought his Emma to Yorke Peninsula to farm a few acres at Penang, ten miles from Moonta. They had a two-roomed hut, a bucket to carry water, a plough to turn the soil. There were no fences, and kangaroos arrived nightly to feed on the young wheat. Emma and George took turns on watch armed with a blunderbuss, and saved enough of the crop for the next sowing.

Sea-water, distilled and still steaming, was carted from the coast to water the stock. A couple of cows, fowls and turkeys kept Emma busy. Dingoes and wandering natives were part of the life. Baby Maud, born in 1875, disappeared from home, at the age of two, late one afternoon. Her parents searched all night and men from the copper mines at Moonta joined them next day. At nightfall there was still no trace of the child. The sun rose again and George came on a ragged shoe. Shortly after Maud was found, clutching the kitten she had gone to find. Alive and whole—Emma was luckier than other pioneering mothers whose children were not reached in time.

* * *

Land under water—that was Millicent 'before the drains'.[4] Ellen Dalton knew it then, her first home a tent on the hill where Millicent town is. Three months from Adelaide by bullock dray to camp in the swamps, native companions so numerous that they must be chased continually from the crops, wheat spread out on a tarpaulin for threshing, were features of Mrs Dalton's early life at Millicent.

Her husband died and she had five children to rear. Little 'time to stand and stare' then. Life was a continual round of milking, setting milk for cream, making butter to sell for sixpence a pound, raising a few cattle to sell for thirty shillings each. ('We get £55 for the same quality today,' says her granddaughter, Mrs T. W. Kealy.)

A neighbour killed the pigs she turned into bacon and hams. The candles and soap, the bread and cheese—all to be made, and yet any time at a call for help she would set off to nurse a neighbour in sickness or childbirth. Nothing daunted her, not even a four-mile pull through raging seas to the lighthouse at Beachport. Another woman needed help, and help was something Ellen Dalton never refused.

* * *

Slowly inland and northward the settlers' tracks were laid, pushing into the country where hope whispered there must be water, the country where Sturt had gone because he saw the bright flash of parrots passing overhead, the land of clay pans and sandhills, where the distance between water and the next soak was important to know. A land of long, quiet miles where Mrs Arthur Treloar in 1886 travelled eight hundred miles north of Adelaide; by train to the railhead at Marree, then by buggy and horses on the last three-week stretch. The second white woman in the area, she had calico windows and slept on a bed of green hide stretched across rails. Stores came twice a year, white sugar and dried fruit were Christmas luxuries.

* * *

A strange, puzzling country, beloved mistress of its ruler, Drought. But when the rains did come, green shoots of grass appeared overnight and wildflowers grew gorgeously.

It was part of the lonely inland where a few women made life easier and kinder for their men and the families they reared with little or no help. It was a land which demanded courage, competence and character to cope with its moods and conditions. Its history is full of women who had those qualities to a superlative degree.

In the 'eighties the Price family moved by train and buggy into the Hundred of Erskine. Backed by Black Rock Peak, timbered with pine and mallee, the property grew wheat, but was hit hard by the Seven-Year Drought.

> It started in 1896 and lasted seven years. During those years we had scarcely any rain, no wheat (or at least very little), no feed for stock, and nothing but red dust everywhere. Scarcely a week passed without a terrific dust storm. You could see it

coming, a huge black cloud, and when it reached the house there was nothing to do but go inside, shut all the doors and windows and light the lamp.[5]

Lean, hard years that took their toll of livestock and courage, but brought out the spirit of neighbourliness, the great prop by which life in the outback is supported.

We had a little well on our property. It was only twelve feet deep, filled from a spring in the rocks. During the drought there were at least six families carting water from that well, not only for themselves, but for their teams of horses. They came as far as twelve miles with tanks on their waggons, and drew up the water from the well. When it emptied, they sat down and waited till it filled again from the spring. Although we had no money, the water was free to all.

Short rations in those drought years. Biscuits made without eggs or fat, and bread spread with black treacle were all that could be mustered to serve guests at afternoon tea. 'Meat, of course, was very scarce, and sometimes we were without it for weeks. Then perhaps we would get a rabbit, or my brother might shoot a wallaby. That was a real treat.'

Guests were always welcome, but how did one feed them when 'there was no meat, and no fat or dripping to make a pudding'? Somebody had an inspiration for one such meal. 'My sister, not to be beaten, cut up a tallow candle very fine like suet and made a plum pudding which everyone enjoyed immensely', except the cook, who that day had no appetite for pudding.

Repairing the waggonette

13
The Pathfinders

THE WAKEFIELD SYSTEM designed to make South Australia a model colony was less streamlined in practice than on paper. One and sixpence in an iron safe at one time represented the amount Governor Hindmarsh possessed to carry on administration. His successor, Governor Gawler, tried to solve the colony's problems with an ambitious programme of public works, later acknowledged as sensible, but paid for not out of revenue, but by bills of promise. When the Exchequer called a halt no one was more surprised than the Governor, or more indignant, when the sun-tanned, blue-eyed young naval captain, George Grey, arrived and tabled credentials authorizing him to take over from Gawler.

Grey's policy of stringent economy made him at first as unpopular with the colonists as his predecessor had been with the government at home. But the colony slowly stabilized, helped by the discovery of copper, the spread of agriculture and stock farming.

Some early arrivals bobbed serenely over the choppy seas of the first years. After three months in a marquee which was both residence and place of worship, the Reverend Thomas Quinton Stow could still write to the Missionary Society in London: 'What a land is this to which you have sent me! The loveliness and glory of the plains and woods, its glens and hills! The same may be said of its climate, salubrious and delightful!'

The Reverend Stow and family reached Adelaide in 1837. They saw tents give place to pisé houses (earth sometimes mixed with straw) roofed with reeds from the Torrens or the Reedbeds, thatch or shingles and palings imported from Van Diemen's Land or cut by Vandemonian splitters who crossed the water and went to work with their axes in the Mount Lofty Ranges.

Makeshift materials finished off interiors of the first small homes: 'A ceiling was improvised out of calico, which flapped noisily on windy days, and calico, also, was generally used in place of glass for windows.'[1]

Well sinkers revealed the existence of good building stone, mostly lime, and clay suitable for bricks. By the 'forties most houses were built of one or the other.

Bullock or horse-drawn drays carted water from the Torrens for so much a cask. Settlers who hauled their own attached ropes to screws at either end of a barrel and trundled it to and from the Torrens: 'The water was execrable, what with tadpoles and other living creatures; the longer it rested the worse it became, and it was expensive as well.'[2]

Adelaide of the 'forties has been described as 'quaint and unreal'. Sawn timber leant nonchalantly against a gum where the *Advertiser* office building now stands, castor oil plants grew out of a heap of debris a little further on, and a small mud or sod fort, complete with 'embrasures and carronades', was falling into ruins on North Terrace.

Isabella Grant arrived in the middle 'forties and looked at it all with something like horror. Empty spaces, few houses, natives begging for bacca and tucker, gum trees and still more gum trees, unpaved roads dusty in dry weather and muddy in wet—to her homesick eyes it was too unlike Scotland and her birth town within sight of Balmoral Castle. A harsh, unfinished country, she decided. At the first possible opportunity she would leave it and be on a ship going back across the seaways to the beckoning Highlands.

But Isabella never went home. Family history says her mind was changed one Sunday while she sat in the little Congregational Church and listened to a sermon preached by Thomas Quinton Stow.

Looking at his congregation on that long-ago Sunday the Reverend Mr Stow told them they were the pathfinders who must go before and prepare the way for those who would come after. On your labours, he said, rests the promise of tomorrow.

He was eloquent and persuasive, and Isabella's mood changed from discouragement to one of high purpose. One by one she shook the dreams of homecoming from her mind, turned her back on the Highlands, and faced squarely into the new land. Here she was and here she would stay and, come what may, with the help of God she would see it through. Amen.

Then, fortified and uplifted, she stepped out from the little building on to the path she would follow in the land of her adoption.

Dreams can sometimes be a long time dying, and the regions of high purpose are heady heights for a woman's everyday walking.

Isabella was probably homesick over and over again, but a bit of Scotland entered her life and gave her company and support. James Sim from the hills near Aberdeen arrived in Adelaide in 1847 and met Isabella at the home of her sister, Mrs Croy.

Family records tell that James set aside each week something from his minute wage as a Scottish shepherd to buy farthing dips so that he could study Latin and algebra at night. He married Isabella on his Australian wage of 10s. a week, and in four years, with the help of his thrifty wife, had bought and paid for a four-roomed house.

The gold-rush fever reached Adelaide and infected James, who determined to try his luck on the fields. There was no money to buy transport by ship or waggon; James, like many another, trudged overland across the Grampians to Ballarat.

He turned up no bonanza on the diggings, but he did come back with enough in his pack to buy a holding of some three hundred acres at Sandy Creek, five miles from Gawler, and a bit over to load a bullock waggon with food and a few essentials for life and living in undeveloped country.

At Sandy Creek Isabella hung her baby Anne in a tree out of harm's way, and worked with her husband to clear the thick scrub. It does not require much prescience to guess the holding would have a Scottish name. It was called 'Balmoral'.[3]

A mud hut roofed with rushes from the creek was the first home. Flour bags, carefully washed, were tacked over the window frames and ceilings to keep out wind and weather. When those on the ceiling rippled and shook, the family knew that yet another snake was slithering above them.

Bullocks hauled the household water casks up from the gully. Sometimes a thirsty calf licked the cork out of the bunghole, and down to the creek again went the patient beasts for another load.

Isabella made butter and walked into Gawler to sell it—barefooted for the first part of the journey, but on Gawler hill she would sit and put on her precious boots brought along so that she might keep her Scotch pride and come shod into town. Her produce sold, she made a few purchases, not many for the land was hungry and every penny saved went to feed it. Then she climbed back up Gawler hill, stopped at the top to take off her boots, and return home as she had started out, with bare feet.

'Perhaps a lark rising from a golden field, or the young green of growing corn, or the yellow glory of a furze patch on the back road to

Gawler helped that beauty-loving soul over the long miles of road', writes her grand-daughter,[4] looking down the years with love and pride at the trudging figure of Isabella Sim.

Six daughters and two sons were born to Isabella and James, and one by one became part of the unit working Balmoral. Anne, the eldest, was five years old when she first took the cows to graze. Day after day she stayed on guard, her only playthings through the long hours a handful of pebbles or a bunch of wildflowers. Helen, the youngest, enjoyed being shepherd when her turn came. It gave plenty of time to read, she said, lying with her head in the shade and her feet in the sun while the sheep grazed.

Life was not all work and no play for the children of the pathfinders. The bush and gullies were their playground, Yatta Creek burbling by on its way to join the South Para was their paddling pool. The seasons added colour and variety to the setting: blue and yellow broom, bush orchids, pink and purple heath, wild lilac twined round tree trunks, full-grown gums and slender saplings showing pink, mauve and yellow (who ever called the gum monotonous?), sheoaks feathery and mournful, wattle signalling spring's coming, brown clay almost purple in winter.

The children absorbed bush lore as they wandered and played. No need to tell them the reason when bird song hushed and the valley stilled. Their eyes instinctively looked up to the dark shape etched against the blue sky, a sparrowhawk hovering for the strike.

Harvest time meant flashing sickles and reapers in the fields and the scent of hay newly mowed. One of the girls always rode out through the heat of midday (side saddle, of course), a basket of food in one hand and a billy in the other. Too bad for Helen the day her horse shied at a large black snake on the way; she landed on the ground close beside it. The snake vanished, no bones were broken, and the only casualty was the reapers' meal.

Finches darted about the garden and bushland, grey gallahs flew over the paddocks with a flash of rosy breasts, and Isabella moved into a large new home that replaced the little thatched cottage where she had washed flourbags to cover the windows.

The children grew up and found paths that led away from Sandy Creek. Helen was the first teacher at Copperhouse, near Burra. She drove to a later appointment at Barossa one winter's night with Yatta Creek running a banker, the road under water, and the horse plunging and rearing as she guided it between boulders swept on to the path by the flood. Her niece, Miss Anne Hoffmeister, remembers visiting her aunt's little three-roomed cottage of wattle daub close to Barossa schoolhouse, and waking to the sound of cattle bells on the ranges above Barossa Valley.

Jean, another of Isabella's daughters, surprised the family by the path she chose to follow. She was an early Salvationist and served her first stint of duty in the red lamp area of Adelaide. When Silverton mushroomed, Captain Jean moved into that 'canvas town of no sanitation, little water, flies, dust and heat'. Inevitably typhoid broke out, and Captain Jean found herself caring for sick bodies as well as souls. She went down with the disease herself, but recovered and lived to marry and return to the pastoral life she had left to become a second-generation pathfinder.

Long before this, harvesters with their sickles left the fields of 'Balmoral' for the last time, the horse-propelled reaper took their place, and tanks succeeded the water casks filled at the creek for household needs. Isabella died at fifty-four. She had lived to see prosperity come along the path she helped to blaze, the path which led to a new Balmoral, far from the Highlands she renounced one Sunday in the little church of Stow.

Threshing by hand

14

Where the Red Cedar Grew

COAL AT NEWCASTLE (New South Wales), and convicts — men and women — to work it. The Hunter Valley open to settlement in 1824, and the settlers duly arriving, to live in small, earthen-floored huts, or in houses of stone quarried out of the valley cliffs.

Segenhoe, still standing on the flats near Scone, was one of the early ones. Crops were growing, sheep grazing, and the first mistress taking her baths in milk, it was said, when explorers Cunningham and Mitchell made the valley a base for the push north and west of north.

But not all settlers had assigned servants to fetch and carry, quarry and build fine houses, or wait on a well-spread table. In 1830 Commissioner Parry went through the district and reported:

> Nothing in the shape of description can possibly convey any adequate idea of the state of dirty wretchedness and want of comfort in which they (the settlers) live for several of their first years. Mr. Graham's father kept his hunters in England; they now live in a miserable slab hut of their own building, open to admit wind and rain, in most parts; badly thatched with reeds (of which the colour is not to be seen within for the smoke and dirt with which it is covered). No floor; the fireplace a recess made with slabs; their beds a sort of cot slung with bullock hide to the rough rafters, and everything giving the idea of filth and wretchedness. They wait entirely upon themselves, chop their wood, boil their kettle wash their cups and pannicans, plough, reap and everything else themselves.[1]

Another family he found 'in a worse hut than Graham's', although the wife was 'Colonel —'s sister, a woman accustomed in Scotland, I understand, to all the elegancies and comforts of life'.

The distress of the Commissioner might have been less could he have seen those unfortunates in later years when hard work and endurance of 'inelegancies' had won them, not a small plot of land, but a large station, or even several runs in the land which Cunningham and Mitchell found further on, where the flocks and herds found rich grazing on land watered by the northern rivers where the mighty cedars grew and the timber cutters worked.

Mary McMaugh might have told him, for she knew the Upper Macleay and the people and features of its early phases: 'wild' blacks, squatters, cutters at work in the rain forest, and the cedar logs floating downstream to the river's mouth.

A seventy-two-day voyage brought Mary to the colony in 1849 to wed Jack Vaughan, grazier, of the Kempsey district. A small coastal vessel took her to Port Macquarie (its arrival announced by 'a salute from a field piece'), and there Mary married her Jack 'in a round stone edifice which served as a fort as well as a church'.

From Kempsey the young couple rode home on horseback along tracks that 'would take no other kind of transport', Mary revelling in the novelty of bush flowers, kangaroos, and her first billy tea drunk at the midday halt by a mountain creek. The night was spent at a station on the way, where Mary received advice on colonial housewifery, bathed next morning in the station's creek, and ate a hearty breakfast before they set out towards 'a never-ending range of mountains—great piles and pinnacles . . . blue and purple in the far distance. A quiet dreamy charm surrounded them and seemed to beckon us towards them'.[2]

Dingoes slunk away at their approach from the carcase of a dead brumby, then the track mounted steeply; 'with difficulty I kept my seat, and all conversation was to me impossible. I clung to my saddle and horse's mane, expecting every minute to slip back over his tail.'[3]

Down into the valley, across the ford and they were at Myall Station—giant figs, winding river and the mountains rising behind. Cattle dogs rushed noisily to greet them, and station hands in clean moleskins and 'the inevitable Crimean shirt and cabbage tree hats' welcomed Mary home.

She slid smoothly and happily into the waters of colonizing. When her husband died, Mary, a widow with nine children, capably carried on the station with the help of her sons, until it was time for them to seek fortune on their own account. Then the place was sold and Mary, left with memories of the busy days she had spent in the country of the great cedars, wrote her account of station life as she knew it from the days when she came ashore at Port Macquarie to marry her bearded Australian bushman.

Into her story come descriptions of perils by fire and water, which the children of the pioneers know only too well.

The Drought Breaks

After a very severe dry season, when bush fires raged all round, and cattle were perishing for want of grass—and wild apple and oak trees had to be constantly chopped down for food to keep the poor starving stock alive—we welcomed the signs of a coming thunder storm, hoping it meant a break up of the drought. . . . Rain set in gradually, and continued till all the creeks were running bank high, and the river came down like a torrent, sweeping all before it. In the low places cattle were surrounded with the rushing waters.

It was dreadful to hear the poor creatures lowing in distress. As the water rose and submerged the land to which they were clinging, they would try to swim. But the logs and branches of trees rushing past in the force of the water so bewildered them that there was no escape. Some were caught in the branches of trees, and drowned there. When the waters receded their carcases would remain suspended forty or fifty feet above the earth.

The flood did not do us much harm, as most of our cattle were on high ground. Lower down the river (settlers) fared worse, owing to the land being flat and swampy. Many were washed away with their houses, some clinging to the roofs and floating timber. One woman was swept into the branches of a large tree to which she clung, and remained there for two days and a night—her cries for help being drowned by the roar of the water. She was exposed to continual rain and surrounded by hundreds of crawling things that had lodged in the tree for safety, while the force of the water pushing against the tree made it shake and tremble. Her position was truly appalling, and when rescued by the boats that had been sent out for the purpose, she was in such a pitiable condition that for some time her life was despaired of.

Mary McMaugh, 'The Days of Yore'.

Loss by Fire

The season has been . . . very dry and my husband in consequence started a large mob of cattle away for the Maitland market. The distance overland was four hundred miles, and he could only accompany them part of the way and then leave them in charge of a trustworthy man, and return home. He had been gone about a fortnight when, after a close, sultry night, we were awakened by the smell of burning timber. We soon found that the kitchen, a detached building, was in flames. Calling my young sons and the men employed about the place to help me, we did all we could to save the house. My eldest boys fought valiantly against the heat and smoke and endeavoured to spread wet blankets over the roof, but the weight was too much for their strength. The wind rose and blew the flames towards them, so, with scorched faces and blistered hands, they gave up in despair, and came to my assistance to save what we could from the house, while there was time—but the fire spread so rapidly, fanned by the strong wind, that a few clothes, valuable papers, and a little food was all we secured. The store room held two years' supply of necessaries, with a good stock of ammunition, guns, saddlery, etc. When the flames reached here the explosion was terrible and shook the very earth on which we stood. The fire was carried for yards right across the river, setting alight to the grass and bushes on the other side. My eldest son had a pet monkey chained up at the rear of the building. At the risk of his life, when he remembered his pet, he rushed through the burning grass, etc., and rescued the poor animal, and held it, singed and almost frightened to death, in his arms.

As I stood gazing at what was once a happy and comfortable home, now fast being reduced to ashes, my poor children homeless, myself alone and unprotected with a young child in my arms, my heart for the first time in my life failed me, and for some time I hardly knew what I did and wept bitterly. But my children gathered round me and for their sakes I collected my strength and began to look round for shelter.

The horse stable was in a strong, comfortable building and, being some distance from the house, had escaped the fire. With the man's assistance we made it as comfortable as possible with the few things we had rescued from the fire. The food supply was the worst—but with vegetables, young corn, wild honey and the small quantity of flour we had, we managed to subsist till my husband returned. A few days later I stood sadly by his side as we gazed on the ruins of our happy home, and felt at a loss for words to express my sorrow and regret that such a sad catastrophe should have happened in his absence. He comforted me by saying that he was thankful that we all escaped unhurt, and was very proud of the presence of mind in rescuing as much as I did, and acting so bravely. As to the boys, they were real little men to show such courage in such a trying time, and they should have brand new saddles apiece to reward them for being such a comfort to their mother.

No time was lost in sending for supplies and in a few months' time a new home was built a short distance from the site of the old one. Before the rainy season set in we were comfortably housed once more.

Mary McMaugh, 'The Days of Yore'.

A picnic on the Snowy

Hat made from the Cabbage Tree Palm, worn by early settlers.

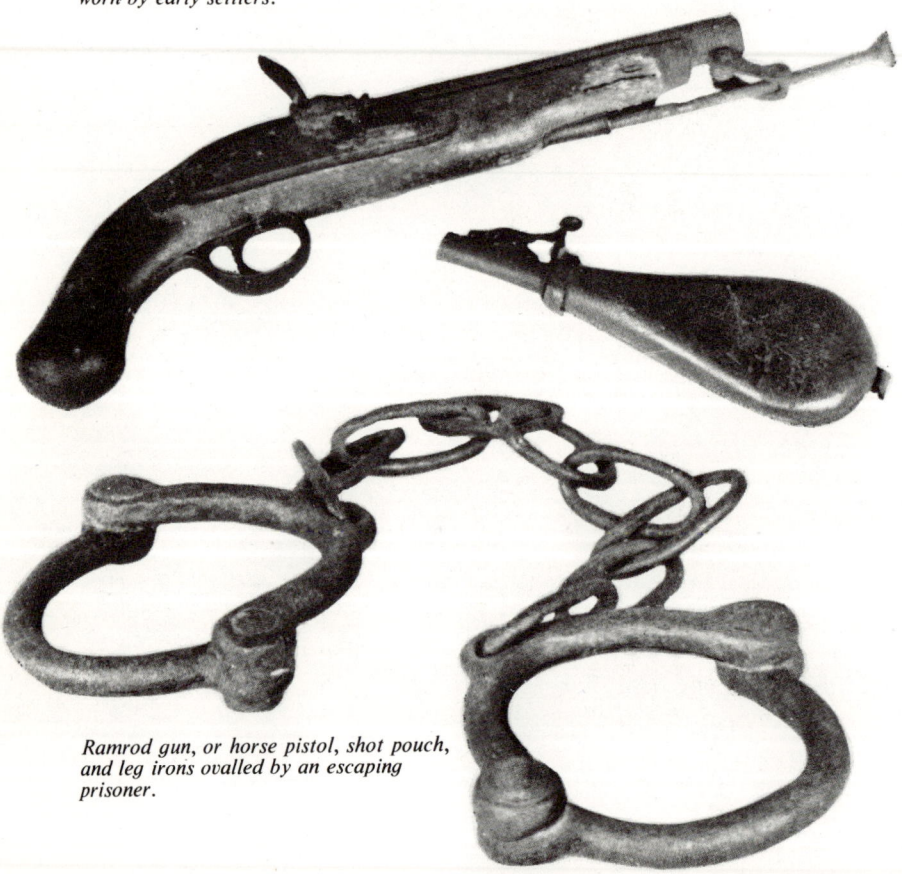

Ramrod gun, or horse pistol, shot pouch, and leg irons ovalled by an escaping prisoner.

15

Pioneer on the Move

IN 1891, the year before she turned eighty, Louisa Anne Meredith was on the high seas between London and Tasmania, with the manuscript of her last book tucked in her travelling trunk, an exploit she describes as one 'of less wisdom than valour'. That was probably a modest concession to public opinion of her day. No one who has read of her jaunting around the colonies will believe for a moment that she doubted her own capacity to see the voyage and its purpose through to the end.

By strictly applied standards, Louisa Anne was no pioneer. She arrived on the second wave of settlement in the wake of her husband's family, and found their enterprise an established fact at Cambria in the Great Swan Port District, where they had sheep, cattle and horses, grew wheat, and had at one time a whaling station on nearby islands.

But Louisa came very close to the early days and saw what may be called the second phase of colonizing, observing it so vividly that she seems to have made her several journeys through the colonies clutching her sketch book in one hand and clinging with the other to the carriage as it bumped over the roads and tracks she describes as 'colonial and therefore execrably bad'.

Louisa Anne was born into the Twamley family of Birmingham in 1812, and published her first book when she was twenty-three—*Poems by Louisa Anne Twamley with Original Illustrations, Drawn and Etched by the Authoress*—written between sessions of miniature painting. What is more, she was interested in the newly-born

Chartist movement and wrote articles on it for the local paper which, it is said, influenced a young man named Henry Parkes. All this in pre-Victorian England when young ladies were not expected to understand politics, much less voice opinions about them. Definitely a young woman of mental stature was Miss Louisa Anne Twamley of Birmingham.

In 1838, when she was twenty-six, she married her cousin, Charles Meredith from Australia, then visiting England, and sailed with him to Sydney.

A quick trip—it took only three months—and at the end of it Louisa Anne was glad to walk again on firm earth instead of a tilting deck, eat from a plate which stayed where it was placed, and set down her glass without first looking for the safety tray to hold it steady.

From Sydney, Louisa Anne made her first overland journey in the colony—a trip across the mountains to Bathurst. She was not impressed by 'Major Mitchell's road', considered he could have selected much easier grades, and found the scenery wild and monotonous.

She was disappointed in Bathurst. It looked dry, yellow and quite unlike the tales she had been told of the rich, western plains. She saw it during drought, when meat was lean and corn and hay scarce. There were no vegetables, butter or milk, and the heat was very trying to Louisa, now pregnant.

With relief she returned to Sydney, to a house at Homebush above the Parramatta River. Here Louisa heard the haunting cry of the curlew and became acquainted with 'possums. The household water was brought daily from two or three clay pits which were also used by the cows and horses.

Louisa had her first baby at Homebush, and spent her first colonial Christmas there. This she could not treat seriously: bright sunshine instead of snow, and flowering shrubs in place of holly were not her idea of a Yuletide setting.

In April the family departed for Great Swan Port, Tasmania, and Louisa left New South Wales with few regrets. True, there was her garden (Louisa was a garden-maker of skill and imagination) and New South Wales had certain advantages (an excellent library, for instance, which she missed in Tasmania), but to offset these there were 'dust, flies, mosquitoes and other detestabilities'. The mother colony was very clearly not Louisa's spiritual home, but it had served its purpose in her life: it broke her in to colonial living and it gave her material for her first book about Australia, *Notes and Sketches of New South Wales*.

The second of her colonial voyages, the trip to Hobarton, was made in a small schooner which sailed at half rig, made her seasick, supplied woodlice in the cabin and 'dirty water dropped through the chinks of the deck planks on to the bed'.

Mutton birds dipping and diving round the ship were entertaining, but a storm at night terrified her as she thought of the iron-bound coast so close at sunset. The ship made Storm Bay on the wings of a gale which carried the mainsail and topmasts overboard. But the wind soon dropped, the heavy fog lifted and there was Hobarton,

> on . . . the noble Derwent, with green meadows, gardens and cultivated land around it, interspersed with pleasant country residences and farms; and above and beyond all, the snowy mountain peaks soaring to the very clouds.

Louisa, in fact, fell in love with Tasmania, the snug little island tucked under the bosom of Australia like a joey in its pouch. She wrote ecstatically of the

> cool breezy climate, . . . the cool moist greenness everywhere, . . . the little gardens before and between houses . . . with their bushes of geraniums . . . Sweet English spring flowers looking happy and healthy, the stout, rosy children that everywhere remind me of Home.[1]

And the hawthorn hedges brought joy to her heart. 'They were the most English and therefore the most beautiful things I saw there.'

She stayed at Newtown, 'where many of the wealthiest merchants, government officers and professional men have tasteful residences', she visited Government House and observed Lady Franklin's uphill fight against apathy towards art, science and literature.

But soon Louisa was embarked on her next colonial journey: to her father-in-law's house on Great Swan Port, at the head of Oyster Bay, riding in a 'broad, stout colonial-built conveyance, an ingenious variety of the big species, with a seat behind for the servant'.

Designed to take the stress and strain of colonial roads, it was put to the test almost at once. The family was scarcely out of Hobarton when Louisa took the baby on her own knee in case the nursemaid, terrified by the severe jolting, should drop the child.

A halt in the afternoon gave Louisa a chance to describe 'Sticker-up' cookery—orthodoxly, kangaroo divided nicely into neat cutlets, spitted on a double-ended stick rammed into the ground close to the fire, a piece of bacon fastened on the end dropping fat on the leaner steaks as they cooked. This time there was no kangaroo in the provision baskets, and the party used ham as 'sticker-up'.

Baskets repacked and stowed away, the carriage bumped and

swayed on, over deep, loose sand, stones and rocks where the horses could only go at walking pace, and were often steered into the uncleared bush to bypass a tree fallen across the track. Sometimes the passengers alighted and went on foot to relieve the load. To Louisa the way with its obstacles became a constant source of wonder.

> Sometimes the banks (of the gullies) were so precipitous that I could with difficulty descend one side and scramble up the other on foot. How the carriage was lowered down and dragged up again, I cannot divine.

At some of the pinches the descent was braked by a rope tied to the back. Sometimes ropes fixed to the sides were all that prevented the carriage from toppling down the cliff.

It was rugged, lonely country. In two days' travel Louisa saw only a couple of shepherds with their dogs. Then came marshy land,

> all splashy with water and alive with unimaginable legions of frogs ... inhospitable country used for nothing but sheep runs ... mountains, hills, valleys and ravines—all are wild and trackless as they were thousands of years ago, except where a rude fence of brushwood indicates the boundary line of different properties, or the narrow thread of a sheep path winds away amidst fallen trees and spreading reedy tussocks.

Mountains fringed the Swan Port district, and the way over Sugar Loaf rose so steeply from the trout stream at its foot that Louisa preferred to walk. High up the hill a bridge ('little more than a network of holes') gave a view of valleys and hills. The untamed gums marching up and down the slopes had an eerie quality for Louisa. 'Like a Walpurgis dancing party', she said.

The road went up and over the crest of the hill, and a very steep track led down the other side. Commented Louisa: 'We young country folks never take the mean middle courses and go sneaking round a hill half way down; if a thing is to be done, we do it manfully, in the most difficult possible manner.' Too exhausted to walk, Louisa made the down road in the carriage 'crouched on the foot rug, clasping the baby with one arm, whilst I held tightly on with the other, not daring to glance ... at the abyss below'.

But terror and discomfort did not prevent her being aware of the wide sweep of Oyster Bay, Maria Island and the Schoutens lying offshore, and the Pacific stretching broadly beyond.

By evening they reached an inn on little Swan Port—distance covered in eleven hours' travelling just eighteen miles. Dinner was toast, mutton chops, eggs, fried ham, 'a mighty teapot ... and a comely mountain of home-baked bread' with English bottled ale. It was served in their bedroom, with the bed as a sideboard, the table in turn washstand, dressing table, dining place, and finally, padded with cloaks and shawls, a bed for the baby.

Next day's journey was along the sea coast, with backward views of the bush and forward and side views of the surf. In the bright waters of Oyster Bay Meredith pointed out the rocks he had known as a boy, where he had seen seals come sleepily from the sea to meet and mate, and the great bulls rear and roar in battle.

Louisa walked, or rather stumbled over sharp stones, rocks and fallen trees on Rocky Hills. She felt safer on foot than in the carriage, but admitted to a sense of inferiority when she encountered a settler's wife jogging calmly over one particular bad stretch on an old white horse, a baby on one arm, another before her, and many bundles hanging from the pommel.

The Merediths rested a while on a fine sandy beach, sitting on huge whale bones, bleached white by sun and weather. More rugged hills, the little settlement of Swansea at their foot, then another stretch of bush, the ford over the Meredith River and they had arrived at Cambria, the large, well-built, cheerful-looking house of Meredith Senior, with its flowers and fields, barns and stables.

After the strenuous journey Louisa found pleasure in resting on the verandah and gazing past the roses and jasmines embracing its pillars to the hawthorn hedges and gorse in flower, sheep, cattle and horses grazing in the rich pastures, the distant road where bullock and horse teams went by, and an occasional gig or jaunting car took settlers to shop at Swansea.

Sometimes a merry cavalcade of family and friends set off to picnic on the beach, some riding, other in an open cart spread with straw, the children in poke bonnets and the ladies supported and protected by cushions, shawls, cloaks and parasols.

Louisa delighted in the shore and the waves washing the cliffs, now gently, now breaking into soaring jets of spray. She collected sponges, seaweeds and shells, a hobby which interested her for years and brought her recognition both in Van Diemen's Land and overseas. She became fond of sea-bathing, and when the hottest days made a trip to the beach a burden she used the family swimming pool, 'a snug bath, built near the house, over a nook of the sea water creek, sufficiently deep to afford a good plunge'.

Swimsuits? She doesn't mention them.

Louisa sketched the shore and the trees, wrote up the diamond bird ('a tiny, flitting fairy'), the robin whose crimson breast seemed brighter than his cousin's under England's weaker sun, the blue cap (wren) with his coat cut from the same velvet as the robin, the seabirds, gulls, redbills, gannets and the stately blue crane. But, most of all, she admired the black swans on the lake near the house, which came at a call to be fed, and flew overhead at evening, their cry 'like . . . music from the clouds that framed their flight in the dusk'.

An excursion to the Schoutens, with silver fish darting through a translucent sea, giant starfish and shells to hold her absorbed, and a view of the Pacific for drama—Louisa uttered no word of homesickness and contentedly adopted the pattern of Tasmanian life.

Pioneering? Well, perhaps not, but it is an attractive picture made by a woman who, in place of the intellectual world she had left, with no Bush Book Service to bring her the contact of minds in other centres, found a substitute and stimulus in observing and extending her knowledge of the natural life and background of the developing colony.

These sea-scented years went into Louisa's books. They saw her first experiences of colonial housewifery when Charles Meredith acquired 1,200 acres north of Cambria and moved his family to a temporary home there. For Louisa this meant supervising the store room, distributing rations to servants and workmen, keeping accounts of all the nails, glue, oil, paint and material used on the farm, and coping with the convict women servants, who were, she said, 'of a far lower grade than the men'.

Louisa, busy indoors, still had time to report outdoor activities where men cleared, ploughed and sowed, while others quarried stone for the new homestead (outer walls twenty inches thick, inner ones eighteen) and burnt shells for lime. Trees were felled (often bringing a plea from Louisa that their life be spared), saws ripped them into lengths and carts jolted them to the building site. Then it was spring, and Louisa recorded the sheep and cattle 'feeding in the deep, long, green grass of the marshes, and the pretty little soft white lambs stepping about'. So different from the dry parched ground of Homebush and Bathurst, commented Louisa with relief.

Summer passed, another child was born, and Louisa sketched native flowers and trees and kept up her hobbies. Small coasting vessels plying between Swan Port and Hobarton took farm produce to town, brought back supplies. Their comings and goings were events of importance. High adventure was supplied by numerous snakes which appeared anywhere at any time: under a chair while the baby was crawling about the floor, in the courtyard where an

Above: The Australian kitchen, from an early edition of Mrs Beeton.
Below: The colonial kitchen, a modern re-creation.

Left: Receptacle with cone-shaped recess which fitted over a candle to heat a nightcap quickly.

Right: Simple lantern: candle shielded by glass.

Middle right: Old-time wick trimmer, used to prevent candle wick from smoking.

Below left: This well-used mould made a dozen candles at a time—a boon in an age when candle-making was a never-ending job.

Below right: The slush lamp was a simple lighting device: a piece of cloth used as a wick in a tin or mug of melted fat.

Above: Milk setting dish, a familiar part of every household. A ladle skimmed cream when milk cooled.

Right: Wooden butter keg with heavy copper bindings. Used to store or transport butter to market. A forerunner of today's cream can.

Below: Butter churn. Separated cream was placed in this through top opening. The handle turned paddles inside the churn and beat buttermilk from the cream.

Right: Dripstones of hollow sandstone stood in many early homes, with a basin below to catch the purified water.

Below: The heavy charcoal-burning iron was hot to use, in spite of the steam-escape hole.

Below right: The iron with removable handle was more often used. Heated on top of the stove, its rounded points were supposed to make goffering easier.

Right: The Colonial Stove of yesterday's bush homes. Cooking was done on the camp oven principle.

Above: Camp or Dutch Oven. Set in a bed of coals with more around and on top.

Left: Frying pan with handle 3′ 6″ long, for use on open fire, helped prevent burns.

Right: Tinder box complete with tinder. Flint struck on iron or stone made the spark to ignite this.

Cast iron pots or skillets of the camp oven family

Nardoo stones used by Aboriginal women to grind grass seeds into coarse 'flour'. Moistened with water, this was made into Nardoo cakes and baked lightly in hot ashes.

English-born nursemaid, carrying the child in her arms, tried to pick one up, thinking it an eel escaped from the cook.

Tales of fatal snakebite were only less numerous than accounts of savage attacks by aborigines on early pioneers. Louisa could not understand why the original inhabitants of the island should oppose the white settlers who, she said, only wanted to farm and depasture their flocks. She genuinely thought the natives were unreasonable.

The homestead, Riversdale, was finished, moving day arrived, and goods and chattels went off, the piano—well padded with bags of straw—on a dray drawn by six bullocks. Declared Louisa:

> The very carts and drays as they started off, loaded with the heterogeneous contents of our abode, had, in my eyes, quite a cheerful and jaunty air as they went nodding along; and the promiscuous arrangement of chair and table legs looked as if they could scarcely be restrained from dancing on the spot.

They were followed by 'the children, the mamma, the nurse and the cat . . . tied up in a bag', to begin unpacking, hammering, scrubbing and polishing in the new home. The garden and lawns were laid out and Louisa 'with strong gloves on . . . enjoyed lending a hand'. She had the children, 'chickens, ducks and turkeys to rear, butter, cream, cheese and other country comforts to make; calves to pet, mushrooms to seek and convert into ketchup'. So the days went by, with visits to the fields to see the wheat and oats growing, to cast an eye on the turnips and potatoes, and take long rambling walks or rides when old Don, the pointer, might start up a brush kangaroo.

Written for the overseas reader, Mrs Meredith's books are full of Australiana, facts about its native people and wild life. The appearance and habits of the aborigine vaguely revolted her, and she voiced the common judgment of her day that the dark women were nothing but slaves. Bandicoots, echidnas (porcupine to Louisa), wombats and the rest were much more interesting. For a time the family had a pet 'possum, a bundle of mischief that scampered on tables and shelves each night in the sitting room, wreaking havoc as it went. A favourite trick was to hitch its tail to the handle of Louisa's workbasket, and tumble the contents on the floor. During a heavy thunderstorm it was discovered asleep, curled up inside a top hat. Unpredictable but endearing, it was quite a character in the household. It escaped through an open door one night and never returned.

Louisa worried greatly at mustering time ('collecting the cattle' she termed it), and was always relieved when the men returned from rounding up strays in the ranges. Shearing took place in December. The sheep were first washed in the current of the Swan River, then sheared in the stables, where hurdles made temporary pens and yards.

After shearing, the reapers moved in with gleaming sickles to gather the harvest, and 'portly stacks' were set up.

Bushfires were fatiguing campaigns waged sometimes for days by every able man on the property. Then Louisa, as a good bush wife, supplied the weary fire-fighters with food, tea and cool cider made from apples grown in her own orchards, and processed on the farm.

Riversdale garden was in full bloom when rains flooded the river, and brought a raging, roaring torrent through the trim beds. Two menservants and their wives, washed out of the cottage they shared, spent the rainy night perched in a tree, one woman holding her baby, the other a cat.

Another mighty storm ripped thatch from the barn roof, exposed the threshed corn to the weather, stripped hay stacks, damaged pigsties and cowsheds, brought down fences and laid low the cornfield.

But the storm passed, the damage was repaired and life moved once more in its ordered cycle—the children, the dairy, the sewing and mending, riding and sketching. Trout, blackfish and fine bream were caught in the river. Bushrangers were reported in the district, but the household never saw them.

The picture has the quality of a pastoral idyll, but now enters the bad fairy, Misfortune. The price of wheat fell sharply, Meredith's affairs in New South Wales suffered through what Louisa indignantly called 'the unprincipled conduct' of an agent, and the family was thrown into financial difficulties. Leaving Riversdale in charge of an overseer, Meredith took a salaried post as police magistrate at Port Sorrell, a hundred and fifty miles away. He left immediately to arrange accommodation, and Louisa found the long winter evenings tedious with the children asleep, no Charles to talk to, and floods keeping 'the post' late.

During the day she packed and despatched the furniture, a few cases at a time, by bullock team to the coaster which would take them to Port Sorrell. Gradually the rooms emptied. When the baby's cot went, he was put to sleep in a drawer; when drawers left, he slept in a clothes basket.

Meredith returned to take his family overland in a jaunting car of his own invention. They forded the river, climbed the mountains, crossed bogs, mudholes and quagmires; spent the night at a settler's house, and drove the next day through a valley of snug farms and cottages. Beyond that was more rough country, and everyone walked while the carriage was taken up and down a steep gully. Sometimes Louisa and the servant built a footbridge of logs, or placed steppingstones in brooks or creek. The carriage plunged into a 'horrible black morass . . . a sable sea of something like bird-lime' which reached almost to the shafts, but the next stretch, though rough and rocky, was reassuringly firm.

Tasmania's snow-clad Ben Lomond towered over plains where they saw nothing but wild birds and a few scattered sheep.

They stayed at a lonely inn, crossed 'some unpleasant creeks and water courses' next morning, and by noon were on a broad metalled road. Twenty-four hours later they had passed 'sheepruns, farms, pleasure grounds . . . and Ben Lomond lifting his snowy head above all the eastward scenery', to the flourishing town of Perth.

At Carrick Louisa stopped to sketch an early mill because it looked so old: everything else in the country was raw and new, she said, nostalgic for her own mellow land.

Cloaks, shawls and furs came out for the next stretch. Boggy roads, swept by wind from the snow ridges, brought them to an inn where George, their son, slept on a pillow stuffed with mutton bird feathers and was 'very odorous' as a result.

It rained next day, and Louisa, now riding, 'jumped' her horse over a flooded creek while the maid edged her way along a fence that ran through the stream.

Avenue Plain was under water, and led into the bush. There were long detours round fallen trees, and even the fire lit for the midday halt could not brighten or cheer the cold, damp, dark scene.

The car jolted, bumped and splashed over logs, rocks, 'lagunes' and bogs. The sun set and horses arrived for all the party. They rode through the dark, among gaunt, bare trees to the cold little house shut in by the forest where they spent the next few months. Louisa kept fires going in every room and complained the furniture was 'maimed, wounded and disfigured for life' by the careless handling of an intoxicated crew on the coastal vessel.

Louisa was appalled by the poverty of the district, the wretched huts and hovels of the 'cockatooers' working land bought dearly or rented highly, trying to clear the densely-packed trees and existing on as near to nothing as she had seen in the colony.

The winter at Port Sorrell was one of almost incessant rain. Each day Meredith mounted his horse from the verandah to avoid the mud and slush which surrounded the cottage. But Louisa had something to look forward to: they were building a house near the sea.

She paid a visit to Hobarton to stay with the Lieutenant-Governor and his wife. 'A neat little vessel' took herself and the children to Launceston, a coach carried them to Hobarton—one hundred and twenty miles in sixteen hours. Louisa had one complaint. 'The fearfully fast driving was the chief drawback' and prevented full enjoyment of the journey.

Two or three months of city junketings—regattas, balls, dinners, parties and picnics—and she was back in Launceston in January 1846. Westerly winds prevented the Port Sorrell boat from berthing, so the party took the rough overland track. Miles of bush and swamp led to the uphill road over Badgers Head. Menservants carried the children, Louisa clambered and climbed, and at last the ocean and beaches looping away east and west were spread before them.

Next morning they reached Poyston, the new house, unfinished but snug and warm even if candles would not stay alight in the house when nor'-easterlies blew in from the sea.

There were goats for milk and meat, stables and barnyards, and bees busy about the hives at Poyston. Vessels putting into port gave life and interest to the ocean view, and Louisa had her garden; shells and marine life to study by the sea; dragon flies, frogs and birds to sketch and classify on land.

She pretended no regret, however, when Meredith resigned his post and the family, its servants, furniture, dogs, bees and favourite fowls were packed aboard the coastal steamer bound for Swan Port. The children were seasick, so was their nurse 'and nothing but the most resolute determination saved me from . . . the same fate', observed Mrs Meredith. But the wind was too strong, the vessel put back to port, and the family took the mail coach to Campbell Town. From there a weary, three-day journey by spring cart brought them to Riversdale, very dilapidated and needing attention. Louisa busied herself with garden-making, additions were built on the house, and soon all was well in the blacksmith's forge, the mill and the barn. Doves cooed in the dovecote, 'portly porkers' grunted in their sties, bees buzzed among the flowers, the dairy cows took their leisurely way among the rich pasture and Louisa's 'Island Home' was restored to order.

*   *   *

Some years later Mrs Meredith rode again over The Tier (the range of hills near Riversdale) with her husband and young son to visit Melbourne and the diggings at Ballarat.

In gaslit Melbourne Louisa found more art and literature than she had known since leaving England, but her trip to the goldfields by Cobb & Co. coach exhausted her, and she thought the diggings depressing. 'Dreary, sleepy plains' had no interest for her, even plains from which some men wrested fabulous fortunes. Their efforts looked, she said, like so many attempts to turn the earth inside out.

But the bumps and hazards she endured gave her copy for another book, *Over the Straits*, the last of her travel reportings.

* * *

Back in her island home, Louisa Anne Meredith wrote, sketched and led a full and busy life for many years. At eighty she contributed to the *Australasian* a well-marshalled case against the plays of Henrik Ibsen. By that time she had half a century of colonial living and many achievements behind her. Books for children, drawings of marine life (she discovered several species of east coast seaweed, and some of her coloured drawings of Tasmanian fish are now in the Hobart Museum); nights of light and laughter at Government House when she bowed to the audience as actor, author and producer. The gardens she built around the homes she made, journeys over the rough roads and tracks of early Tasmania, her children, her husband, her busy housewifely days—a rich hoard of memories they made. But possibly her thoughts turned most often to Riversdale, her island home, where the cattle stood deep in pasture, the bees raided her flowers, doves called in the cote and the breeze came in from the bay carrying the salty tang of the Pacific.

Louisa Anne Meredith has been described as a woman of physical and mental strength. If she appears to have done her pioneering from a cushioned seat, it is possible that as a woman of character she glossed over the knocks of fate, and as a writer and artist showed only to the public what she deemed fitting and interesting, leaving behind a picture of one who went pioneering with dash and style.

16

Home at Worlds' End

IN 1832 explorer Oxley, back from the north, reported a new river: the Brisbane, flowing into Moreton Bay. The following year convicts sentenced for offences committed after arrival in the colony were moved to the new area and began clearing the region which afterwards became Brisbane.

At first government edict forbade settlement within fifty miles of the penal camp, but fifteen years later pressure from settlers moving north on the tracks of the explorers forced a change of policy. In 1839 prisoners came out of the Moreton Bay district and settlers went in.

* * *

Two of the earliest were the McConnel brothers, David and John, who established a prosperous run at Cressbrook on the Brisbane River shortly after its proclamation.

After eight or nine years, David returned to Scotland and found himself a wife. Mary McLeod was young, only eighteen at her wedding in Edinburgh, and her parents consented to her marrying David only on condition that she was not taken to 'faraway Australia'. But when letters from his brother made it clear that affairs in Australia needed his presence, David prepared to return, and Mary went with him, although 'he honourably left me free to go or stay', she wrote later.[1]

In December 1848, on a cold night of high wind, the McConnels sailed in *Chasely*, 'not A1, but considered quite good enough to go to the Antipodes'.

Most of the passengers were bedded in the cuddy or saloon, but the McConnels had a large cabin in the stern which they furnished with a chest of drawers, table, folding washstand, 'a well-filled bookshelf', a sofa which opened into a double bed at night, two swinging candle lamps, comfortable chairs and a carpet.

David kept a terrier in the cabin to cope with a major shipboard pest—the rats. But the dog was hopelessly outclassed, and Mary ate all meals with her feet tucked up on her chair. She reports a bout between the mother of the ship's doctor and a large rat which climbed on to her supper table and made for the cheese. 'There was quite a tussle, but the old lady came off victorious.'

The McConnels shipped poultry and sheep to ensure fresh meat on the voyage. The livestock, except one sheep, were washed overboard in a storm soon after sailing; after that the menu was salt beef and pork covered with bristles, bread heavy and dark, and ship's biscuits 'old and musty'. Vegetables, milk and butter scarcely appeared once port was left behind, and three pints of fresh water a person a day had to meet all needs except baths, for which salt water was drawn from the sea.

The voyage passed pleasantly enough. Passengers gathered daily on the poop; Mary had her needlework, someone played the harp, or David told about the country they were going to pioneer. Mary helped give daily lessons to the ship's children and Scripture classes on Sundays, while the ship sailed down the map, across the Southern Ocean, and came in five months to Moreton Bay. Said Mary: 'It seemed to me we had come to the end of the known world.'

Her heart fell further when she landed with her 'traps' near the present Customs House jetty to be asked in astonishment by a young woman resident: 'What will you do with all those things?' 'I'll require them when I travel', replied Mary. To the further query, 'And where will you travel?' Mary could find no answer.

A room in Brisbane's only hotel without handle, lock or bolt on the door, and no blind at the window (Mary could not spare the one towel to hang there) was too much to endure, and David took over two rooms his brother John kept in George Street.

Mary found the table appointments appalling: 'cups without handles, steel forks with missing prongs, no apology for the absence of cruets, no glass, only pannikins, and oh! if only they had been a little brighter!' The cooking was bad, but the food was unsalted and fresh. 'Flying cockroaches' appeared at dusk from behind the chest of drawers, and smelt even worse than the animal skins John collected and kept in arsenic-strewn casks in the room.

As soon as possible the McConnels moved again, to a small rented cottage on the south of Kangaroo Point. Its weatherboard walls were unlined and its shingled roof leaked during rain and required an assorted line of jugs, basins and pitchers to collect the drips. There was a narrow kitchen, sitting and bedroom for Mary and David, small back room for the 'married couple', and an even smaller upstairs room for Mary's maid, Hannah. No scarcity of domestic help, but how in that confined space did they work without bumping?

Most of the furniture brought from home was stored in a shed, but the wedding-gift piano was kept in the house. Placed against the door between sitting room and verandah, it completely blocked the front door and all visitors came through the kitchen.

But in spite of all inconveniences, Mary recorded: 'How happy we were in that rough little place!'

While their permanent home was being built at Toogoolawah (now Bulimba), David and Mary visited Cressbrook, travelling in the Albert phaeton brought from England, its springs reinforced with green hide to take the hazards of the road.

Rowdy little wayside inns housed the McConnels at night, along with noisy crews of teamsters whose dray tracks were the only paths through the bush. Mary closed her eyes and prayed at 'impossible-looking gullies', walked to relieve the horses at the steeper pinches, and clung to the side of the phaeton as it zig-zagged its way around trees fallen across the track.

She found time to enjoy the wattle-scented air, but used her favourite adjective to describe the bush in general: it was 'a dreary place'. When her husband bade her welcome to Cressbrook as they crossed its boundary she thought he was joking, she could see 'neither white man nor black . . . nor hoof of stock'. But soon they were greeted by cheering stockmen who unharnessed the horses and pulled the carriage to the homestead—'a pretty, neat cottage', with a grapevine walk, a flourishing garden, and a great banyan tree planted years before by David.

Mary poured tea from an enormous tin teapot 'that I think held at least eight quarts; it took two hands to lift it,' into large cups and saucers patterned with fiddlers, bagpipe players and dancers. Sugar was 'as near black as could be', and the fat lamp smelt horribly, but gave a fairly good light.

It was shearing time at Cressbrook and preliminary wool-washing was in full swing. Bleating sheep were driven into the river, lathered with soap, scrubbed, rinsed, then turned out to dry on a grassy clearing—a study in green and white. Clicking shears went to work, men called, sheep injured by an inexperienced hand protested plaintively, and the fleece piled up in the large shed. It was a long way from the quiet Victorian household less than a year behind the girl who had been Mary McLeod.

Mary tried her hand at interior decorating. She had the carpenter turn a large box into an ottoman, and candle boxes into stools. Then with Hannah's help she upholstered the ottoman and an old sofa in grey unbleached linen found in a corner of the storeroom. The stools she covered with crimson silk handkerchiefs which she found in David's clothes chest.

But the empty vastness of the 'interior' awed Mary, and she returned to Brisbane with relief. The first wing of the new, white, freestone house was finished, and Mary insisted they move at once. A curtain down the centre of the large living-room gave them sleeping and eating quarters while the rest of the house grew around them.

Mosquitoes bred in the nearby swamp in 'intolerable' numbers. To escape them, Mary often tucked herself on her bed under the nets to sew, read or write.

Immigrant ships swinging into Moreton Bay supplied the McConnels with gardener, farm manager and dairy hand whose wives and daughters were nurses to Mary's babies, looked after the large poultry yard, and helped with the milking.

McConnel bought and sold land (at special rates to his own people) and Mary records 'a busy time—clearing, draining, ploughing, planting and everything growing like mushrooms in the virgin soil' with 'my good husband the centre of all'.

There was always Sunday School for the children of the employees, and whenever possible a minister was brought across the river to conduct a service. The farm bell rang to signal his arrival on the opposite bank, and the workers' families streamed out of their little homes to gather at the homestead.

A strange experience befell Mary in her beautiful white house. David had planted pineapples and the crop was so prolific that Mary decided to make jam for friends back home. Working all day in the storeroom, she pulped and set in earthenware jars pound upon pound of the tropical fruit, and went to bed thoroughly tired.

But about one in the morning she awoke to find herself standing on the floor of her room. 'I rubbed my eyes,' she said, 'and wondered how I came there.' Something impelled her to enter the nursery where her children slept, but everything there seemed quiet and still. Moonlight spilled over the river and into the room. Perhaps it shone too strongly on Harry's cot. Mary went to draw the curtain—and

The station billabong

found the child in the throes of convulsions. Thankful then for Mrs Hamilton Macarthur's advice given in her first days in the colony, that a household should always have hot water ready for an emergency, Mary had the child in a steaming bath in a matter of minutes. Gradually he grew less rigid, and then—up came the pineapple pulp he had been taking by handfuls all day, unnoticed by his preoccupied elders. Unnoticed? It was the days before Freud, and there was no one to tell Mary what her subconscious mind had absorbed while her hands and energy were busy elsewhere.

The episode passed, day followed day contentedly, and life seemed fair in the white house at Bulimba. It was not to last. A 'tightness' behind Mary's knee did not respond to treatment. The family tried a change of air at Cressbrook, but Mary grew worse. One night a 'gangrene wound' was discovered on her leg. In a few hours the family was on the way back to Brisbane—four days in incessant rain with the country a swamp and the phaeton held back in places by ropes. Near Ipswich there was nothing for it but to take Mary out of the carriage and lower it down a steep, muddy bank, while she slid down as best she could.

The puzzled Brisbane doctor could give no relief. Mary went from one fainting fit to another, growing gradually weaker as she lay on a couch while the scent of hay and the sound of the German farm servants singing in the fields floated in through the windows. In desperation David hired a river steamer, had Mary's bed carried on board, and took her to a German doctor at Ipswich. He thought the case hopeless and refused it. The McConnels pleaded, he yielded—and suggested amputation.

When a horrified Mary said she would rather die, he shrugged and began treatment—liquid caustic poured over the leg twice daily. Mary felt no pain; her leg was quite numb. She lay all day in the open air on a Chinese lounge fitted with wheels, ate little but 'bread dipped in champagne and herb tea made by the doctor', and the weeks passed. Then one day during treatment she felt 'a little red hot cinder . . . rolling down my leg'.

It was the caustic, the leg was healing, and Mary steadily improved. Even the death of her baby son did not retard her recovery. She accepted the loss with pious resignation and eventually moved about on crutches. When she suggested a high heel on her shoe would give her greater mobility, her doctor said: 'You are young and you shall compel your leg to get straight.' Sound psychology. Within eighteen months Mary walked as well as ever.

Today's physicians would diagnose Mary's illness as an infection, and might treat it by the methods which cured her: rest and good

Home at World's End

nursing. But Mary's own doctor declared the climate of Moreton Bay the cause of the trouble, so David sold the beautiful white house, left Cressbrook in his brother's care, and took his family to England.

Seven years there and on the continent, and four more children for the family (only three survived), then David's interests recalled him to Australia. Mary's English doctor declared her perfectly healthy and able to accompany him, so in 1862 the family was back in Moreton Bay, now separated from New South Wales and greatly changed. In some ways it was better, said Mary, but she still found the country crude and unfinished.

To the children everything was new and exciting—the slow journey to Cressbrook over rough roads, walking to relieve the horses, camping at Sandy Creek (now Esk), the women and children sleeping in dogcart and phaeton, the men round the fire, its flickering flames making the bush shadows darker and the far-off howl of the dingo more melancholy.

Splitters, sawyers, carpenters, builders and bricklayers moved on Cressbrook to alter and add to the little cottage until it could house the larger family comfortably.

Years later it was described by Mary's daughter, another Mary,[2] who coming as a child to the colony adopted it whole-heartedly in a way her mother never could. She tells of the river fronting the house, the long line of hills beyond—blue by day, purple at dusk—covered by tall pines and scrub. She speaks of the giant eucalypt near the homestead, the banyan tree planted long ago by David, the chain of lagoons that joined the creek edged with dark trees, its water falling lower down into the river. Gold-centred lilies rested on the surface of the lagoons, and a platypus sunbaked his furry back in the creek.

> Behind the house lay the outbuildings, stables for the horses and the pure-bred stock, barns for the hay and corncobs, sheds for the ploughs, a school house, a store where a morning and midday bell was rung, a blacksmith's forge and a little row of wooden houses ('the huts') where the stockmen, the ploughmen and the blacksmith and an old Irish carpenter lived with their wives and children.[3]

This was home to the children, and here Mary the elder gave her time and energy to the welfare of her family and employees. A 'female teacher' provided with rooms, food, firewood and £100 a year to which each pupil paid sixpence a week, taught school where 'the little girls learnt to sew very neatly and make samplers'. (Where are they now, those little specimens of patient stitching?) The men had a library and reading room with pens, ink, blotter on the cedar table, a kerosene lamp to light it, and a fire during the winter.

Sunday School at 10 a.m. was followed by a service, David reading prayers and a sermon unless a minister was available. Mary the younger, delighted with the adventure of the occasions, said: 'Nurse curled my hair . . . for these events. I was decked with gay ribands and wore a crinoline, which was extremely difficult to control when I knelt.'

Household life centred round the verandah shaded with green cane blinds from Java or Japan. There

> peaches were stoned for jam, oranges peeled for marmalade, and quinces were carefully pared and cored for jelly. There was a wide table where the many kerosene lamps were washed and trimmed every morning, and set ready to be carried to their respective rooms at night. There was the indispensable treadle sewing machine, and in a cool corner, in a draught, stood a filter with a tap and tin pannikin, and near it a large porous water jug swathed in damp flannel for evaporation.[4]

In the dairy pans were set for cream, and butter (long in coming when the weather was hot) duly churned. There were usually visitors in the house, and travellers from the Upper Brisbane or the Burnett made the house their first stage on the way to town.

For a time the station employed Kanakas who lived in small cottages with fenced gardens. Mary the elder taught them to read, bought them copy books, and slates, and copies of the Gospels written in their own language: 'In winter we had school at night . . . in summer at 5 a.m. on the verandah.' Their copies and sums she set the night before with David's help.

The children's lessons still left them plenty of time to visit the yards, watch camp drafting, or sit on the fence while a buyer purchased stock. They saw the working bullocks take off for town with hides and tallow, they visited the itinerant hawker's team to buy sweetmeats, jew's harps or hair ribands, and knew the leathery smell that was part of branding time.

Sometimes mother and daughter visited shepherds' wives in their small huts some miles from the homestead. They had few visitors, and were grateful for the magazine or book Mrs McConnel always took them. In return they served boiled eggs and home-made jam for tea. Young Mary enjoyed these visits. Although 'the little phaeton in which we drove creaked its reproaches as we jolted over ruts and stones', there were frequent halts to gather wildflowers, purple sarsaparilla, small white jasmine and dog violets beside the bush tracks.

Shearing was followed by the Shearing Shed Dance, opened with a quadrille, followed by sets of lancers, polkas and country dances, with a caller to 'instruct us when to set partners and swing'. Occasionally an Irishman obliged with a jig, and Mr and Mrs McConnel's piano duets were an indispensable part of the entertainment.

The elder Mary's character and authority were deeply respected by her family. 'My mother was equal to any emergency and never lost her presence of mind,' reports her daughter, and instances an occasion when a party from the household went bathing in the river. One of the maids lost her footing in a deep pool, and Anne, the laundress, cried in panic: 'I can't help you. I can't help you.'

> My mother leapt into the water, her crinoline making a great splash, and called, 'Anne, Anne, you foolish woman, stand up and hold my hand at once,' This Anne did, her knees shaking under her, while my mother went to the edge of the pool, holding out her other hand to the sinking girl . . . We watched, awe-inspired . . . It seemed as if the end of all things had come when my mother, the ruler of the house, upholder of seemliness and order, was seen making her way through the river, a wide wake following her, her shady garden hat still on her head, her crinoline only half-submerged and moving up and down with each step forward.[5]

It goes without saying that she brought the girl safely to shore.

In 1873 the family bought a town house: Witton Manor, six miles up river from Brisbane, where they lived when not at Cressbrook.

Immigrants were still flocking into the new colony. 'How hard they worked!' commented the older Mary. They felled trees and cut slabs to build small houses. Wives took their place at the end of a cross-cut saw and kept fires going to burn out the roots of fallen trees. Until the hut was ready, families lived in tents lent by the government. Children soon learned to be useful, did chores and looked after younger ones. The climate favoured outdoor life, but Mary was often called on to help sick women and children. She used a household medicine book plus her own sense and experience. When these failed, a stockman was sent at the gallop for the doctor. But a serious case meant a patient travelling over rough roads in a springless cart, often a long wait in town for examination, then back to the tent which served as home. The mortality among children under these conditions distressed Mary. She rallied sympathizers, and made representations to 'all in the colony we could reach, personally or by letter'. The concerted effort brought about the founding of Brisbane's Children's Hospital in 1878, to the great satisfaction of Mary McLeod McConnel.

The younger Mary delighted in the life at Cressbrook. She loved the garden and gravelled walks leading to the house, the croquet lawn with 'its wide hoops and still wider crinolines of the players spread bravely on the grass'; the yellow jasmine, lilac Duranta and white spiraes, the wistaria sprawling over the woodshed and dairy, the hedge of pink baby roses

> which we plucked to arrange with violets for evening buttonholes. My parents, our governess and various visitors played when the day had grown cool, crinolines swept the lawn, balls rolled briskly from the mallets, contending voices argued the points of the game.

Often she climbed to the loft above the hall to look over the horse paddock and see travellers arriving, hear whips cracking, horses champing at the bit, buggies rolling in. Then darkness closed over the lagoon, stars blinked in the sky, and through the stillness of the bush a mopoke called. No wonder that in the evening of her own life the younger Mary's homing thought should fly to the river which her mother had once called 'the end of the world', and remember with gladness her youth at Cressbrook, for there life had been full and interesting, at once energetic and gracious.

1867 saw the rush for gold at Gympie, Queensland. Housing went from canvas to bark humpies and, later, homes built of shingles.

Margaret Cockburn (afterwards Mrs Robert Gibson) was nine when she walked with her mother and brother and a group going to join their menfolk on the diggings. One evening on the way salt meat was cooking over the camp fire when Margaret picked up from a dray a dark block-shaped object, and tossed it at a friend. It missed and ended in the cooking pot where it bubbled away unnoticed. Dinner was served—and thrown away. Margaret's 'block' had thoroughly flavoured the beef. It was a cake of soap covered with dirt and grease.

Rewritten from *Gympie in the Cradle Days*,
85th anniversary publication (1952).

17
Mary of Maranoa

THEY RUN A PLANE service now in south-western Queensland above the land where the first settlers' waggons rolled.

Like as not, if you go that way they will point out the town of Roma and talk about its oranges. The first time I heard these mentioned I thought of a girl, tight-bodiced and full-skirted, who galloped her horse over the place a hundred years ago. No streets or houses there then, no oranges. I wondered what Mary McManus would think of the prosperous town today, Mary who saw the first oranges grow there, who rode over the district before there was any thought of a township, when there was a spring in the grass and a give in the turf which goes when settlement comes.

Mary was the daughter of Stephen Spencer of Iron Bark Station, near Barraba, New South Wales. When she was fourteen and her brother eleven, her father led his wife and family, his herds and household effects into what was then the wilderness, to Mount Abundance Station, the new land he had purchased west of the Darling Downs.

To the Spencer children the exodus spelt excitement and adventure. To their father it was a considered risk which enterprise, hard work and fair seasons could turn into good fortune. To their mother —here we can only guess. Mary gave only an occasional glimpse of her mother when she wrote her account of the early days of Maranoa.[1] 'I fear my dear mother did not enjoy the trip or her stay very much, although she murmured not,' was one comment. It gives the impression that the pioneering life and existence far from friends and amenities would not have been the personal choice of Stephen Spencer's wife.

It was the era of Victoria, when order and seemliness were no idle words stitched on a sampler, but the desirable basis of living. To women reared in such tradition, the untidy nature of pioneering must have been anathema, so if they enjoyed the strenuous life and raw beginnings less than their daughters, if their hearts and minds yearned often for a gentler, more settled life, praise them higher, for they gave up more. It takes character to cope with life when duty rather than excitement is the sustaining force.

* * *

It was March 1858 when Mrs Spencer climbed into the spring cart with her children by her side, settled her skirts and faced the four-hundred-mile trek to the new home.

Four bullock drays carried food, clothes and household goods. Thirteen men helped Stephen Spencer drive the thousand head of cattle and sixty horses which went with the family into the wilderness.

They travelled at the pace the beasts walked, and the long, slow journey took four months. Food and water were scarce in the first half of the trip, so the stock were often kept plodding through the night to the next watering place. Day after day the teams swayed and bumped their loads northward. Week after week the wheels of the spring cart turned and the bright eyes of Mary and her brother looked out on new scenes.

For most of the journey the party chose its own path over uncharted country. They had covered many long miles before they picked up and followed two old dray tracks that marked the path other men had taken through the wilderness.

On the few stations they passed only stockmen were living. One or two properties were completely deserted, and there the Spencers rested a while. The stock was spelled and clothes washed, while the children roamed and explored, or staged mock attacks in rooms with 'shooting holes' in the walls, proof that the tribes of the western districts did not take kindly to the loss of their hunting grounds.

Along the Balonne River the cattle fed fat, for here, says Mary, there was 'tall grass waving in the wind nearly over our heads like a field of wheat ready for reaping'. It was so tall that the bullocks were almost lost to sight as they drove through it, and everywhere wild carrots, crows' foot and native plants grew profusely.

Two drays capsized crossing the Balonne, so the party rested to repair the damage and dry out clothing and goods. About two hundred natives joined them when they set off again, and all went along together. A cavalcade of patriarchal white man with his herds, and stone age natives with spears and yam-sticks—what a subject for a mural on inland settlement! Eventually Stephen Spencer called a halt and the two groups parted, only twenty natives remaining to help with the white man's stock.

A bush fire had destroyed the previous head station of Mount Abundance on Muckadilla Creek, so while huts and stockyards were rebuilt, the family camped in a large tent and under tarpaulins which had covered the drays. The weather was so cold that water left in buckets overnight could be turned out solid next day.

Mary made her first damper—'by no means a success'—and helped with the chores of camp life. But Stephen Spencer had no mind to make this the site of the family homestead, and in a few weeks they moved to a more central position on Bungerworgorai Creek.

For six months they lived in two V-shaped bark humpies, twelve to fourteen feet long, six to eight feet wide and six feet high in the centre. 'All available space was filled with boxes and household effects, leaving a narrow gangway down the centre.' It was very crowded 'and the place was swarming with fleas . . . out of the bush'.

At Christmas time ('hot and steamy') thunder rumbled and rain fell every day, the creek ran a banker, and the ground turned to bog. Work on the homestead came to a standstill, since the horses and drays could not move to bring in the timber cut on the hills.

But in time the house was finished, and the family settled in. Spencer planted the first wheat, and grew grapes and figs. Mrs Spencer planted a rose tree which bloomed when spring came. The family was setting its mark on the new soil.

Many districts reported trouble between newcomers and the country's original inhabitants; attacks by natives and retaliation raids by settlers engendered fear and ill-will on both sides. At Mount Abundance Spencer laid down a few simple rules to cover his household's dealings with the natives. No black of either sex, said Mary, was permitted near the white's quarters after dark—a wise precaution, since much of the inter-racial trouble stemmed from white man-dark woman relations. The family treated the natives 'kindly but firmly', and expected the station staff to do the same. Arms were always kept ready, but were never used. An occasional company of native police (six or eight dark troopers under a white officer) called in on patrol, but was never required to restore or maintain order between white and black at Mount Abundance.

Meeting the mailman

How much this was due to mother and daughter is difficult to say, but the presence of white women on a station usually meant kindlier treatment of the natives, and higher standards of behaviour for the household generally. In the pioneering pattern, their role was not only helper, but civilizer.

The flocks which had walked from Barraba flourished at Maranoa. Shepherding, yarding, washing, shearing, consigning the clip by dray to Brisbane gave year-round occupation. Mary does not say whether she played any part in all this. Her duties included sewing (all by hand) and housework, with gins always on hand to make things easier.

The family were 'the most westerly residents in the State', and there were few passers-by.

> The country did indeed look lovely then before it became overstocked and hardened by constant tramping. The ground was soft and springy like English turf. Many a time as I have galloped over the downs I have felt the sward spring under my horse's hoofs like a sponge.

With separation from New South Wales, the pace of settlement quickened and grew feverish: 'Everyone was infatuated with the desire to possess a run in Queensland. The excitement was intense, and nearly equal to the gold rush seven or eight years before.' Mount Abundance, the 'farthest-out' station, the last place where supplies could be obtained, became a depot for men setting out into 'terra incognita'. The rush went on for some years—stirring times, says Mary, who lived in the heart of it.

> Our house was crowded with visitors. I have seen our dining table covered with maps and compasses. Many a time I have made . . . ten beds on the table and some under it. I have often seen as many as twenty riding-pack saddles and other . . . gear, tents and pack-bags lying on our verandah.

To Mary Spencer who had come as a young girl to this, her 'country', the unfolding of the land and the problems of settlement were of absorbing interest. Every facet of development affected her deeply. She mourned for the untouched land itself, for the clear streams and magnificent waterholes which natives said had never been dry in their lifetime, but which became sand drifts when white men stocked the country. She sympathized with the station owners without shepherds for their flocks. She wrote of McManus, whom she later married, bringing stock from Maitland, New South Wales, and shepherding 'by himself 10,000 sheep, using two horses a day and galloping all the time from sunrise to after dark'.

The lonely shepherd in his hut, visited only by the overseer and the man who brought the rations (often late); the enterprise of settlers coping with broken equipment, taking a fractured wheel in separate parts sixty miles on horseback and rolling the repaired unit the whole way back; land-seekers going singly or in groups to explore, discover and take up new country, racing back by roundabout routes to deceive a rival, waiting in the crowd outside the Land Commissioner's tent, were all part of the district's settlement. So were the natives. Mary declares roundly that the stations would never have survived without the help of their aboriginal stockmen and workers.

Population increased. 'Now two families were living not more than twenty miles from us, and we were beginning to get civilized.'

Travelling, however, was difficult, often dangerous, so the female part of the community seldom went visiting, or saw other women. When they did there was no doubt a mighty chatter and comparing of notes on current fashions: the wide crinolines they all wore, the small pork-pie hats, and the garibaldi jackets. Mary distrusted those crinolines, which must have been a menace in the limited space of pioneering homes. One caught alight when its wearer swung round close to the stove.

There was little variety in dress material. 'Brown holland was used for everything.' Streamers of different-coloured ribbons fell from hats almost to the feet; velvet neck ribbons joined the cascade. Hair was dressed over the ears, padded out at each side, with a huge bow behind adding long trails to the collection, down the back. Mary liked the style no better than a later one, when hair was stuffed into heavy chenille hair nets, black or coloured, 'some large enough to hold a cabbage'. When they hung to the waist, Mary thought them 'horrid things', and added: 'The state of one's dresses at the back need only be imagined.'

After the long, dry summers there was usually rain to flood the creeks, bog down drays from Ipswich, sometimes for months. Rations ran short more than once. 'Many stations were reduced to pigweed and fat hen, which grew plentifully everywhere, and was a good substitute for cabbage.'

Once Mount Abundance was a month without flour and down to its last two pounds of sugar. However, they had plenty of vege-

tables, including some outsize swedes, which Spencer shared freely with neighbours. Everyone agreed the most-missed item was salt.
There were other discomforts.

> Fever and agues were very prevalent then; nearly all of us had them ... Mosquitoes and sandflies were in swarms driving the horses frantic. Fires were made of manure and kept burning day and night to allow both ourselves and our horses to rest.

Flies were so bad that 'it was almost impossible to ride a horse with any comfort or to get him to stand still an instant to be saddled and mounted. Grasshoppers, too, were in clouds, myriads of them', and maddened horses reared and bolted when the insects whirred and flew in their faces.

At all times the horses, fed on rich grasses, were spirited and difficult to manage, but not too much for Mary. She rode everywhere and accompanied her father and the Government Surveyor when they went to choose a town site for the district. (The town was called Roma.) When her parents visited other properties Spencer took up, Mary rode all the way, wearing a heavy habit which swept the ground when she stood. On this journey her horse decided to lie down on a high sand ridge with Mary still on his back. She struggled free—'No easy matter with one's habit on'—scrambled to her feet, and used her whip to prevent the horse rolling on the saddle. Another time her horse bucked violently during a thunderstorm, 'but', says Mary unconcernedly, 'after a time he went quietly'.

In 1864, after seventeen days of almost non-stop rain, came the great flood. Carcases of thousands of sheep, horses and cattle floated on the swollen waters. Many shepherds and stockmen were drowned. Others stayed for days in trees or on roof tops, or floated to safety on trunks uprooted by the flood. Water lay around Mount Abundance for miles like a great sea. It was awe-inspiring and unforgettable.

Waterfowl benefited. They came in hundreds, built nests, hunted and dived in the water. Black swans drifted along, the males' scarlet heads turning from side to side; native companions trod quadrilles along the ridges, herons and wild duck dropped down from the skies to partake of Nature's lavish banquet.

Natives took refuge on the sand ridges, swimming through the flood, mothers carrying piccaninnies on their heads. One old gin found it beyond her strength. She drowned in the rushing waters.

The flood marooned shearers gathered to clip Spencer's flocks: 'The station was like a small township. Our house, too, was as full as it would hold with weatherbound travellers, no less than fourteen or fifteen extra sitting down to table every meal.'

One of the stranded was Mrs Dolman, of Ipswich, who had ridden out of inspect a property in the district. When the creek seemed 'crossable' she mounted her grey horse, Clarence (a big horse for a big woman) and set out with Mary to show the way.

At the creek's steep banks ('a positive quagmire') the horses floundered at every step. They plunged in, the water half way up the saddle flaps, and Clarence reared and struggled until Mary feared his rider would be thrown. But Mrs Dolman was a superb horsewoman and managed to ride the grey splendidly up the opposite bank.

At Cattle Creek Mary turned back. In mid-stream her horse swerved and almost lost its footing in deep water. Mary used whip and bridle vigorously and the mare bounded ahead to firm ground, but it was so near a swim, said Mary, that the pocket of the saddle was wet.

The flood receded and Stephen Spencer made an inspection of his properties. His wife and daughter travelled with him through the devastated land: 'thousands of tons of sand washed from the ridges on to the plains and into the river bed, filling up magnificent waterholes.'

The flood had submerged even the highest trees and dead beasts were everywhere: sheep, cattle and horses as well as kangaroos and other wild life—all victims of the floodwaters. Debris was piled high against trees and fences; large trees had been uprooted and lodged in the forks of others. But over the almost uncanny scene of desolation, covering grasses were springing up and wild flowers were blooming.

Several times the Spencers missed the track which had been obliterated by the trampling feet of passing flocks; thunderstorms caught them without shelter; the glare from ridges covered with fine white sand hurt their eyes. They travelled all day and sometimes far into the night, occasionally putting up at a homestead for a meal and a bed, but more often camping out. One stormy night the wind 'was so strong that it was all we could do to hold our tent from being blown away.' Once the Spencers shared a shearers' camp. Wives and families travelled with some of the men, sleeping at night under carts and drays.

The tour of inspection took three weeks. 'We were delighted to be once more at home, though on the whole it was rather a pleasant journey.' Four hundred miles there and back, over loose and unmade roads. No wonder 'the horses were very tired, and one was lame.'

So Mary's life ran through the busy years of Queensland's beginning, when men were absorbed in the search for runs, 'The forming of stations, the purchasing and driving of stock and great efforts and striving to secure these precious holdings.'

Station routine and the long miles kept them from their fellows, and few had wives to keep them company. Says Mary:

> The fact is there were so few marriageable girls in the district that there was no opportunity of indulging in the tender passions ... squatters and run hunters were too busy to spare the time to seek sweethearts and wives. Runs were all they sought after.

Women were few in those early days, but even in the farthest west and north some were making homes for husband, sons or brothers, softening the roughness of raw beginnings, sharing, encouraging, enduring all that pioneering meant.

Mary herself married McManus of Tyrconnel Downs, the same McManus who had shepherded his stock alone in the first days on his run. But Mary says nothing of their life together. When she sat down to write of her youth it was the busy days of settlement and land-hunting in Maranoa that she described. These and the comradeship between neighbours, often thirty and forty miles apart, and the help they gave each other in need were vivid in her mind, long after the spring had gone from the turf where she galloped her horse before the first orange grew in Roma.

Fashions for the Gentlemen

The men all wore great turbans ... on their hats called puggeries. Some were very large, some were twisted, some were pleated over the crown of the hat. Some wore plain book muslin, while the majority wore ... scarves with red or blue ends or long fringes hanging over the brim of the hat behind. Some hung down six or eight inches, some a greater length, in order to protect the nape of the neck from the sun. ... When too large they had a heavy and clumsy appearance, which strongly suggested the slang name for them, 'poultice'.

In winter heavy rugs were worn over the shoulders with a hole cut in the centre through which the head was thrust. ... They were very warm ... a good protection from the rain

. . . and often gaudily coloured and resembled the skins of the tiger or leopard or some other wild animals. They were called ponchos, and were introduced into the colonies by the Spanish gold diggers. . . . When wet they were very heavy and troublesome to dry.

Mary A. McManus, *Reminiscences of the Early Settlement in the Maranoa District.*

Settler's home, Queensland, at the turn of the century

18

Beyond the Nineteen Counties

FAR-RIDING land-seekers journeyed well beyond the areas of government control and roused official anger by their practice of taking up unsurveyed land for pastoral purposes.

Governor Darling tetchily called a halt. He drew a line around the surveyed portions of the map (the Nineteen Counties). Inside its borders, he declared, land could be bought and sold legitimately; outside the line it was illegal to take and use it.

But before the order went down on paper the Nineteen Counties were outdated, their boundaries pierced, and the tide of settlement flowed out north, south and west. It was the squatting age in motion and almost every area came to know the plodding hooves, the cracking whips and the shouted orders as the cavalcade of the land-hungry went by, seeking pastures and still more pastures.

The Shelley brothers found their way to Brombowlee and took up a tract of country watered by the Tumut. William, the elder brother, pressed on to seek other land; George, the younger, stayed. In 1835 he brought his bride, fairhaired Amelia Waddy, to a small slab hut and the lonely life of pioneering in the country where the rivers fill each spring with snow melted on the Monaro Range.

They were three years in the little cottage before they moved to a brick house on land between the Tumut and its tributary, Little River. Amelia's first son was born there one night with the floodwaters lapping over the verandah.

George, unwilling for Amelia to repeat her child-bearing under such conditions, moved the house uphill and added another wing. Over a hundred years later their grand-daughter, Mrs Florence Stacy, sat there to write the story of Amelia who saw the beginnings of the district where winter comes early and stays late, and the town of Tumut stands in a bower of trees.

Amelia was thirty-five when George died of typhoid while droving cattle to the Melbourne market. To rear and educate her eight children Amelia carried on the run in the same way as she brought up the family—with firmness and decision. Her affairs prospered, her family throve, and she left behind a reputation of good motherhood and first-class land management.

* * *

Eliza Dulhunty of Dubbo House was under forty when she found herself thrust into the same circumstances as Amelia Shelley.

Eliza was the daughter of Collector of Customs, Lieutenant-Colonel J. G. N. Gibbes, of Point Piper. Her marriage in 1837 to Robert Dulhunty had been the wedding of the season, held at St James' Church and performed by the Bishop of Australia.

Dulhunty's run was far inland—at Dubbo, taken up soon after Sturt went down the Macquarie in 1829. The station buildings of mud, logs and bark, staffed by assigned men bearing a broad arrow over a number tatooed on their arms, Robert considered no place for his bride. Eliza was installed at Claremont, Emu Plains, close enough to town for friends to drive out in their carriages and crinolines, for music and dancing in the cedar-lined rooms.

Robert moved between Emu Plains and Dubbo, keeping an eye on the stock, the clip and the house he was building. It was finished in 1847 and the family moved inland.

It must have taken several drays and conveyances to move seven children, servants, furniture, goods and chattels, provisions and livestock, but the only record of the journey spotlights Eliza's carriage, evidently the last word in fashionable transport. It was the first of its kind to cross the Blue Mountains, and was hauled up and down the steepest pinches on ropes. Presumably at these times Mrs Dulhunty proceeded in the traditional pioneering manner: she walked.

There was the usual self-contained community around Dubbo House: blacksmith, carpenter's and saddler's shops, yards, barns and quarters for the stockmen. Horses were scarce, and only the owner and head overseer rode about their duties. Wheat was grown for the family and workers. Every outstation had an iron handmill fastened to a central post to grind the grain. Wool was pressed in a hole in the ground, a tree lever or wooden spade was the mechanism for bale packing. Cowhides spread over stumps about two feet high dried in the shape of a cask. They were used to hold tallow. Two-wheeled drays with six bullocks apiece hauled station produce to Sydney and brought back supplies. A year on the road was not uncommon.

For several years the Dulhuntys of Dubbo House were the holders of the farthest frontiers. Robert died in 1853, and Eliza, only thirty-eight, was far from the fashions and entertainments of Point Piper. She remained on the run with her nine children, the eldest thirteen, but found it hard going. Dubbo township by-passed Dubbo House, workers drifted away, and the estate dwindled. The Dulhunty boys grew to manhood, sought their own pastures, and carried the family name as far afield as the Logan River and Dunedoo.

But Dubbo House passed from the family. Thirteen years after Robert's death it was sold to meet the mortgage, and Eliza spent her last days with her son John at Bathurst.

* * *

Sun, dust and long distances were established very early as the key words in Australian pioneering. But cold weather and snow also had their place on the canvas. Frost moved with the pioneers even in sub-tropical Queensland. It met the early settlers on the highlands of northern New South Wales and supplied a climate favourable to the elms, oaks, poplars and linden trees they planted. By the late 'thirties and 'forties landseekers arrived in the districts where winter paints Christmas card scenes in June. At first their households were exclusively male, but in 1845 John Everett wrote home:

> Within the last few years many ladies have ventured to try the bush life, and none I think regret the experiment; on each side of us, and far beyond us, petticoats are to be found, and pianos . . . considerably out of tune. I don't think drays and stony ranges improved musical instruments.[1]

Some of the petticoats belonged to Mesdames Charles and Matthew Marsh, whose families, by the second generation, had a ring of properties on the tablelands. Terrible Vale, the most central, was a long wooden homestead lined with plaster, its french windows shaded by cedar shutters.

Lucy, Lady Crofts, was one of its daughters, and remembers well the pattern of her growing days in the highlands: household bread from the baker's oven, sheep killed for the table hanging in a gauzed meat house, dishes of milk standing overnight in the dairy to be skimmed next day and churned for butter, lessons with the governess, rambles in the orchard, and riding.

Plumbing may have been limited, but an iron fountain and several huge kettles were always bubbling on an open fireplace. They supplied hot water for making tea, washing up, and for the hip baths taken in the bedrooms.

At jam-making time the children cut up fruit at a table set out of doors under a spreading tree. The copper preserving pans, brought from England, are still in use. The jam was stored in large earthenware crocks protected by paper pasted over the top.

Bushfires were uncommon in that district of plentiful rainfall, but one stands out dramatically. The seven small children of Terrible Vale clustered together awed and frightened as it swept close to the house. It was only checked after a stern fight lasting two days and nights. Half a century later Lady Crofts still remembered the children's distress when they saw the burnt skeletons of stock which had not escaped the flames.

Growing up in the highlands was full of pleasures: gay gatherings of young folk at Terrible Vale, riding to visit neighbouring properties with habit skirts frozen stiff in winter, the sound of horses trotting, buggy wheels rolling, the clop of balls on racquets, afternoon tea on the lawn on Saturday afternoons, dancing after the evening meal, each girl taking her turn at the piano, and the last waltz always over before midnight brought in the Sabbath.

A young Englishman often came to tennis parties at Terrible Vale. His grandfather, Matthew Marsh, owned Salisbury Court from 1845, and the families were related through their grandparents. Romance grew in the clear upland air, and in 1900 Lucy Taylor of Terrible Vale was married to Hugh Crofts at her parents' home.

Today the fifth generation lives in the old homestead established by the Marshes, one of the pastoral dynasties made by pioneers who shaped a new life in the district they nostalgically called New England.

To their descendants it has another connotation. To them it is simply home.

19
Homes South of the Murray

BETWEEN THE RIVER MURRAY and the coast which faces towards Antarctica there was no settlement or permanent home until well into the 1830s. Sealers, with aboriginal women brought either forcibly or voluntarily to help them, had rough quarters on a few islands off shore. Smoke seen by passing ships showed where native people camped, but white settlers' herds had not yet appeared on the ancient hunting grounds. Explorers reported rivers and watered lands below the Murray, but the government in Sydney turned a cold glance on all would-be settlers. Any more territory to police would be much too much; Port Phillip and its environs were placed firmly out of bounds and all requests for land refused.

But tides are difficult things to control, as a king named Canute once proved. In due time the tide of colonization broke over the square miles destined one day to be called Victoria, the State which was not planned, but, Topsy-like, 'growed' just the same.

Its first settlers came across the straits from Van Diemen's Land. The vanguard was the Henty brothers, already working their trim little settlement at Portland Bay when John Batman of Launceston made his famous real estate deal with the natives of Port Phillip area in 1835, paying over blankets, beads, flour, sugar and what not with all solemnity. John Fawkner and others trod hard on his heels, axes rang, ploughs were yoked, and on the Yarra a township was born.

Immigrant ships four months out from England disembarked at William's Town, but more numerous at first were overlanders from north of the Murray who followed the tracks of explorers Hume and Hovell, and the energetic Mitchell. Into 'Australia Felix', with its rivers and running streams, rolled the tilted drays, Australia's version of the covered waggon, coloured and exciting, though they lack a Hollywood to give them publicity.

Women? They were few, but there were some. Mrs Stephen Henty, for instance, was housekeeping at Portland Bay soon after Major Mitchell, to his great surprise, came on the pastoral-cum-whaling enterprise of the brothers from Van Diemen's Land.

Upcountry men came with flocks, but mostly without wife and family, treating the country, as Margaret Kiddle said, as a huge cattle camp.[1] They lived uncomfortably, according to Thomas Walker, who saw them in 1837.

> I think no class of people live in a rougher way than many of the settlers do here at present. Mr Mollison (his host) is erecting a hut, which will be well enough when finished, but in the meantime it is open and comfortless. No furniture has he, except a bench or stool, a broken cup or two, tin pannicans, a couple of knives and forks, and a plate or two. All he has to eat is Irish salted pork, damper, and tea and sugar, and the light we had was produced by burning rags in pieces of fat pork.[2]

He gives a different picture where women are present. He found another settler 'with his wife and daughter, very snugly placed, and with a comfortable and well-furnished cottage, quite a contrast to the other habitations'.[3]

On some future day movie cameras will turn their lenses on reconstructed versions of our pioneering past. There are paying lodes waiting them in many a homestead history. One ready-made for filmcraft is the trek of the Docker family from Clifton, New South Wales, where James Docker, clergyman of Windsor parish, left the church to turn farmer. Docker, disgusted with the untrustworthiness of his convict servants, determined to follow 'the Major's track' southward, 'taking like the patriarch Jacob, all his possessions'.[4]

One four-wheeled waggon, two bullock drays, a light cart and gig, horses and working bullocks carried the parents and six children, men and women servants, tents, food for the journey, clothes and belongings. A flock of almost three thousand sheep were part of the cavalcade which set out.

It was autumn 1838 when the waggon wheels began rolling from the Hawkesbury Valley; it was September before they came to rest at the place chosen for a new home. Ten-year-old Mary, the eldest daughter, kept a journal of the trek; the slow-pacing bullocks gave plenty of time for writing, twelve miles a day was the most they ever covered. At Yass all settlement ceased. From that point 'the only guide the party had was Major Mitchell's wheel tracks on his return trip from Portland Bay. One of the men went out ahead daily to note these tracks and act as scout for the rest of the company'.[5] As jam and other luxuries were soon used up, all shared the same diet—bread and mutton.

They were still north of the Murray when lambing time came and the party camped until it was over. Provisions ran short, so two men were sent to Port Phillip for flour. Flooded streams delayed them and it was ten weeks before they were back. The party was then down to its last bag of flour.

Snow waters from the Monaro Range were swelling the Murray (then called the Hume) and the ford was impassable. Mary Docker (later Mrs Read of Wangaratta) described how the party crossed to the other bank.

> My father had a long rope fastened to a tree and then sent two men across in the boat to secure the other end to a tree on the opposite side. He had a strong brush fence made on the farther bank, where there was a good landing place. Then, stowing away in the boat as many of the sheep as they could, the men worked the boat across by the rope hand over hand. When a few boat-loads were thus taken over, the sheep were secured in the brush yard at the landing place in view of the main flock. Then with a great deal of shouting, and with the help of some natives, the main flock was driven across with the loss of a few sheep only, which the blacks were allowed to have. The next undertaking was to get over the tilted carts. These were floated on a couple of empty casks and towed across, and a camp with the tents was made on the Victorian side. A heavy waggon and drays were a more serious difficulty, but the waggoner, 'Cranky Bill', had provided a scheme of his own. He proposed to place the empty casks beneath the heavy waggon, the drays being lashed behind, and with a team of four bullocks to attempt a crossing. We children stood on the bank eagerly watching the proceedings. As long as the water was shallow things went on very well, but as soon as they got into the stream the carts began turning over and over, then the waggon, Bill climbing up to the highest part. The poor bullocks were in great danger with their yokes and bows on. Fortunately the men in the boat with the aid of some black-fellows managed to get Bill and his cavalcade ashore with the loss of one bullock.
>
> My father and I walked ahead as far as Black Dog Creek, now Chiltern, and camped there . . . and next day we ascended a hill from which we saw the beautiful Bontherambo Plains in the dis-

tance, and my father determined to ride over and examine them when we should come nearer. Two days further brought us to the Ovens River . . .[6]

George Faithfull had taken up a run at Bontharambo, but abandoned it when natives killed some of his men. Docker determined to try the place and dare the danger. He never regretted his decision.

My father was glad to find a hut at Bontherambo, which he occupied with my mother and as many of the family as it could contain. I and some of the other children slept in the covered carts until father had the hut enlarged for a temporary residence.[7]

Mrs Docker was exhausted by the journey and took months to recover, but the children thrived.

In later years the first dwelling was replaced by a two-storied stone house with a tower. There the family grew up, crinolines billowed, guests were welcomed and music flowed, while outside the flocks roamed and increased. The cycle of life and the years went peacefully on in the country where the first little hut had stood.

This is the door of the first house—this little green door in the wall of the garden. There are the square-headed nails they used in those days—nails without points—and the mark of the adze that shaped the door. It belonged to the brick hut where they first lived, but that is gone now. The door is all that is left. There is a picture of the first hut on the dining-room wall. The tutor painted it. Yes, it has a brick chimney—they look dangerous, but they were often used . . . The girl in the blue dress is Mary. Yes, those wide skirts must have been awkward in the bush, but she probably wore a riding habit, with a long skirt, of course, but not as full. She was a great rider. Her side saddle is still . . . resting . . . on a beam in the huge stables . . . a beauty, sewn and quilted with fine craftsmanship.[8]

It belongs to the past now, like Mary who used it, her family who trekked from the Hawkesbury to the Ovens, and the waggons and tilted carts which brought them all to Bontharambo and the beautiful land of the plains.

20

Pastoral Partners

The squatters of Port Phillip were by no means confined to the male sex. The names of some very plucky women are to be found in the records as licensees in their own rights. Some of them were single women, some were widows who took up land, thinking to benefit their children, and many a woman carried on her husband's work after his death—caused perhaps by a falling tree, a riding accident, or a well-aimed thrust from a treacherous black.

R. V. Billis and A. S. Kenyon, *Pastures New*.

ON 1 MARCH 1841 Georgiana McCrae arrived off Williamstown with her children and her talents.[1] Three days later she went up the Yarra in 'a scrubbish grinding little steamer', sheltering her children from the rain under her plaid.

Melbourne's population at the time was between five and six thousand, Collins Street had no pavements, and was 'only a rough road, with crooked gutters—the shops built of wood, and raised on stumps.'[2]

Georgiana's first colonial home was Argyle Cottage, Little Lonsdale Street West. It had

> one tolerably large room, with four closets, *called* bedrooms, opening out of it. The walls of wood, about half an inch thick, and the ceiling of the same. The building raised on stumps to about two feet from the ground, and three wooden steps, like those of a bathing-machine, led up into a french window, which is the front door.[3]

The rental was £100 a year.

There Georgiana lived for about four years, went on foot to evening parties 'to which ladies walked in their husband's Welling-

Georgiana McCrae

tons over their dress shoes',[4] made tartan trousers for her sons, drew miniatures (but not for payment: her husband disapproved of a working wife) and saw the city increase in size before moving to her next home, fifteen miles from Captain Collins' landing place.

Her diaries, carefully annotated by her grandson, Hugh McCrae, give colourful pictures of the young city and its housekeeping problems.

Potatoes, never less than sixpence a pound, came from Van Diemen's Land, with carrots, turnips, and other vegetables. Small Victorian cabbages were ninepence each. Water from the Yarra was delivered to the door in large barrels carted by dray. It cost from seven to fifteen shillings and was barely a week's supply.

Georgiana's family often dined on pies from the baker. Beef-steak puddings cost 5s. each, pies of spur-winged plover shot in the swamp were 7s. Native turkeys, kangaroo tail and fish, occasionally mentioned in the diary, did not appear on the table so regularly.

In 1843 Georgiana was paying 'three ha'pence' a pound for beef and mutton, fourpence for veal and pork. The butcher delivered a side of mutton twice a week

> with a shin of beef for soup. The driver invariably added a sheep's head and pluck for the dogs, but Ellen prepared these Scots fashion for the master and allowed the dogs the leavings. The mutton was so fat, Ellen used to make candles for her own use and for the nursery of it. On Friday afternoons, troops of blackfellows and their gins used to assemble at the slaughter-houses to collect sheep's heads and plucks which they roasted at their fires by the Merri Creek (afterwards called Dight's Falls).[5]

Some of the mutton might have come from the run worked by two women partners. The elder, Ann Drysdale, forty-eight when she reached Australia, had capital and experience for the enterprise, while Caroline Newcombe, younger by twenty years and described as high-spirited, had drive and a gift for management. Both had what appears to our smug twentieth-century outlook, fed on the idea that woman's emancipation is of very recent origin, quite surprising backgrounds: Ann had farmed in Scotland on her own account, and Caroline grew up in Spain where she 'roughed it with her father in the Peninsular War'. The same reason, ill-health, brought them separately to Australia and the new settlement at Port Phillip. There they met, became friends, and conceived the idea of working their own run.

Boronggoop, their first property (there are other versions of the spelling), stood on the Barwon four miles south of Geelong, among the wattle, sheoaks and acacia 'scattered about like a nobleman's park'. It was praised by several visitors to the colony, including the much-travelled Dr Lang, for its groomed appearance and the contented and particularly well-cared-for look of its livestock.

The Misses Drysdale and Newcombe handled their venture with great competence. They rode astride, mustered and tended their stock, managed the servants, coped with natives and the many perils and problems of early squatting, and, it is said, could turn their hand to almost every kind of work required to run their property.

Their home was a model of neatness and comfort. 'Got a tolerably good piano,' wrote Ann Drysdale in her diary, 'nine American chairs, and the floor covered with Indian matting . . . The walls are covered with bagging whitewashed, and the wood painted.'[6] Glazed, latticed windows, a garden and one of the first gravelled paths in the country, pinpointed a snug, comfortable homestead and successful estate management.

When the township of Geelong was proclaimed, the run's licence was cancelled. The partners then established Coryule on Indented Head (1849) and ran that as efficiently as Boronggoop.

Ann died in 1853, leaving the run to Caroline, who remained in management until 1861. Then she married and, as a clergyman's wife, apparently went no more a-droving or stock-running. Her death in 1874 ended an intriguing episode, the story of two women's ability to take a portion of a raw world and shape it into a successful enterprise.

* * *

The discovery of gold brought consternation to the pastoral industry as shepherds left their flocks and stockmen abandoned their charges to follow Lady Luck to the diggings. But some graziers found a pool of labour right at home.

> It was in the early 'fifties when the excitement of the gold rushes was at its height that the women helped so splendidly to carry on the pastoral industry. All hired labour had left for the fields, and in those days the pastoralist was regarded as a lucky man who had a wife or a daughter to help him with his stock. James O'Malley Walshe, who held a large scope of country from Barwon Park running to Lake Connewarra, declared that had it not been for his daughter, then just a young girl, he would have been unable to continue.[7]

* * *

Swamp hens, spoonbills, sandpipers and wild ducks still nest along the shores of Lake Terang, but the lake, like the district around it, has seen many changes since the white men came.

The pastoralists made the district, the men who followed made the town of Terang. Mrs Elizabeth King was its first white child, born in the tent of Thomas Wheatley and Ellen his wife. The first house the family knew had kangaroo skins tacked over its glassless window frames. Domestic water was carried from Terang Lake and tipped into the water barrel at the back door. Local amenities increased, a town pump was installed, and household chores included a trip to the pump with buckets hung from a shoulder yoke. An enterprising tradesman gave the town its first water supply carted to the door at one and sixpence a barrel.

Large mobs of brolgas danced by the lakeside when Elizabeth was young, and kangaroos bounding and feeding were common.

Washday was an occasion. Elizabeth helped carry the family's clothes to the lake, where a busy crowd of women and children converged each week with scrub-boards and home-made soap. There was gossip and chatter as clothes were soaped and rinsed in the water, children played, and the natives came out of their mia-mias along the banks to join the entertainment.

The drag to Geelong was replaced by Cobb & Co.'s red coach with its four horses, the little town grew and the lakeside laundries ceased to function.

Elizabeth married John King, and in the years that followed saw the district opened up for selection, saw superphosphate and new fertilizers bring in another kind of pioneer, saw the cream separators come to farms to relieve the drudgery of those who worked long hours with the dairy herds.

Did mechanization take away as well as give something? Mrs Stan Coad of Blackwoods, Cobrico, thinks it did.

As the daughter of an early pioneering family (Thomas Cowley, a great-uncle, was a member of Sturt's inland expedition) she grew up in the district, and from childhood was responsible for so many cows on her parents' farm. She says the old ways gave one a special understanding of the animals. Any ailment was speedily apparent and effectively treated with time-tested remedies.

Marriage took Mrs Coad to a small property which, she declares, was mostly dry paddock. Child-bearing was only a slight pause in the hard routine necessary to put the farm on its feet. She was back at the bails when her daughter was only eleven days old. She drove a horse and dray with her year-old son lying across her knees while her husband shovelled out 'super' to feed the soil. The day's work began at 6 a.m. and stopped, but did not finish, at nine at night.

A heavy schedule, but it brought its reward: the small two-roomed house of the first hard years has given way to a comfortable, rough-cast cottage with modern amenities.

It is a prosperous district, this corner of south-east Australia, with the humps of the Otway Ranges standing clear inland on fine days, and farms fronting the lake about thirty miles away from the coast, lapped by the sea which brought the first-comers to the area.

The Shearer's Wife

Before the glare o' dawn I rise
To milk the sleepy cows, an' shake
The droving dust from tired eyes.
I set the rabbit traps, then bake
The children's bread.
There's hay to stook, an' beans to hoe,
Ferns to cut in the scrub below.
Women must work, when men must go
Shearing from shed to shed.

I patch an' darn, now evening comes,
An' tired I am with labour sore,
Tired o' the bush, the cows, the gums,
Tired, but must dree for long months more
What no tongue tells.
The moon is lonely in the sky,
The bush is lonely, an' lonely I
Stare down the track no horse draws nigh
An' start . . . at the cattle bells.

LOUIS ESSON

21

Observer in Blue Serge

CHALK THE YEAR 1851 large and round on the blackboard of Australian history, for this is the year of high water in the tide of pioneering. A fever broke over the young settlement, in the search for and discovery of gold, and a struggle that set back more than a few. The eaglehawk saw it beginning as he rode the winds above the mountain road—a long, moving trail on the hills Elizabeth Hawkins had crossed. It was the spearhead of the army of diggers rushing to the fields near Bathurst, where Hargreaves and his companions panned gold in the creeks. In a matter of weeks the yellow sorceress was working her magic, reaching into shops, homes and factories, on to farms, orchards and sheep runs. It radiated over the waves and drew men to Australia as surely as the power of the moon draws the tides to and fro across the world. It was a magic that lured shepherds from their sheep, and sailors from their ships.

> The road to Summer Hill Creek was literally alive with new-made miners, some armed with picks, others shouldering crowbars or shovels, and not a few were seen with wash basins or cullenders strung round their shoulders. Some had rushed from their homes provided only with a blanket, a damper and a pick or garden hoe . . . Perhaps the strangest party on the road was a group of women who went out to earn an honest living at the washtub.[1]

Gold—was it curse or blessing? The State of Victoria gambled on the latter and offered £200 reward for the first gold discovered south of the Murray. In a few months the reward was paid and the yellow goddess was enshrined on the Castlemaine and Ovens, and at the great fields of Ballarat and Bendigo.

It was a male world at first, and largely remained so until mechanical mining took over the fields. But gradually women appeared to share the tents and the little huts and help with the puddling and cradling. They found their way through the maze of claims, the unhygienic conditions of gutters and 'streets', going up hills and down gullies to shop at canvas stores distinguished by fluttering flags.

For some it meant hard work, disillusionment, loss of all they had owned, ill-health, even death. To others it was an adventure which ended successfully, or was its own reward. Mrs Charles Clacy, by her own account[2] we place in the second group with thanks for a piece of clear reporting on a setting where other women lived and worked.

Mrs Clacy came out from England with her brother (she was unmarried at the time), and seems to have looked on the whole affair as an adventure in navy serge. Her brother and his friends walked to the fields from Melbourne beside the dray where Mrs Clacy rode in state. The dray (it cost £20), drawn by two cart horses (£90 and £100 respectively), was laden to the axles with food, tents, camp ovens, cooking utensils, tin plates and pannikins, blankets and 'opossum skin rugs'. Mrs Clacy, walled in by tents and tent poles, leant against a bag of flour and used a large cheese as footstool. She wore 'common dark blue serge, a felt wide-awake and a waterproof' which she thought 'made a ludicrous assortment', but found her transport 'tolerably comfortable'.

The party camped out at night, avoiding inns and halting places where bushrangers operated. When it rained they built a fire inside a hollow tree and boiled or roasted eggs and made damper.

It was spring, with wattle (mimosa to Mrs Clacy) and wild flowers along the way. Mount Macedon beckoned across the plains where the only roads were tracks made by carts and drays. 'We crossed a swamp, now a rocky place, here a creek, there a hillock.' At one swollen creek the dray lurched and swayed so tipsily that one of the party pick-a-backed Mrs Clacy across.

At last Bendigo came into sight.

> Never shall I forget that scene, which well repaid a journey even of 16,000 miles. The trees had all been cut down; it looked like a sandy plain, or one vast unbroken succession of countless gravel pits . . . The earth was everywhere torn up . . . men's heads in every direction were bobbing up and down from their

holes ... The rattle of the cradle, as it swayed to and fro, the sound of the pick and shovel, the busy hum of many thousands, the innumerable tents, the stores with large flags hoisted above them, flags of every shape, colour and nature from the lion and unicorn of England to the Russian eagle, the strange yet picturesque costume of the diggers themselves, all contributed to render the scene novel in the extreme ... thousands of human beings engaged in digging, wheeling, carrying and washing, intermingled with no little grumbling, scolding and swearing.

The cost of living on the fields was the same as in Melbourne. Mrs Clacy quoted the price of meat as 4d. to 6d. a pound, and flour ('the most expensive article in housekeeping here') as 1s. 6d. Butter was very scarce, and when obtainable sold at 4s. a pound. The stores (large tents, either square or oblong) fascinated her. They stocked everything, from 'sugar candy to potted anchovies; from East Indian pickles to Bass' pale ale; from ankle jack boots to a pair of stays; from a baby's cap to a cradle; and every ... article for mining from a pick to a needle.' There was no attempt at order or arrangement in the stores:

> Here lies a pair of herrings dripping into a bag of sugar or a box of raisins; there a gay-looking bundle of ribbons beneath two tumblers, and a half-finished bottle of ale. Cheese and butter, bread and yellow soap, pork and currants, saddles and frocks, wide-awakes and blue serge shirts, green veils and shovels, baby linen and tallow candles all heaped indiscriminately together.

It was 'no joke to get ill at the diggings; doctors make you pay for it', said Mrs Clacy. 'Their fees are—for a consultation at their own tents, 10s.; for a visit out, from one to ten pounds, according to time and distance.' The common complaints of the diggers were sore eyes and dysentery brought on by the dust, flies and primitive sanitation of the goldfields.

The average digger's tent was a dreary place, said Mrs Clacy. The bedding usually lay on the floor and the only furniture was a table—a block of wood balanced on a box. There the digger ate his monotonous meals: mutton, damper and tea.

But where there was a woman to cope with the housekeeping 'things are bright as silver, there are sheets as well as blankets on beds; and perhaps a clean counterpane ... dry sacking or pieces of carpet on the ground ... and a pet cockatoo chained to a perch to keep the Missus from feeling lonely when the man is at work'.

And 'the Missus' often was lonely, finding adjustment to conditions on the diggings anything but easy. Women often became

> scared and frightened, then cross, and commence a 'blow-up' with their husbands; but all their railing generally ends in their quietly settling down to this rough and primitive style of living, if not without a murmur, at least to all appearances with the determination to laugh and bear it.

The masculine angle on goldfield domesticity Mrs Clacy gave in another part of her book. 'Here is one man grumbling because he has brought his wife with him, another ditto because he has left his behind, or sold her for an ounce of gold or a bottle of rum.'

But even the roughest miners seldom injured a woman, and Mrs Clacy concluded her book with this advice to

> my own sex who desire to emigrate to Australia: do so by all means if you can go under suitable protection, possess good health, are not fastidious or 'fine lady like', can milk cows, churn butter, cook a good damper and mix a pudding. The worst risk you run is getting married and finding yourself treated with twenty times the respect you may meet with in England.

As a propaganda writer for migration in the 1850s, Mrs Clacy stands high and probably influenced more than one settler to try the country where she had her own blue-serged adventure.

Oh, who would paint a goldfield
And paint the picture right,
As old Adventure saw it
In early morning's light?
The yellow mounds of mullock
With spots of red and white,
The scattered quartz that glistened
Like diamonds in the light.

The azure line of ridges,
The bush of darkest green,
The little homes of calico
That dotted all the scene.
The flat straw hats, with ribands,
That old engravings show—
The dress that still reminds us
Of sailors, long ago.

The rattle of the cradle,
The clack of windlass boles,
The flutter of the crimson flags
Above the golden holes.

HENRY LAWSON

A successful digger and his family: lithograph by S. T. Gill

22
Pioneer in Disguise

MRS CHARLES CLACY met Harriette Walters on the diggings in 1852 literally by accident. She sprained her ankle one day while out walking, fainted, and came to in a strange tent tended by an attractive young woman. Mrs Clacy described her in detail:

> She was young and fair; her step was soft and her voice most musically gentle. Her eyes were a deep blue, and rich brown was the colour of her hair, which she wore in very short curls all round her head and parted on one side, which almost gave her the appearance of a pretty boy.[1]

The fact that Harriette Walters looked like a boy was no coincidence, but something she had deliberately cultivated. At home in England she had been married only a year when her husband's firm closed its doors. With such funds as he had, Walters decided to try his luck on the Australian diggings.

His young wife waved him good-bye and returned sadly to live with an aged aunt, her only relative, until her husband should return with pockets stuffed with gold, or summon her to join him in the land of El Dorado. But his ship was hardly out of English waters when a sudden illness carried off the elderly aunt and Harriette was alone, with very little money and no connections to offer her shelter.

To Harriette, young, confident and in love, the solution was obvious. She would join her husband at his fortune-seeking.

All Australian-bound vessels were crammed with gold-seekers and migrants, and Harriette had no trouble hiring herself as children's nurse to a family going to Port Phillip. In a short time she was at sea, certain she had taken the right course, and happily looking forward to the journey's end and reunion with her husband.

But she had not foreseen that her ship would sail faster and bring her into Port Phillip Bay three weeks ahead of his. The family with whom she had travelled went on to their destination some miles up country, and Harriette found herself alone once more, this time in a strange city. And what a city! Full of seekers after fortune at Ballarat and Bendigo, Castlemaine and the Ovens—Europeans, Americans, Chinese with pigtails and loose 'trowsers', aborigines wearing at the most a blanket apiece, pickpockets, prostitutes, the virtuous and the vicious—everyone, in fact, from the successful digger in his blue serge shirt and green veil still dangling from his wide-awake to 'the fashionably attired, newly arrived gentleman from London who stared around him in amazement and disgust'.

Lodging was so scarce that people were sleeping on planks in the streets, and more than one expectant mother bore her child there. In any case, Harriette had no money for board and lodging, so in order to live and be safe she cut her hair and then, dressed in 'loose trowsers, full, blue serge shirt, fastened round the waist by a leather belt, and a wide-awake—passed very well for what she assembled to be—a young lad just arrived from England'.

In this role Harriette sought employment and obtained light work near the waterfront: wages, a pound a week, with the right to sleep in a tumble-down shed. Here she worked and slept for three weeks, until her husband's ship berthed and she rushed into his unbelieving arms. Now they would woo Dame Fortune together and face whatever that unpredictable wench might send their way.

A tent on the south side of the Yarra housed them while preparations were made for the journey to the diggings, and Harriette kept to her youth's clothes until the party reached Bendigo. Then she went back to petticoats, cooked for her husband and his companions, and kept house in a neat tent painted on top to make it rain-resistant.

The story had a happy ending, for Walters and his companions found a paying lode. It did not bring them wealth enough to indulge in one of the fabulous shopping sprees some successful diggers conducted in Melbourne, lighting cigars with banknotes and loading their comfortably-figured wives with the latest London finery, tight corsets and shoes usually too small. Instead, the Walters quietly turned their nuggets and gold dust into currency that was sufficient to buy them a dream, or at least set them on the way to realizing one. For the last Mrs Clacy saw of them was on the wharfside at Port Phillip about to embark for South Australia to buy land and become settlers.

A hut on the diggings: sketch by S. T. Gill
Women and children helped to work the claim

23
Advice for Migrants

WITH THE DISCOVERY of gold, articles about Australia broke out in British magazines like measles during school term, and publishers produced a small flood of books and pamphlets on colonial life to meet the demand for information about the land where golden nuggets were supplying a new motif for legend.

John Capper's *Emigrant's Guide to Australia*, published 1853, was typical of material produced to meet the market. Capper discussed the country as a whole and New South Wales, South Australia and Victoria in particular, their minerals, metals and goldfields, and made out a case for emigration. Two chapters were addressed directly to prospective emigrants, one giving details of what to take to the colony, how to travel, and what to do on arrival; the other was titled: 'Who Should Emigrate and How, with a Few Words to Those Who Had Better Remain at Home'.

The government paid the passages of certain emigrants, Capper pointed out, but not for young women under eighteen 'unless with their family, or in charge of some near relative'.

Even then they had better be the right kind of young woman.

> Young unmarried women, unacquainted with any kind of farm or agricultural occupation would be of little use in the new colony . . . The drawing-room accomplishments of singing, dancing, painting, crochet would stand no shadow of a chance against the highly-prized virtues of churning, baking, preserving, cheese-making, and similar matters.

A wife and family should spur on the right type of male emigrant.

Should an intending emigrant be married, so much the better, provided the wife be frugal and industrious: such a helper will not only be no expense, but she will actually often earn nearly as much as the husband. Children ... too ... are so many valuable assistants to the farm settler ... Children of ten or eleven are of the utmost use in tending sheep, whilst a lad of fourteen is quite as good as a man either as shepherd, stockman, or hutkeeper.

So go ahead, urged Capper. Apply for information at your regional emigration office, or at the headquarters of Mrs Chisholm's Family Colonization Scheme. If you satisfy requirements of character and fitness, you pay a sum varying between one pound and six as a guarantee of good faith that you will be ready when the ship sails.

As a set-off against these small sums, the emigrants have the use on the voyage out of a new mattress, bolsters, blankets, and counterpanes, canvas bags to contain linen, etc., knives and forks, spoons, metal plates and drinking mugs, which articles will be given after arrival in the colony to the emigrants who have behaved well on the voyage.

For those who financed their own passage, Capper offered practical advice. Such passengers he divided like Gaul firmly into three classes: cabin, who had the poop and stern cabins and dined with the captain and officers in the cuddy on 'unlimited fresh meat, poultry, beer, wine, etc.'; intermediate, who had 'cabins built up ... between decks, about 8 feet by 6 feet, with four or six sleeping berths in each, though four is ample for the space,' and whose 'dieting' consisted of 'beef pork, preserved and fresh meat, flour, biscuits, raisins, rice, pease, preserved potatoes, tea, coffee, sugar, butter, etc., with three quarts of water daily', and the steerage or lowest class for whom

> sleeping places are put up on either side of the lower deck, though for married people separate berths are erected. Bedding is sometimes added, and always cooking and mess utensils.

Their 'scale of dietary' was less than for intermediate passengers.

Capper advised young settlers, especially married couples, to

> avoid the cost of cabin or even intermediate passage; engage a space between decks at the steerage price, £20 to £15 each and employ the ship's carpenter to run up a little cabin, fitting it with a few useful things, such as a common filter, tin wash basin and jug, two quart hook pots, one pint ditto, tin plates

and dishes, knives and forks, tea and coffee pots, small water jug, and a ship candle-lamp. Before sailing everything should be safely lashed to prevent their rolling about and doing mischief. In addition to the above, a supply of provisions will be found acceptable, as the ship's dietary may not be such as the emigrant and his wife have been accustomed to; say 1 cwt. of flour, 1 cwt. of potatoes, a few pounds of tea, coffee, and cocoa; some candles, a hundred eggs, greased and packed in salt, some suet, butter, cheese and biscuits; a dozen or two tins of preserved provisions, a side of bacon and a couple of hams, with a little wine and some bottled beer. The whole of the above may be bought for about £20, which, added to the cost of the steerage passage for a couple, say £40, will not amount to more than the cost of a single cabin passage.

He gave some warning that intending travellers should take a look at the ship they would sail in, and not believe all they might read in certain advertising by ships' agents who painted the lily beyond recognition; he quoted one traveller's letter:

Trust nothing to owners or their agents. I would not believe one word they would say. Just take the ship we came out with, for example. In printed bills she was said to be 1000 tons burthen. She was in reality under 500 tons. She was said to be fitted with patent ventilators, which on examination I found to be an old sack with the bottom out! The agent told us the very morning we went on board that the ship was fitted up with all sorts of baths—cold, warm, and shower—which would be such a grand thing for the children. Well, after being a few weeks at sea, I began to wonder where the baths were, as I could see them nowhere. At last the Captain was asked 'Where are the baths?' 'Oh,' was the reply, 'there is an old cask up at the forecastle, which any of the sailors will fill for a consideration'! When I mentioned what the agent had said, he laughed and said 'Do you really believe all that a ship's agent says?' adding 'There never was a bath on this ship'.

As to what should be taken to the new country, Capper warned the migrant that he was going on a long voyage with the possibility of a rough journey at the end of it. Too many belongings were a nuisance, besides being expensive to transport. Cull out your possessions, he urged. Even food for the mind was rationed. Books were heavy, so apart from the Bible he suggested 'a book or two of instructive tales should there be children, and, if possible, a few volumes of standard English literature, with a few lighter for the wife'.

Ship's regulations allowed one box or bag only to be taken 'into the sleeping berth, sufficient to contain a month's clothing, at the end of which time they (the passengers) have access to their chests in the hold, replacing the clothes used by clean'.

Capper has much to say about clothes. First and last, they must be strong and serviceable.

> Let men, for instance, avoid all sorts of fancy waistcoats, dandy boots, or costly cravats and ties; let women shun the idle vanities of silks and satin, of lace and ribbons, of many flounces and fashionable bonnets; and let both men and women forget that there are such things in the world as kid gloves, lavender water, and toilet tables.

A minimum outfit for a married couple was based on the fact that

> it is not possible to wash on the voyage, unless it be a few very small things, the supply of water being limited to three quarts a day.
> For the wife:—three cotton dresses, one pair stays, four petticoats, sixteen chemises, two flannel petticoats, twelve pairs cotton stockings, four pairs black worsted ditto, six nightdresses and caps, six pocket handerchiefs, four handkerchiefs for the neck, six caps, two bonnets, cloak and shawl, one pair boots, two pair shoes, and eight towels.
> For the husband:—two fustian jackets, waistcoats, and trousers, three pairs of canvas trousers, one over-coat, two felt hats, one Scotch cap, sixteen striped shirts, two Guernsey shirts, twelve pairs cotton half hose, four pairs worsted hose, six handkerchiefs, eight towels, two pairs boots, and one pair shoes, strong but not heavy.

Children's needs he dismissed in four words: 'Children in like proportion.'

Other suggestions for articles needed on the voyage were

> a flock mattress and bolster, one pair blankets, one coverlet, six pairs cotton sheets, two or three table cloths, six pounds of yellow soap, three pounds of marine soap, metal wash hand basin, knives and forks, one quart tin hook pot, one coffee pot, comb and brush, besides a supply of string, sewing essentials, tape and buttons, etc.
> Should a little extra means be at command let it be expended in laying in small supplies of calicoes, brown holland, camlet, fine canvas, etc.; and it will always be desirable that the wife makes as many of her clothes on board ship as possible as the

occupation serves to pass away many an otherwise idle, heavy hour.

In fact, said Capper, every emigrant should find himself

some regular occupation during the voyage for some portion of the day, especially before and after dinner . . . (then) there would be fewer unpleasantnesses occurring on the outward voyage than often take place.

The voyage over, Capper assured his readers work was easy to find. He wrote knowing that labourers had left rural areas for the goldfields, and that pastoral workers would find plenty of employers. The demand remained high for years. Even after the gold fever lessened, the glare of Eureka's fire faded, the diggings became settled towns, and the mining industry stabilized, conditions were favourable to emigrants. Gold and increased population added to primary production gave Australia its next prosperous cycle. The emigrant in his fustian jacket, Scotch cap and canvas trousers, his wife in her cotton dress, shawl and bonnet, and their children 'in like proportion' could step ashore confident that, with will and enterprise, comfort, if not luxury, awaited them in the new land.

Emmigrants on their way to Sydney, 1849

24

The Northward March

The unfolding of Queensland is the settlement of the other States multiplied by x—the excitement of great distances against which it happened and the exotic flavour that belongs to a land set largely in the tropics.

From the 1840s on, the cavalcade of pioneering moved away from the south and spread north and west, reaching a peak in the 'fifties and 'sixties when separation from New South Wales speeded the pace of settlement. It was a mighty tapestry of action and adventure, enterprise and endurance on the scale of the Biblical wanderings. 'It was as in the days of the patriachs,' wrote Rosa Campbell Praed of the people who pioneered her birth State. 'Men travelled with their flocks and herds and, like Abraham and Lot, fought the tribes for land and water.'

Men alone, in pairs, or with families and drays, and always with stock, were goaded on to conquer the map which in many places was shaded in only by guesswork and hearsay. Through the seemingly never-ending distances they moved—up the coast into the tropics where the trade winds blew, into the centre where the coolibahs and banyans stood guard, into the west where the sandhills rose and fell and lignum grew along the yellow waters snaking lazily through the gibber plains. They journeyed through lush country where their cattle fed fat, and they laboured over drought-sculptured land where dead trees mocked their courage as foolhardiness.

Ahead of them beckoned the jade, Fortune. Discomfort rode on the flank, and Death grinned from the following dust as the cavalcade advanced—muscles strained and breath panting in lungs that worked desperately to feed the pounding heart for the tasks demanded of the body—the lowering of buggies into gullies and the haul up the other side, plunging into swollen rivers with roughly-made rafts, riding at the head of terrified cattle. It was a cavalcade which marched to the beating of invisible drums and the music of the spirits of distance, the Lorelei of green pastures and rich lands where stocks could graze.

The tapestry of settlement which stretches across Australia's second largest State shows immigrant ships turning into Moreton Bay, small schooners plying up the coast to anchor in unmade harbours, or be stranded for days, even weeks, on the Barrier Reef till high tides set them afloat. Horses and buggies are driven into the water to bring settlers ashore, and wheelbarrows are used to push carpet bags and wooden trunks to townships that are merely a huddle of tents and slab huts against a background of scrub.

Look along the rivers where the overlanders camped. They have travelled up from Goulburn and Maitland, from the New England Highlands, from the Riverina, from Melbourne. Some have brought a bride from the snow country around Cooma, some from a snug, long-established farm in Tasmania.

Sometimes in the tapestry there are families banding together for company and greater protection, the waggons loaded high with goods for the months' long trail—and the first to think of including a pair of cats was inspired, for rats were a major problem. Kittens were later valued as highly as a couple of steers.

Through humid rain forests with their creeping vines and waterfalls, over the range to the high lands of Atherton, into the Gulf Country with its lagoons and mosquitoes, its fevers and the long, long communication lines, went the pioneers.

Hostile blacks and hostile nature both threw hazards in the way. Spears and gunfire appear in many an encounter, and not every woman escaped like Mary Costello, who outfaced an attacking tribe and drove them off with the aid of Sancho, a great watchdog.

Unnumbered cattle fell beneath the black men's weapons. One grazier assessed his first year's loss at not less than a head a day. John Atherton's young daughter, journeying home from Cairns with her father, grieved one morning over the remains of her pony discovered in the ashes of the blacks' cooking fire.

Steep hills lay across many a pioneer trail, and the picture shows mothers toiling up the slopes with children in their arms, while native helpers place stones behind waggon wheeels to brake the gravitational pull as horses scrabbled for a foothold.

Long days were passed on rain-sodden banks in rain-sodden clothing, waggons were floated across flooded streams, cattle were swum. Goods stacked on poles across waggon tilts were often in danger from plunging, rearing horses. Sons, husbands and native stockmen rode at the head to hold them on course in swirling waters. No one had time to interview the mother on the matter of her feelings as she watched her son, aged nine, swim a pony across the swollen Burdekin in the strenuous 'sixties.

Mary Costello would have paid handsomely for some of that flood. It might have saved her two-year-old John who begged for water on the long, dry stretch where he died.

Lush pastures in the Gulf Country excited the cattlemen. They were unprepared for the Wet and the Gulf fever which claimed many victims. Mrs James Cassidy lay desperately sick in her house near the Leichhardt River. She went to Sydney to recover, but it was too late. She never again saw the northern sky or the pelicans afloat on the northern river.

Mosquitoes came in clouds, snakes appeared everywhere. John Macartney and his men destroyed ninety which invaded the stockyards during one cyclone.

While fathers and brothers mustered at the cattle camps, daughters were often shepherds, walking by day, yarding the flock at night, catching and killing a wether when meat was needed.

First homes were all of a pattern—small huts of slab walls, bark roof, earth floor, wooden pegs driven into verandah walls for bridles, verandah rail where pack saddles were always spread. Windows had rough wooden shutters, doors were rough slabs, beds were made of saplings. Furniture, including cradles, was fashioned from packing cases with occasionally some attempt at upholstery.

Almost every house had the ominous round holes, large enough to take a gun muzzle, and the armoury always stocked and ready. The inland blacks did not take tamely to dispossession of the land where they had lived so long on kangaroo flesh, the lily roots in the lagoon, and the nuts of the banyan tree, before the white man's fire added smoke to the miles where only the tribal firesticks had functioned.

In places there were wild ducks, turkeys, pigeons, cockatoos and parrots to lend variety to the cooking pots, and fish to be caught in rivers and lagoons. The Costellos had a fine vegetable garden at Kyabra, but Anne Macartney had few additions to her monotonous diet in the first years at Waverley when she was often ill. Sometimes her husband brought home small wild cucumbers from the scrub, and occasionally a few eggs from the nest of the wild turkey or plover. Anne always remembered with gratitude a kindly traveller who gave her a cabbage.

The vastness of Queensland was a challenge to the men who settled it. They were always in the saddle, seeking lands farther and farther on. Mrs Nat Buchanan, born in Port Macquarie in 1842, moved to Glen Innes as a child, and later to the Burnett district. There she married Buchanan and went with him four hundred miles to Bowen Downs. At forty-eight she was on the move again—to join Nat and the Gordon brothers who had overlanded to Flora Valley Station, near Hall's Creek, Western Australia. When she came to rest after that trek across the top of the map she was two hundred miles from the nearest white woman.

Women, too, undertook long trips almost casually. The Costello girls went to school in Goulburn, and their mother visited them from Rockhampton each year.

The long, long tracks, the heat, the loneliness, sheep and cattle were the themes of letters that went back across the seas. They have come to mean the 'real' Australia to those who have never seen it, though this ignores our mining towns, our industries and life along the coast, and is almost as unfamiliar to many Australians as it is to the citizens of Bradford, Dublin and the Isles of Skye. Australia to the non-Australian is still spelt in terms of the long, sunburnt miles that the pioneers covered, though along their tracks have sprung up towns, industrial centres and tourist resorts. On the land they saw only as grazing places, crops they never knew are growing, planted and tended by men and their mates who became latter-day pioneers, working with textbook knowledge that did not exist in the days when the first women passed that way, having their babies in lean-to shelters, fortunate if some member of their family were present; if not, lucky if some faithful gin lent a hand to bring one more white into the country her people no longer owned.

The cavalcade has long since passed, the bullock teams jogged their last load home, the dust faded away from their wheeels. They have gone into the distance, into time and history, leaving behind a legend of endurance, a saga of achievement which will feed the pens of our poets and novelists for generations to come.

25
Childhood of a Pioneer

ROSA CAMPBELL PRAED has been called 'the most distinguished novelist of pre-Federation days'. Time has whittled down her literary stature, but cannot rob her character of its strength and resilience, qualities which stemmed, if the psychologists are right in their theory of 'formative years', from her happy, colourful childhood.

Born in Queensland eight years before it became a State separated from New South Wales, Rosa knew life in a pioneer's humpy and in the suburbs of Brisbane when that city's population was only seven thousand. Her childhood was lived against a pastoral background; her girlhood brought her close to the world of governments through her father, Queensland's first Postmaster-General. She was the first woman author of her State, and, although little more than a quarter of her long life was lived in her birthland, she can on several counts be called an Australian pioneer.

Her father, Thomas Murray Prior, came to Australia in 1838 and worked on various properties in New South Wales to gain pastoral experience. Bringing wool or droving stock to Sydney on occasions, he came to know the Harpurs of Cecil Plains on the Parramatta River, and was engaged to Matilda Harpur when he took up Bungoroopin Station on the Logan, Queensland.

The letters her parents wrote while separated came into Rosa's possession later, and gave her a picture of a prim courtship that seldom went beyond the most demure prose.

The house at Bungoroopin where Matilda went as a bride was a bark-roofed slab hut, with gum saplings holding up the awning of the earth-floored verandah. Roses, passion flowers, sweet verbena and many trees flourished in the garden which sloped away to a waterhole the natives always avoided. 'Debbil debbil sit down like it that place', they declared.

The Logan was a lonely place in the 1840s for a girl still in her teens, with no near neighbours and cut off completely when the flood waters were out. 'For two months . . . the river has been bank high, and four drays are encamped on the other side waiting to cross', she wrote in a letter to her family.

She was nineteen and the river was in flood when her first child was born in the little slab hut. Matilda apparently had a difficult confinement, for her husband wrote that she had been in great danger, that there was 'no doctor within sixty miles and in any case the rivers were flooded so no one could cross'. Her next child lived only six months; then in 1851 Rosa was born.

Bungoroopin failed to establish the family fortunes, so Murray Prior went in search of better pastures. He inspected Naraigin (later Hawkwood) and wrote his wife to 'have grass cut for packing and the harness of the American waggon oiled' for the family was about to move.

The journey to the new property is almost the first thing Rosa remembers of her childhood.

> It seems to stand out like a sort of Hegira . . . scenes rise from it, vividly illuminated for an instant, and the next a blur,—vistas of giant gum trees and of a buggy toiling among them along a bush track with a small retinue of blackboys and packhorses before and behind, and two figures always prominent in the picture—one a dark-whiskered, bronzed and resolute person . . . who is mixed up in my child's mind with a bright Crimean shirt and pancho, a carbine, and with long cantos from 'Childe Harold' and 'Mazeppa' which he taught us to recite of evenings by camp fires; and the other a frail, delicate complexioned being, helpful and gay, dimly (seen) . . . against a background of forest, wearing a large hat, bending over packbags, and holding horses, with two babies clinging to her skirts. . . . The terror of wild blacks blending in imagination with the eldritch shapes of the old gum trees. . . . Shifting glimpses of great plains, of stony hills and gullies, and of lonely bark huts. . . . Rain and . . . roaring waters, for we were stuck up for weeks by floods.

When she looked back down the avenue of years she heard again a dingo howling and saw a child snuggling deeper into the blankets, taking comfort from the camp fire's flickering flames.

At the new home in the wilderness ('almost as far north as one could then go') she saw herself 'a small child dressed in a holland overall with rows of wavy red braid . . . and a sunbonnet dangling from my bare neck', sitting with Tommy, her brother, 'dipping into the bog which the horses made . . . when they were run up to be saddled'. She remembered her mother reading aloud 'The Ugly Duckling' while a kangaroo bounded 'in ungainly leaps over the hurdle fence and cleared patch of the stockyard, where lucerne and pumpkins and fat-hen plants grew', and fact and phantasy seemed equally enchanting.

Blue lilies floated on the lagoon which had

> that deep, dark clear look lagoons have; and the blacks' gunyahs and camp fires by the edge of it, and the cart track leading off to the woolshed, losing itself over the stony pinch among the iron-bark gums. There was Naraigin humpey and the sugar loaf shaped hill behind, with long, brown, blady grass, and bare white trunks of dead gums.
>
> I can see the slab hut with its sloping bark roof fringing raggedly over the verandah eaves. The slabs stand apart as though they had not been introduced to each other, but you don't notice that inside, for the walls have been lined with canvas. The verandah has an earthen floor and log steps, and is supported by gum saplings on which the bark has been left. All along it are rough squatters' chairs and slab settles, and there are saddles and bridles and stockwhips hanging from nails in the walls, and a canvas water bag slung from one of the rafters. These rafters, and those in the parlour, I recall as the home of tarantulas, centipedes, and sundry uncanny reptiles, as well as frogs which had an uncomfortable way of flopping down on one in rainy weather. Centipedes used to live, too, between the canvas and the slab wall, where they would in their perambulations make eerie scratchings, and many a long hour have I been awake in cold horror, listening to the sound of the hundred feet on their travels, and getting as near to the outer side of the bed as was possible. For in the bush we slept mostly on bunks made of sawn saplings nailed against the slabs.

Naraigin was a wonderful background for active childhood, in spite of periodic scarcity of rations when drays were flood-bound for months on end, the store was empty of flour, tea and sugar, and mutton and pumpkin appeared on dinner plates day after day.

The woolshed out of shearing time provided 'the most delightful playground that the heart of a child could long for, with its many pens, its empty wool bales and presses, its slanting log floor, and all its queer nooks and corners'.

Over: a farm in the forest, Victoria, in the 1880s

The children visited the native camp with Billabong Jenny, their aboriginal nurse, but by parental instruction they gave the 'possum rugs and their millions of lice a wide berth, and steered clear of festering pieces of bandicoot, snake and iguana lying round in the dirt.

The native women showed them how to plait dilly bags and make drinking vessels out of gourds. And white children and dark splashed happily together in the lagoon where the gins dived to pluck up the blue water lilies whose yam-like roots were roasted in the camp fire.

These were features common to many a Queensland pioneer's childhood. So were grisly tales of massacres and retaliation raids, for at this period the Burnett district was a trouble spot where white settlers and natives were in frequent conflict. Who was to blame? Rosa could not say. She was not proud of the whites who gave poisoned cakes and puddings to aborigines; nor could she recall without horror the spearing and tomahawking of whites by natives.

But her own family's relationships with the tribes were good, and half-caste Ringo was Rosa's special companion in the native camp. He chopped 'sugar bag' (wild honey-comb) for her from the trees, and under his tuition she ate fat white witchetty grubs, iguana flesh, and eggs of the black snake. It was a happy black-white association with one macabre side effect: through it Rosa is certain she saw a preview, a rehearsal in corroboree, of a station massacre which is now part of Queensland's history.

* * *

A generation later, in foggy London, Rosa wrote of her Australian childhood. Then the remembered heat of those summer days beat up at her from behind the years, heat so intense that the children fried birds' eggs in the sun on a sheet of zinc, water in the casks 'tasted as though it had been boiled', and the lagoon was a warm bath.

Insects were many and varied. Legs of the dining table stood in billies of water to discourage the ants, which climbed up in a black stream and swarmed over food. Flies were a scourge. One species caused sandy blight, and drove 'shepherds in their huts and women in the head stations blind and wild with pain'.

Snakes, centipedes and scorpions were everyday visitors. After forty years Rosa could still recall the agony she suffered from a scorpion bite. Her swollen finger turned black, and ached excruciatingly until her father lanced it with his razor, sucked out the poison, and completed the cure with arnica and bread poultices.

There was no financial gain to balance the ledger of discomforts;

the smell of the stock 'boiled down' for tallow surrounded Naraigin, and debts mounted up. Murray Prior sold the station and the family moved again. This time the new home was a small cottage among lantana and hibiscus, a banana plantation on the Brisbane River. 'One could write a whole essay about the delights of a banana field,' said Rosa, remembering the green hands of the fruit under the ragged leaves.

A little later she was exclaiming over a farm on 'the Bay' (Brisbane Harbour) where Murray Prior tried to raise sugar and cotton. Rosa loved it.

> For pure joy, nothing comes up to a canefield. Perhaps a grown up person might find it a little difficult to walk in, but for a child it is paradise . . . the shoots of sugar cane are most toothsome, and sweeter than store goodies. Better than to walk is to lie at full length between two rows of canes, which meet again over one's body, and one can look up and see the tassels flirting with one another, and the sunbeams shooting arrows through leaves which make flickering shadows till the whole baby wood seems alive. I think that lying in the cane field was the thing I liked best.

Besides the delights of the farm, there was the discovery of the sea, excursions in cutters to little islands, swimming (in a fenced area because of sharks) and all the fun childhood finds by the seashore.

Separation of Queensland from New South Wales in 1859 took Murray Prior into the government as Postmaster-General, and life for the family became very civilized. No more acting in the theatre of the saw-pit, no rides along the sandy isthmus, no splashing on the shingle. Instead, there was school in a Brisbane suburb, music lessons—'one, two, three and thumb under'—French, dancing.

A change of government and the Murray Priors 'went bush' again —to Marroon Station on the Logan River, between New South Wales and Queensland. It meant jolting over the Dungadine scrub where the train now runs to Boonah. One of the native boys went ahead to chop vines and remove logs, others led horses which were buckled on as leaders when the buggy came to a deep gully or a slippery pinch, and the elder children carried sticks and stones to set against the buggy wheels as required. Campfires at dusk and the children coo-eeing as they played; edible berries, chucky-chuckies and wild purple plum, vines winding like coils of a boa constrictor around tree trunks, flame tree like a burning bush, flowers everywhere, and bird calls Rosa never forgot: the ringing notes of the bell bird, the decisive flick of whip birds, and the tender hoo-hoo of the wonga pigeon.

Wallabies came in the late afternoon, curlews wailed sadly at dusk, and the night was haunted by the dingo's howl, the mopoke's call, or the faint cry of the native bear as the family went farther out.

On Coolin Plain they passed a lagoon covered with blue and pink lilies, and bottle trees stood bulbously along the way. Beyond the plain were the Marroon Mountains, heights, gullies and plateaux, and here the trek ended.

At Marroon Rosa's girlhood slipped by, marked by the sheoaks' sighing, by the shining husk cast by a cicada, by hawks above the killing yard, the crack of stockwhips rounding up the cattle, by haymaking, and kind Kanaka Peter's garden whose flowers and colours signalled the months of the year.

Like sand drizzled through the fingers, events and incidents of her youth ran through Rosa's remembrance when she wrote the story of her Queensland youth. She recalled picking grapes to place in large basins on the verandah, figs and melons set for jam, milkpans scoured in the dairy, bins cleaned of weevily flour, a boiling water crusade against cockroaches and spiders, walls in the Bachelors' Quarters papered with *Illustrated News* sheets. When that was done, she could turn to binding saddle cloths, copying branding tallies for the station log, preparing prickly pears for jelly; or putting corn through the cutter and the crushing, crackling sound of the orange grain rolling out of the machine's red mouth.

Travellers on the road were invited to 'spell' their horses and stay awhile, and Rosa began her writing career as editor and correspondent of the family paper *Marroon Magazine*, read at night round the fire burning in a huge slab chimney-piece almost the size of a room.

Full years, rich years—they gave Rosa source material and background for many novels which she wrote in London after her marriage. That took place after gay seasons in Brisbane, where she was beau'd and squired to a round of parties.

Her mother died and Rosa was still single. Then she met a young Englishman, come to make his fortune in Queensland. Their marriage from Government House was a brilliant social event, a contrast to the opening chapters of their married life, spent on Curtis Island, where Campbell Praed leased a property.

Rosa's first impression of the island was a pillar of cloud hovering over it—actually a swarm of mosquitoes which were ever present, and only controlled by green twig fires.

Rosa and her husband rode along a sandy path, seated on a board

Childhood of a Pioneer

in a two-wheeler dray, with the cloud of mosquitoes escorting them the whole three miles to the homestead

> a hideous modern sawn wood erection . . . built on the crown of a treeless ridge with the full force of the western sun pouring upon its verandah—not a creeper, not a flower bed, not a tree close by, except the blanched skeleton of a dead gum.

Dust came up through cracks in the floors; so did the fleas. It was weeks before these gave up the battle and retreated from the gallons of boiling water poured through the crevices.

The Campbell Praeds arrived near Christmas-time and the staff promptly departed for the mainland, leaving the young couple a wedge of salt junk and a large three-corned loaf of camp oven bread. The house had not not been cleaned for months, and the best bedroom, said Rosa, was knee-deep in mire.

Rosa found it an odd Christmas, gathering sticks for a fire to cook sweetbreads of the calf killed in honour of the day and the crabs brought in by an old lubra.

The staff eventually returned, but servants seldom stayed long on the isolated station, and endless pan-cleaning was part of Rosa's stint as an island housewife.

Every six weeks a bullock was killed, salted, and hung in a meat house till it was almost as hard as iron bark. Between killings they lived like patriarchs 'on the flesh of kids'. Stockmen fished occasionally in the creek, and on one occasion landed a huge turtle after a tremendous wrestle.

After two years Campbell Praed sold out, and on a soft, clear March day the family, including their infant daughter, boarded the Customs' House schooner and returned to the mainland. As the shores of Curtis Island fell behind, Rosa felt she had turned the final page of her Australian girlhood.

Her life thereafter was spent in England. But she was fifty before she set down the record of her pioneering youth,[1] a potpourri of sounds and scents of her early years, shot with colour, and laced with personalities she had known in the days she spent in what she called her 'eucalyptic cloisterdom'.

In literary and social London Rosa knew success and acclaim as well as tragedy and frustration, but in that book about her growing years, one senses the riches she drew on, the reservoir of strength which helped her survive life's buffetings. At the end, her unsuccessful marriage behind her, when she had outlived her children and her dearest friends, she could still return in memory to the mountains and lagoons, feel the wind of June sweeping down on Naraigin from the west, and know a lift in the heart when she remembered the banana stalks turning royal purple, and the rustle of the cane as it met above her head in the days when she and Queensland were young.

Rehearsal for Murder

In 1857 Hornet Bay Station in the Burnett River district (Queensland) was occupied by a widow, Mrs Frazer, and her four sons and four daughters. One night a party of blacks descended on the station when the family was sleeping (except one son, who was away at the time). The house dogs gave no warning, being reassured by a native employed on the property, and the blacks entered the homestead. A blow from a waddy stunned seventeen-year-old Sylvester, and knocked him between the bed and the wall. Here he lay, dazed and unable to move, while the blacks killed his brother and their tutor, and speared another brother, a mere child, as he tried to escape. Then they went to the room where the mother and daughters slept, and, in spite of Mrs Frazer's appeal that they remember the many kindnesses received at the station, the women were all murdered. The blacks spent the night feasting and drinking from the store room supplies, and the next morning slew the remaining white men on Hornet Bay—two stockmen, whose quarters were some distance from the homestead—as they went to the stream for water.

Eventually the injured Sylvester, dazed with horror, escaped to tell of the massacre. White settlers in the district organized a retaliatory raid on the blacks and many were killed.

A few nights before the attack on Hornet Bay, Rosa Campbell Praed had gone with some playmates from the blacks' camp to watch from a distance a corroboree which she was afterwards certain enacted the planned murder.

> The moon was near the full. One day Waggoo told me, in strict bond of secrecy, that there was going to be a corroboree that evening across the river, and promised that if I were willing he and Tombo would take me to a spot from which I might look unseen.
>
> There was a horrible fascination in the prospect. I had listened with bated breath to Waggoo's tales of wonderful corroborees, and for months—years—had yearned after the sight. I trembled and longed, but dare not ask for permission, which I know would

certainly be refused. Towards dusk, I sneaked surreptitiously out of the humpey, and Tombo and Ringo conveyed me across the river to a little stony pinnacle on which was a patch of scrub, whence we had a good view of the little timbered flat where the Blacks were assembled in a wide circle illuminated by many fires.

The fires burned at regular distances, and in rows of three or four deep were gathered, in line, first the naked forms of many warriors, pipe-clayed and painted, their heads bristling with parrot and cockatoo feathers, their necks wreathed with rush beads, their spears brandished above their heads; then the old men, and behind them the gins, who kept up a monotonous, discordant chorus to the accompaniment of a kind of tom-tom and a few jew's harps and the beating of boomerangs and waddies.

Now the chant dies in a long wail, now it swells into a fierce shout of triumph. The chiefs in front seem to direct the performance. Some of them are painted to represent skeletons, others in spiral stripes as though huge snakes were coiled round their bodies. They wave their spears and utter harsh cries. Presently a little party of braves steps into the arena. They hold their shields in front of them and make sinuous movements, glance from one side to the other, vigilant and cunning, stoop as beneath imaginary doorways, and whisper together.

Clearly it is a rehearsal of a night attack upon some white man's station. Then there is a dash sideways upon a cluster of mock sleepers, who rise with drowsy gestures, give signs of horror and alarm, and after offering a feeble show of resistance, beg for mercy. A pantomimic struggle follows. Spears are pointed, nulla-nullas aimlessly hurled...

Now the chant becomes still and mysterious, as if it were an invocation. There are three wild shouts, and four or five rude effigies of women, made of saplings and draped with red blankets, are dragged in to the circus and stood upright with gestures of derision. Then the black forms thicken round them. They are thrown down, stamped upon, beaten with nulla-nullas, and at last hurled upon the central bonfire. The boomerangs clash louder, the saturnalia is fiercer. But I feel faint and sick, for I am convinced that a human sacrifice is about to be offered, and I turn and flee. Tombo and Waggoo follow and lead me back to the humpey, where I creep into my bed and lie shuddering. I did not dare go to my parents, who, believing us all long ago in bed and asleep, are in the verandah watching the red glow. I have often thought that had I described to them the ghastly performance I had witnessed, the Hornet Bay tragedy might have been averted.

A bullock team outside the homestead, about 1910

26
No Medals for Mary

THE BROAD PATTERN of settlement was established in New South Wales by the 1860s, and hills and gullies had long known the rumble of waggon wheels and plodding teams making the long trek into the land of the west. But in each decade other districts opened up, and newly developed areas required work and devoted toil equal to that of the early pioneers.

Mary Blattman, married at seventeen, helped John, her husband, clear and fence a small farm in the mountains around Jenolan Caves.

They built a little four-roomed wooden house, plastered and whitewashed it inside and out, hung shutters at the windows, and thatched the roof with grass from the creek bank.

There were children in the cottage, magpies in the gums and goslings on the creeks near the house. Mary baked crusty bread in a camp oven, churned butter, made cheese, and sewed for the family by hand. After twelve or thirteen years, the little farm looked well with its standing crops and a few cows and horses grazing about it.

Then John was brought home one day badly hurt. 'An accident with horses,' says the family.

Before her thirtieth birthday, Mary was a widow: owner, manager and workman of the little farm that must support herself and her six young children. Life became one never-ending round of duties. She worked in the fields by day, washed, baked bread, cured bacon and did the dairy work late at night. Her eldest daughter, aged eleven, worked beside her until sleep slowed her hands and set her young head nodding. The eldest boy chopped wood, fed stock, carried buckets of water from the creek, and helped where he could. Eight years old is young to shoulder a man's work.

Mary drove a heavy, old-fashioned cart to Oberon, ten miles way, for groceries and supplies. In winter, when carts bogged down in swollen creeks, she went horseback, riding along the tracks (there were no roads), picking her way over creeks (there were no bridges), and dismounting to open and close the gates. (The swing gate had not yet come into existence.)

The farm pigs fattened on potatoes, turnips and boiled rye. A neighbour killed and butchered them, but Mary herself did the curing. This was the way of it:

> She stabbed the rind with a bootmaker's awl, then, with a little board, rubbed coarse salt into the holes. The pieces were then turned over and salt sprinkled liberally on the fleshy side—covered with a cloth, it was left for two days, then the process was repeated—three times altogether. It was then hung in the kitchen to dry. It kept a long time and was good bacon.[1]

In the large dairy she made cheese. Rennet tablets placed in fresh milk formed thick curds after an hour or two. They were crumbled by hand, tipped into a vat lined with thin cloth, pressed tightly and the cover weighted. Next day the cheese was turned out and set on shelves to dry, covered with white cloth and turned over once a day for several days. When thoroughly dried it was ready for market—a mild cheese that always sold well.

Three or four times a year Mary harnessed a spring cart and drove forty miles to Bathurst, with eggs and dressed poultry, her home-cured bacon and cheese. When she returned, there were goods to unpack—a new saucepan, perhaps, a butter churn, tools or supplies for the farm, boots for the family and material for clothes which she made up by hand in the time she miraculously squeezed from the inexorable day.

Working round the clock there was no time for self-pity. Never a holiday in twenty years, rising early to pull on the elastic-sided boots she favoured because there were no laces to tie, a slight figure dressed mostly in cotton skirts and blouses and a sunbonnet, she was out early in the paddocks.

The children must be off to school (half day only; the teacher divided his time between two schools five miles apart), there were the lamps to fill, wicks to trim, melted fat to pour into candle moulds ('make sure the cotton hangs over the edge'), cooking, making bread, housework, sewing—that was the day gone. Winter winds sweeping from the mountains, spring returning with the wattle to the hills, the children growing and helping—the years were flying by.

Mary, used to the old sorrow of a lost mate, now had a new one to set beside it—an ailing child whom she took to Bathurst but could not save. It was a long drive homeward down the lonely road with only a small son and her own thoughts for company, but that was life and the busy years were going—had gone, like last year's snow on Oberon's hills. The boys grew and built their own homes. The daughter, who had worked sleepy-eyed beside her mother, became a bride and moved away.

Mary was tired and the little farm had served its purpose. It was sold and Mary turned her back on the thatched roof and the wattle-clad hills, and moved to Bathurst. She died in her sleep in her daughter's home, aged ninety, joining the great multitude who rate no niches in the nation's remembrance, no banners, no medals for a life of uncomplaining service.

Vale, Mary! May the wattle glow brightly wherever your dust is drifting.

An Australian shepherd's hut in the 1840s

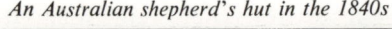

27
Matriarch of Cooper's Creek

IT IS IMPOSSIBLE to write about Western Queensland without running into names and stories of the Durack clan. And no one can write about the Duracks without bringing in the other families with whom their lives were enmeshed—Costellos and Scanlans and Tullys by the dozen. Yet their printed histories amount to little more than a few newspaper articles, most of them dealing with the great saga of the Durack overlanding across the map from the Cooper to the Kimberleys.

But scarcely anything about the women who trod the trails by the side of their men, and that was what I needed.

Friends who knew her kept urging: 'Write to Mary Durack. She'll tell you. She's a giver, is Mary.'

So at last I wrote to Mrs Horace Miller, care of the MacRobertson Miller Airline Office, Perth, knowing someone would take enough time off from getting planes away into the air lanes of the western skies to see my letter reached Mary Miller, née Durack.

In a matter of days she had dipped into the patch box of her tribe and there tumbled on my desk a collection of vivid, colourful personalities accompanied by the typically generous franchise: 'Do what you like with this.'

From such a treasure who should one select? Perhaps Great-Grandmother Bridget Durack, gentle and Irish, who never mastered the reading or writing of English, but had an age-old wisdom in herbs and cures, who could deliver a child, fix a fever, or turn a foal with inspired hands and a goodly dose of prayers, always said in 'her native Gael'. Someone could make a wonderful story of Bridget, and, when he does, let him not forget her trip north with her youngest son, Michael, when she was nearing sixty, driving a buggy behind the dust of a mob of cattle, sharing the camps and discomforts on the way and the pioneering pattern her children established along the Cooper.

There was Mary Durack's other great-grandmother, Mary Costello, who sailed with her husband from Ireland. Four children they had at the start of the voyage, but none of them ever saw Australia. The aides of Death were busy on many an immigrant ship of those days.

Mary Costello bore two more children in the new land, John and Mary, and her great-granddaughter wonders if she wasn't the mightiest old pioneer of all. Neither distance nor danger daunted her. Where her children went, she followed, and kept a watchful eye and a firm hand on all their doings.

And there was Mary Scanlan, who married Mary Costello's son, John, and went with him and their two-year-old boy away from the settled lands of Goulburn and Yass, up into the frontier—the country over the border of Queensland, where the natives fiercely disputed the white man's coming, and the small son was buried along the drought-ridden track.

There was Mary Costello's daughter who married Patrick Durack and bore the men who trekked to the Kimberleys, which is settlement brought to a high-powered crescendo. When the Queensland bank smash took toll of Patrick's speculations, he and Mary went to the Kimberleys to be with their sons and kinsfolk. This Mary Durack and Mrs Nat Buchanan were the first two white women to live in East Kimberley.

A small house built of mud bricks at Argyle on the Behn River, near the Ord, was Mary's new home but it did not know her long. Malarial fever carried her off the following year, 1893, aged forty-nine.

Her sons' wives in time took on the job of pioneering that land of tumbled ranges and from it their daughters, Mary and Elizabeth, drew their knowledge of the north and its people.

But gradually the spotlight focused on Sarah Durack,—'The Matriarch of Cooper's Creek' her great-niece called her, flinging wide the treasure chest that I might dip therein, and telling me of others who might give more information.

So out of the words of Mary Durack with her novelist's sense of selection and her Irish eye for drama, and from others who knew the pioneers of the dry places of Western Queensland, I became acquainted with Sarah Tully, born Durack, for whom the adjective 'indomitable' seems to have been especially coined.

* * *

Sarah was the fifth daughter of Michael Durack and his wife Bridget, who came, stated their great-granddaughter, 'from County Clare, Ireland, where they had been farmers 'way back, of course, to the days of Brian Boru', coming 'like most of the famine-driven Irish of the time, as assisted migrants'. 1853 that was, and Goulburn the place they went to—Michael and Bridget and their seven children, two boys and five girls. A new start in a new land for an energetic, hard-working Irish family. Inside two months they were gathered at the graveside of Michael, dead through an accident with a horse, with the mourning Bridget preparing to bear her eight child. Patsy, the eldest, went off to the goldfields, seeking gold to establish the family financially. Somehow Bridget kept the family together and cared for in the interval he was away. Then he was back with gold to buy land and set up a holding for them all.

And who was the greatest help to Patsy in his venture? Sarah, of course. The same Sarah who, when they left Ireland, was scarcely expected to survive the voyage.

You see her thriving in her new home land, a plant in the right soil, small but hardy and vital, the measure of her character showing in the steel of her grey eyes, in her firm mouth and her purposeful walk. Riding, working with the stock, dancing till daybreak whenever there was an opportunity—that was Sarah when she met Pat Tully, a miner drawn by the magnet of gold out of County Galway, to stand up at Eureka, they say. Pat lost all he had in a claim at Eldorado, but at Adelong, in his own words, 'had some good luck'. Then, with money in his pocket and a new land to see, he dropped in on a visit to his cousin Tully, settled at Gullen. Inevitably in a district where Duracks and their relatives were housed and homed, he met and shortly after 'married on 24 June 1861, Sarah, youngest daughter of Michael Durack of Murmnel'.

Sarah was then sixteen.

Now the years of apprenticeship to the soil of the new land were turned to making a home for herself, her man and the family they reared at Grabben Gullen on Hume's Creek near Goulburn, where Pat Tully was granted a free selection and farming property.

Years later he wrote of their beginnings:

Bought a team of bullocks and first night brought them home and lost them and had to follow them back twenty miles. Got them home and started to grub trees and clear some of the land for wheat. Had a very poor crop the first year. Second year got 500 bushels of wheat but found it was no good for sale as soil was too rich. That year I went to Goulburn cattle sale and bought a mixed lot of cows and calves. These were the start of the splendid cattle herd we afterwards took to Queensland.

Clearing and sowing, yarding and branding, with Sarah doing her share in the fields, her baby lain to sleep in a freshly turned furrow. Then home to cook and bake, scrub and mend, her washing done so late that the night was nearly gone when she finished and crept into bed without disturbing her sleeping husband.

Children came along regularly, their grandmother Bridget's deft hands helping them into the world. But 'the wheat did well', wrote Pat, 'and we were prospering'. The drays which went to Goulburn for supplies came back well loaded, and at times there were family gatherings and local dances, laughter and music, with the babies tucked up in a back room, sleeping through the music and the noise while their parents danced and the night faded into dawn.

Pat could record truly that 'we did well there—till the rust came'. That meant seasons when the grain never ripened, the stalks stood dark and withered, the life cut off from the tasselled ears.

What was the sense of fighting it, of 'staying put' when the tramping feet, the plodding hooves, the turning wheels of settlement were on the march? These were the days when the world was wide, and tales circulated about this or that member of the family back from or going to some land of better pastures. Patsy Durack was over the border with his brother-in-law John Costello, droving cattle and horses right on to the Barcoo. No luck that time, but next year Costello was away again and took his bride into the area to establish Warroo Springs. 'But the blacks speared and chased their cattle, killed their head stockman and set fire to their homestead—and drought hit them hard', says Mary Durack and it was upstakes again, and into the north, sending word down south of land further on, and urging relatives to follow.

Pat Durack lost no time going forward. With his wife (Mary Costello) and their two boys in a covered waggon, the cattle and goods they needed, trail was made to the north.

The families met and stayed a while on Mobile Creek, adventuring and droving on an epic scale. Then Patrick Durack, his younger brother Michael, and an old native were away on to Cooper's Creek, where there was good country for those with the will to work it. Kyabra Creek watered the land where Durack and Costello brought their families and established Thylungra and Kyabra Stations, their joint holdings larger than their birthplace, Ireland.

Babies were born before homesteads were built in the wilderness, the great spacious wilderness that was too good to waste and must be shared by the rest of the clan. So, runs were taken up, and urgent letters went south, pressing the claims of the new country, the endless opportunities, the need for the family to follow.

The call reached the Tullys, now on another selection, between Adelong and Gundagai. Said Pat Tully:

> Sold up everything, and with the best of the cattle and horses we all started out in bullock drays for West Queensland. . . . We took the route through the goldfields and on through 'Bushman Township' now Parkes. We stayed there nine weeks where our eighth child, Francis, was born on 1st April. . . . We then came on through Brewarringer (Brewarrina?)—crossed the Darling and caught some very big fish which we preserved in casks and they lasted till we got to Ray. Then on through Eulo by Hutchinson's Lake and crossed the Bulloo near Morley. Very rough crossing. Wild blacks were everywhere. Camped at Morley homestead for a while (Sarah probably got out the tubs and had a field day), then onwards to Kyabra where the Costellos greeted us warmly. Stayed a while and then on to Thylungra—had a month there, and then on to Ray Creek.

So Sarah came into her kindom; the year, 1874.

'We lived in tents while we were building the house of horizontals and mud and a thatch roof of cane grass. It was cool and comfortable and I was sorry we ever pulled it down. We had to go to Wilcannia, 500 miles away; in bullock drays for supplies. It took three months' at least, nearly six if the the stores were out of supplies. Rather than wait, the dray and driver might push on south. It was a long haul, and there was need for Sarah always to watch the rations carefully, and eke out supplies in the months between loadings. Bread and milk for breakfast and nothing between meals was the pattern of those first years at Ray.

Blacks to help with housework and washing, children to be trained in the way they should go. 'Sit up straight, Margaret'—(or Maria, Clara, Jack, James or whoever offended). Or 'Look at your pinafore, miss. It's a disgrace. What a sloppy Jane you are.'

Meat spicing and preserving, butter making, and the long days and nights when Patrick must be away at Wilcannia. Then Joseph, the eldest, must get the cows and do the outside work, and stand by her side as the tribes passed in a long troupe, carrying firesticks to their meeting ground at Thylungra. Sarah brought the children indoors, grabbed her muzzle-loaded gun, and fired a few warning shots through holes in the wall as the dark people went by.

Baking and cooking—and where were the children? The eldest daughter, Margaret, found little James out of his depth in the creek at two and a half. She reached him in time, but that was enough for Sarah. They must move.

The new home was pisé (puddled mud mixed with straw), its walls two feet thick. In spite of an iron roof, the large, well-ventilated rooms were cool on summer days, but at night the heat drove the family to sleep out of doors. Built round a square, the house looked to the horizon over a wide plain of Mitchell grass, facing towards Thylungra, home of Sarah's loved brothers and their families, eighteen miles off.

What was eighteen miles to Sarah, who sat a horse in show rings until well on in years? Just a comfortable canter with morning tea at the end. Carrying a baby or two, and never without gifts (always butter of her own making, and once a precious broom brought by the dray all the way from Bourke), she was often seen riding across the plain to greet her kin.

Whose turn to bring in the firewood? When the stack ran low, someone went out with an axe and the dray to cut down more of the gidyea trees. Winter, though its stay was short, breathed frostily enough over the plains to make a fire welcome, and Sarah might find time to sit beside it as the gidyea log flamed and burnt away to a snow-white ash. Wonderful whitewash for pisé walls it made, with a hint of blue in its whiteness.

Even in the new house, death claimed his quota of the family—Francis, born on the way north, never had a firm hold on life and slipped gradually out of it; the small Annie wandered away one mid-summer day, gathering wildflowers. Though the whole district searched through a week of violent heat, she was not found until Patrick's horse shied suddenly in the long grass, and the search was over. They carried little Annie home with the wildflowers still in her hand—back to Sarah, from whom that week of strain took some quality she never recovered in full measure.

It is hardly strange that Sarah was the one who withstood brother Patrick when he wanted the whole clan with him in the Kimberleys. Writes Mary Durack: 'He tried to persuade his sisters and their husbands to come along, but Sarah put her foot down for them all. They had buried so many little ones between them in the soil of Cooper's Creek, she said, that they would never leave. They stayed.'

In time, the Cooper country dealt kindly with Ray and gave material return for the man and woman hours of endurance and patient work which went into it. 'Had some fine horses on Ray', Patsy reported laconically. 'Cattle pleuro nearly wiped out the herd, and in the 1884 drought we lost a lot. Before that I bought our first sheep'.

No one thought of the Cooper as sheep country; the idea was widely held that wool would grow as coarse as goats' hair in that harsh climate. But Sarah argued against the theory. Drought might and often did wipe out the cattle man, but sheep could be kept alive on mulga and other growth of the dry land, she declared.

Although time and again the creek rose and flood waters swirled round the house, Sarah's theory was proved right again and again, for drought was almost the common state of the country, and gave the central inland its harshness. Drought, grinning and grimacing, flayed the land till the heart was wrung with pity for beasts waiting for a soak to 'make', and the diseases which stalk dry regions moved in relentlessly to destroy the weak and the young.

> Only those who lived through the recurring droughts can have any idea of the hardships entailed. There were only natural waters in the long ago and many years passed before the boundaries were fenced. Many more years passed before the paddocks were sub-divided and sub-artesian bores were sunk.

wrote a woman who knew the country.

Again and again the drought struck, but hardest of all in 1900, when it was touch and go whether the Bank would take over Ray as it had already taken other stations. But if Ray were resumed, who would work it? No one could pull Ray out of its troubles better than the Tullys, decided the Bank, and one can't help feeling a little sorry for the manager obliged to face the steel-grey eyes and firm mouth of Sarah.

There followed years of privation when the boys lived out in the scrub, felling mulga for the sheep and cattle, camping through the frosty winter nights with but a blanket apiece, and enduring the summers without nets when the air throbbed with the hum of mosquito hordes.

That was the front line of the fight. Twelve miles back was the base—the homestead held by Sarah and the girls. It was their stint to cut bags of beefwood leaves to feed the cow or two left on the station. Kangaroo fat fed their only lights, the slush lamps. They saved the fat from the sheep to bake cakes for the boys.

Every so often the girls rode the twelve miles to the camp on pushbikes, carefully balancing the food and extras they so painstakingly gathered and prepared.

Hard riding? It was worth it. At the end of the trail were the brothers, and at the end of the servitude—Ray Station, won back by teamwork and endurance.

Now the new century had come, the worst of the struggles were over. In 1906 Patsy and Sarah set out on a special adventure along the trail which led back over the seaways to the place of their origin, the soft green land of Ireland. It was fine to have seen it, but it was far from Ray, the waterholes at Erbin and the Three Mile, the vegetable garden and fruit trees along the creek banks, the grapes by the trough that led water from one tank to another, the bougainvillea rioting over the grass dining shed, and the saltbush over the arbour.

Back home, the years raced. Children married, more homes were established, grandchildren arrived. Jack, the favourite of the family, not back at nightfall from his work at the Top End, was found by old Tippo, famed blacktracker, unconscious where his horse had flung him against a tree. The old station buggy brought him home sixteen miles over rough country, then went another seventy to Adavale for a doctor. But with no ice and few facilities for treatment, it was hopeless.

The shuttles of the years flew faster. It was 1911 and golden wedding celebrations and merriment in the old pisé house lasted a month as friends and family foregathered.

Four years later young Patrick was drowned in the tank on Pinkilla and another stone was raised in the old cattle camp that housed the family's dead, its white fence sharp against the red windswept plain.

In 1918 bores were sunk and the sub-artesian water brought from its underground hide-out to feed the upper earth. Windmills for the great lift, and troughing to take it to the stock—it was a new bloodstream for the country so often beaten to its knees by drought.

In Sarah's bedroom, hung with pictures of her faith, she would gather some of her grandchildren. Over the fireplace she cooked maizena, eggs and their favourite dishes, and if grown-ups protested, she swept them aside. The children needed more nourishment, she declared. Perhaps she was remembering back to the days when other children had lived on meagre rations, and there had been nothing for snacks between meals.

But gradually the springs were weakening. Sarah sat by the hour in her rocking-chair, telling her beads. Patsy died and she never realized it. 'How is your father today?' she asked afresh each morning. Her own call came three months later. She lingered a day and was gone—Sarah of the grey eyes—gone from the Cooper and the overland trails, but leaving behind a host of descendants and the legend of one who looked that land in the face in its harshest moments, and never cried quarter.

Mary Durack (Costello)
Left: Patrick (Grandfather Patsy) Durack

28
Spinifex Pioneer

YOU MAY BEGIN the story of Emma Mary Withnell if you choose with a small coastal ship heading north from Fremantle in 1863. Its destination was the land revealed by explorer Frank Gregory, the little-known north-west lying empty and unpeopled.

But perhaps the story of Emma truly begins with a rattle of chains as *Warrior* comes to anchor off Rottnest Island in 1829.

Among its passengers was young John Hancock, come with his parents to pioneer along the Swan. Thirteen years later, John, now a full-fledged farmer, greeted another daughter born to his wife Sophia. The child was named Emma.

I have no description of the house at Beverley where Emma grew up, but it was full of children, five sons and seven daughters. Many hands to help work the farm and the house, and active young minds to be taught by their university-educated father at the end of the day.

Emma passed out of childhood and at seventeen became Mrs John Withnell. She was twenty-one, the mother of two children and expecting a third, when John decided to follow Gregory's trail to the district back of Port Hedland. Golden-haired Emma, daughter of pioneers, was not one to draw back from such a venture, so John chartered the *Sea Ripple*, displacement 100 tons, to take his family, Emma's brother and teenage sister, servants, stores, provisions, 1,000 sheep, 10 draught-horses, 1 saddlehorse, 6 cows and a Clydesdale colt to the new country.

For a month the small vessel, its crew and complement sailed north, with little to mark each day's passing; a quiet trip, said all, until the wind dropped, the sails fell slack, and they lay becalmed off the coast near Cossack (then called Tien Tsin).

It was a week before a breeze came; the crew sprang to the ropes and the ship moved. The great tide which sweeps that coast was rising, the *Sea Ripple* sailed in on its swell, and ended on a reef. And there she lay when the water ebbed, listed so badly that the stock were soon in a sorry state, through lack of care, and cramp.

The ship was eventually refloated and a tarred sheet fixed over the hole slashed by the reef. But the captain flatly declined to proceed to Port Hedland. He was anxious to take the damaged *Sea Ripple* back south as soon as possible and only after much discussion agreed to a compromise. For the consideration of a further £100 he would anchor off Cossack if the company were prepared to alter their plans and go ashore at that spot.

So, deputy for the force of destiny, this skipper of a small coastal vessel influenced the future of a family whose name is woven into the fabric of the north-west.

Two miles off Cossack anchor was dropped, and the ship's dinghies lowered. Into these, somehow, went Emma, her two babies, and the rest of the party. Somehow, too, the stock and stores were taken in relays by those two little boats plying back and forth between the beach and the *Sea Ripple*, until all were landed, the stock reduced by the hardships of the past fortnight to 84 ewes, 2 rams, a cow and a horse.

While the *Sea Ripple* set sail and headed south, the Withnells made a depot for their stores, and, because there was no other way of going, set out on foot to find a homing place. Emma carried her baby and helped the toddler along, the others loaded themselves with as much baggage as they could carry.

A few miles inland they climbed a hill, set down their loads, and straightened their backs. What they saw they liked. This, they felt, was their goal; here they would settle. The hill on which they made their decision they called Mount Welcome, and on its summit they set their first home—inevitably a tent. Stretched canvas, fire licking round the sides of a swinging billy, flour mixed for damper—once again they appeared in pioneering history. It was Sunday, so heads were bowed, prayers said, and hymns learnt in childhood sounded over the spinifex country, where the white man had now arrived with his faith and his flocks.

*   *   *

Emma Withnell lived forty years in the north-west, and for the first twenty of those she did not leave it. Life was too full and time so short for all that must be done.

When the family was grown and the tempo slowed, she had time to look back on the busy years spent in the spinifex country. She remembered the storm which broke over Cossack soon after their arrival and the havoc wrought on the stores at the depot. Only a portion of flour and sugar was unspoilt, so 'we kept the sugar . . . for the children, and fortunately the cow had calved, so we had milk'.[1] She recalled that their spare boots were damaged beyond use, a serious blow in a land where the hot sun makes the earth unbearable to white men's feet. A solution was found by someone in the party who fashioned wooden clogs and covered them with sheepskin. A house was soon under construction—at first but a room or two built of mud and thatched with spinifex. Additions went on as the family grew; so did a wide verandah, centre of family life under these northern skies.

Dark faces and figures were part of Emma's remembering. The local tribes were reputed to be wild and unpredictable, but they did the Withnells neither hurt nor harm because the family's treatment and kindness never violated their sense of justice.

'This our camp', said John Withnell to the dark people, drawing a white line right around his homestead and indicating that no aborigine must cross it unasked or carrying weapons. In turn, the family would respect a white line drawn round the tribal camp. A member of the staff violated the boundary (presumably in search of feminine company) and the white men made no move to interfere when the tribe belaboured him.

'Medicine Woman' the aborigines called Emma, because she brought ointment and mixtures from her medicine chest to treat their sick. Not even smallpox, brought in by Malay ships, deterred her. Compassionately she did what she could, and, when the disease proved fatal, she helped John burn or bury the bodies abandoned by the tribe.

Emma's long, thick, fair hair fascinated the dark women. She recalled their delight when she let them take out its pins and hold out its strands to watch it gleam in the sun, while they danced round like children at a party.

Eight times in the strenuous years at Mount Welcome Emma came to childbed—the first shortly after the family moved into possession. Each arrival meant more work—not only washing, cooking, mending and sewing, but teaching also. There was no library of standard works such as John Hancock's children had known. Emma's children were taught to read and spell from newspapers. She listened and corrected while busy with the endless family sewing.

Her children and the friendly dark people—even these could not cancel at all times the special quality of that land of sun and spinifex: its great, appalling loneliness, loneliness that endured day after day, while the men were mustering at outer camps, leaving Emma and the children alone. As the sun went down, so her heart sank, for then she felt most keenly the isolation from her own kind, the extreme loneliness.

She remembered an evening when she saw from the house a figure lurking in the bushes, silent, still. She called, but there was no answer. Was it a native? If so, what did he want? She caught up a rifle and called again. No answer, so she fired—and still there was no sound, no movement. Cautiously she drew near—then laughed aloud. She had shot at her own dress and hat hanging on a line.

A handful of settlers found the nor'-west. Then gold at Pilbarra started a rush to the diggings. Typhoid struck the camp, and Emma Withnell moved from tent to tent, her medicines and presence bringing comfort and relief to the ailing men.

Pearling became a part of the district's pattern, and a run of bad seasons at Mount Welcome sent John off with the luggers to help the family purse. Emma, left in charge of the station, sold two sheep a day at 6d. a pound paid for in gold over the butcher's block. It was all profit, and, added to John's earnings from pearling, promised a turn in the luck of Mount Welcome.

But who can be sure what will happen in the north-west where Nature is as chancy as anywhere in the world? Fierce heat, rivers of rain in the Wet, or the unfettered fury of a willy-willy scourging sea and coast are all of its texture. Withnell's hopes vanished on the wild breath of a hurricane that wrecked the homestead and killed thousands of sheep. Emma, clasping her baby, staggered from the creaking house into a screaming world. The house collapsed behind her. The force of the wind blew her over, a broken bottle cut her arm, and her baby vanished, carried away by the tempest. When the wind fell, he was recovered against a pile of firewood, which fortunately held firm and protected him from much of the blow.

Prosperity came through energy and unending toil over many years. The children grew and went off on enterprises of their own. Then John, who had chartered the *Sea Ripple* to set them ashore in the north-west, was dead, and Emma gone to spend her remaining years in the south and remember the land of spinifex.

She was eighty-six when Death made her part of its tradition. To those who said the years had made life easier in the land where she had pioneered she always replied: 'But still the work is hard', and reminded them that one thing remained unchanged—the great pervading loneliness that moves with those who tread the miles where the spinifex grows.

A Darwin verandah, at the turn of the century

29
Reporter of the North

JUNE 1870 in the southern cities: a winter backdrop to pork-pie hats with long ribbon streamers, and flounced dresses sweeping the ground at races and theatre. Gaslight on the streets and in the homes of the well-to-do. Train whistles startling the horses clopping along the roads by the railway lines; parliaments in six States; universities and colleges—Australia, almost a hundred years from Cook's east coast voyage, was acquiring an air of sophistication, at least in its cities and some larger towns.

But it was to another world entirely that Captain Bloomfield Douglas led his wife and family ashore that June, to a little settlement in a gully among feathery casuarinas and paper bark growing in a tropic climate. The Union Jack shone bravely, a handful of whites cheered loudly, and the permanent occupation of Darwin had begun.

It was not the first attempt to take white settlement to Australia's far north. Fear of the French, that bogey which haunted governments for fifty years, caused Darling to form an outpost at Melville Island in 1824. Not the French but scurvy and hostile natives drove the soldiers and convicts out, and today only a few ruins and a number of buffaloes (whose descendants still lure hunters north to the Territory) show that they were ever there.

No more successful was the outpost established by Captain Stirling north-east of Raffles Bay in 1827; nor one at Port Essington on Cobourg Peninsula ten years later. Then the British government, all taste lost for colonizing North Australia, recalled officials from Port Essington, transferred any settlers who had a mind for it to

Palmerston on Port Darwin, and left nature and time to deal with the remnants of the abortive northern settlements.

For the next few years white settlement concerned itself with consolidating the south, disregarding the north and its age-old routine of monsoons and tribal living almost as completely as though it were another country (as even today many declare it is). Then came a man who breathed life into the clay of public disinterest, a Scot with a name like a clarion call—John McDouall Stuart, back from his mighty march from Adelaide to the Arafura Sea. Stuart, blinded and broken in health, brought word of fertile miles stretched out across the continent, and South Australia, sponsor of his venture, now planned to settle the land he had uncovered.

But in spite of surveys and exploration by Litchfield (called the Territory's first own explorer), and two shiploads of pioneers (including two women, Mrs Packard and Mrs Bauer), the settlement stagnated until the arrival of George Woodroffe Goyder, Surveyor-General of South Australia and 'Father of Darwin'. In the schooner *Gulnare* he anchored at Fort Hill

> In the glorious harbour of Port Darwin on February 5, 1869—Darwin's natal day. The friendly Larrakeeyah blacks held a corroboree of welcome ... On the narrow neck of land formed by Fort Hill, at the foot of the multi-coloured cliffs in the shade of tamarinds and banyans, Goyder pitched his tents. For want of a better name the area was known as 'The Camp', the headquarters of police and Government officials.[1]

Surveys were made of the land between the Adelaide River and the Finniss, charting it for the men who would work it and officials who would administer the white man's law, now to be superimposed on old tribal rites and rulings.

Buildings went up, their materials bark, log and corrugated iron, with a few of local sandstone, shaded by tamarind and paper barks.

The Camp, facing into the isolated Arafura Sea, now had washing days, housekeeping and domestic chores as well as administration to keep it busy, while the *Gulnare* was away down south again, embarking the Resident, Captain Bloomfield Douglas, his family and staff. In the group came the Territory's first unofficial reporter, Miss Harriet Douglas.

Harriet must have been in her teens when she went to Darwin. She was older and married to Dominic Daly, bushman nephew of South Australia's Governor when she wrote *Digging, Squatting and Pioneering Life*, a history of those early days when the Territory was taking its first, tentative steps as a separate unit of Australian colonizing.

Her book, a mixture of domestic and official events, contains few personal details, and her reporting of the family's experiences is mainly a recital of day-to-day living. Nor does she have much to say of the other women who shared her experiences. Never a word as to Mrs Junior Carpenter's household arrangements, nor Mrs Assistant Surveyor's babies. The only woman outside the family who is mentioned at all is the maid Annie, a gem of price to her mistress, to whom she gave devoted service. Even Annie is dealt with briefly. 'A good-looking, clean, active, Australian-born girl', Harriet described her, with two outstanding capabilities: she was a hard worker and a born flirt who mowed down almost all the ship's crew on the way north, and in the Territory repeated the same pattern until at last she settled down with 'one of the best of men in the Government service'.

But in spite of what it does not say, the book is not only interesting but valuable, because as a daughter of the Residency (at first only two huts in a gully), Harriet Douglas was a reporter in a grandstand seat, in a key position to view the birth of the Territory, and the first thrust into the hinterland and adjoining districts.

The family (five girls and two boys) left Adelaide prepared for pioneering, a spirit rather damped by seasickness in the early part of the voyage north. When they recovered, Harriet had daily housekeeping duties, but, primly, does not say what they were.

A storm which almost piled the *Gulnare* on the shore near Warrnambool was accepted as a routine hazard, but in Brisbane the two eldest girls, Harriet and the sister to whom she always refers frustratingly as 'N', faced tragedy: invitations to balls and picnics, and their party clothes left behind in Adelaide! Tears ran down to bosoms clothed plainly for the pioneering days ahead. But yards of material were ordered, scissors snipped and sewing machines whirred in the cabin, enabling the two Misses Douglas to sweep, suitably attired, into the social whirl of Brisbane for three gay, light-hearted weeks of 'dinner parties, picnics, dances and boating parties'.

Then north again and the excitement of the tropics. The Barrier Reef: Cape York and the pearling vessels: brown-bodied Kanakas diving through translucent waters for the gem-bearing oyster and gleaming shell. A stay off Booby Island to cache stores for exhausted sailors often washed ashore there from wrecks of ships criss-crossing the sea lanes to and from Java, India, China and Australia.

Rough weather in the Gulf, but the wind was favourable and

Gulnare near its journey's end. Port Essington and Cobourg Peninsula dropped behind, and native canoes stood out from shore to warn of the reef near Vernon Island where the *Bengal*, supply ship with explorer John McKinlay on board, was already high and fast. The tide floated it off. and next day the two vessels sailed into Darwin's harbour together. The Union Jack blazed on one headland; the opposite 'literally swarmed with black men and women' of the Larrakeeyah tribe, the men standing like the figure 4 with one foot across the opposite thigh as they leant on their spears to watch the arrival of the white dispossessors now come to claim the North for themselves and their flocks.

The Camp's citizens were brought up to date on personalities and politics of the South, and the rumoured telegraph that would join Australia to Asia and Europe, with Darwin as the connecting link.

Then the family inspected the outpost.

> On closer inspection we found a pretty, well-kept and neatly laid out Camp. The married people lived on the left-hand side below the Larrakeeyah's camp in log huts, with neatly thatched roofs; at the farther end on the same side was the stable, a long shed made of logs, roofed with sheets of bark, and well filled with horses we were glad to see. . . . The quarters assigned to our use were two huts not large enough to accommodate such a large party, but were pleasantly situated close to the sea, and were . . . the best the place afforded.

The family slept under the bark roof of a large log hut divided by partitions and plugged with paper bark; its mud floors soiled dress hems, and added to the laundry.

A breeze-way joined sleeping quarters to the sitting room, twenty feet long, lined and floored with wood. Built of galvanized iron, with sheets of the same for windows, in spite of doors at either end and bark laid across the iron roof, it was always hot. It also held all the furniture brought from Adelaide, and Harriet thought it looked like a broker's shop where 'chests of drawers, sideboards, chiffoniers, tables of every description and shape elbowed each other, seeming as lost as we were at the strange and novel association in which they found themselves'.

The whole settlement was one of contrasts: sixty white people in a land of unnumbered natives; primordial scenery scarcely dented by tribal axes, the soil unexploited, unshaped—and orderly Victorian government and housekeeping, Monday washing day and all; habited misses cantering their horses sedately past palms and vines rioting in tropical abandon; mounted white troopers in royal blue uniform, garibaldi jumper faced with quilted black satin, black and silver braid on the cuffs, silver stripe down each dark blue trouser leg, and more edging their caps—and dark men wearing nothing but a bunch of spears carried in the hand. Domesticity was just as incongruous, mud floors and chiffoniers; dark women, carrying babies in 'an old basket in ... company with a quantity of old rags, and bits of half-eaten food, and general rubbish', helping with the laundry. White men worked through the day, but Harriet thought the natives lazy and improvident, working neither for themselves nor the white community. They could have made money supplying the Camp with food but 'they only infrequently brought in a few fish, yams, or "big one heltpoe" (turtle).'

Even the indefatigable Annie's energy had limits, so the Misses Douglas became the Residency's laundrywomen, assisted by a gaggle of lubras who turned up with piccaninnies for the fun, and enjoyed the novelty of rinsing clothes, emptying tubs, fetching water and 'hanging out'. But Harriet dismayed one dark mother when she

> carefully disrobed (an) infant of its bits of bark and rag which did duty for swaddling clothes, and having filled a bath with nice warm water ... began operations ... The mother thought I was working some deadly spell upon her offspring, as she saw it growing whiter under ... soap and water. She snatched the baby out of my arms, and uttering some doubtless soothing and endearing term restored the piccaninny to the depths of an old basket she carried slung behind her.

The girls sewed for the family and helped with household chores, including the never-ending fight against food decay in the humid tropics. Flour was constantly sifted 'on account of mildew, weevil and damp coagulated masses, which lined the sides of the barrels'. Oatmeal needed the same treatment, and 'the preserved potatoes, tasteless, dried, and granulated, were spread out on a sieve or cloth and carefully examined before being soaked previous to being boiled'. Cockroaches devoured the currants, jam and sugar,—'in fact,' complained Harriet, 'their diet was far more varied than ours, for they made plentiful meals off our boots, the coverings of our books, and any stray pieces of flannel which came their way'. The white ants were even more voracious, and went through several cases of books, clothing, paper, wood and telegraph poles.

Riding was a favourite recreation of the Misses Douglas: 'After a hard day's work it was pleasant to ride out of camp, and along

Over: a bush funeral, sketched by S. T. Gill

the bridle tracks on the tableland above.' An armed trooper escorted them, and revolvers hung at their sides as they rode past paper barks and coolibahs, lagoons and speargrass, on horses trained to canter 'at the rate of five miles an hour, gently and slowly as a rocking horse . . . the climate being too hot to allow of very fast riding for any length of time.'

Sometimes larger parties rode out on longer trips, taking 'refreshments' in packs and saddle pockets. And sometimes a general holiday was declared, when everyone but a few police left the Camp early. Food packed overnight went ahead to the picnic spot by boat. Wives and children of the workmen

> went off in spring drays seated on mattresses; the waggonette took my mother and the children, and everybody else rode, making quite a cavalcade, followed, of course, by a specially chosen escort of Larrakeeyah who never failed to include themselves in what was going on.

The day passed with horse races, shooting matches, rambles along the beach to gather shells and coral and spiky sea eggs, and ended at dusk with huge pots of tea brewed and drunk around fires before returning to the Camp.

Fish caught in the seine net on such outings gave variety to the diet; otherwise its main feature was tinned meat, known as 'blanket'. It appeared month after month, and whether dressed as curry, stew, hash or mince, it was still 'blanket'. Mushrooms were fairly common, but fresh meat was the mark of special occasions. A bullock was killed for Queen's Birthday and Christmas, and shooting parties usually returned from Melville Island with buffalo meat. The only vegetables were tinned until the garden got under way. Once established in that land of luxuriant growth, garden produce not only flourished—it positively galloped. 'The progress of a melon vine could be counted by so many inches a day; we used to put a stone or stick to mark the growth from one day to another.'

Natives dug up the first coconuts, but bananas and pineapples came to fruit, tomatoes grew freely and gave a lift to the 'blanket' dishes. Rosellas were turned into jam and jelly, and Mrs Douglas 'who was very clever at home brewed ginger beer, managed to invent Rosella syrup which was one of the most refreshing beverages.'

Harriet specialized in dishes made from cockles brought into Camp by the Larrakeeyahs: 'I stewed them, made them into soup, and crowned all my efforts by a grand success in scalloping them, deceiving everyone into the belief that they were eating oysters.'

Harriet enjoyed the climate, the 'sense of boundless freedom in the country', the 'inky arch' of a tropical storm sweeping across the harbour, the places she came to know through riding—the waterfall in Doctor's Gully splashing among ferns and creepers, the long white open beach of Fannie Bay—good for a canter at low tide; great pink and white water lilies on a lagoon, creepers twined round tree trunks, orchids in 'the Jungle', staghorn antlers against smooth white bark.

When night fell on the outpost, the family entertained friends on the 'verandah': canvas spread over saplings staked out at the edge of the Resident's quarters. Someone slapped at a mosquito, someone else dealt with sandflies. Camp gossip, yarns innumerable, the possibility of the Overland Telegraph—talk flowed on and on through the tropic night, stopping only when someone sang 'Wait for the Turn of the Tide' or 'Paddle Your Own Canoe' to the accompaniment of concertina or flute, or N.'s fine voice held them still with 'When Other Lips' and 'Ever of Thee'. Nature filled the few intervals of silence with the sound of waves swishing over the shingle, or wind moving creakily in the corkscrew palms.

John MacKinlay took his party of land-seekers into the interior. Three weeks saw them back, enthusiastic about the country and eager to snap up the surveyed blocks numbered on the maps spread over tables in the stables turned land office.

Business finished, the land-owners waited for a ship south. Until that came they rode with the Resident's daughters, shot ducks on the lagoon, came to dinner (' "blanket" cunningly disguised as soup, entrée and joint'), sang while the waves washed over the shingle, and strolled by moonlight round Fort Hill.

Weeks went by with no ship from the south, though searching eyes watched constantly from Fannie Bay. Something on the horizon —was it a sail? 'Alas! nothing but a blackfellow's campfire behind some faraway headland, or at times some . . . tree . . . floated out to sea, its branches against the sky line made us think a sail was heaving in sight.' The natives, anxious to please, often reported: 'Morte (ship) come on.' But it was September before the *Omeo* arrived with a stack of letters, newspapers and books: 'The latter was the greatest boon we could have had. Miss Broughton's "Red as a Rose Is She" had then come out in "Temple Bar", and some kind, thoughtful creature sent us the bound volumes for a year.'

With the *Omeo* came proof that the Overland Telegraph was to become fact. The harbour buzzed with activity as the contractor and his men landed from the ship to begin work at the northern end.

Slings lowered horses overboard to swim ashore, drays were floated in, their wheels following by boat, and on the tableland above the harbour a construction camp went up. A week after *Omeo's* arrival the whole community gathered to see Miss Harriet Douglas ram earth round the first pole and declared it well and truly fixed. Axes cleared away the paper barks to make a track for supply drays hauling food, clothes, medicine, wire and gear to the camps of the line-builders.

It was blue-print planning, done with little knowledge of the terrain. Hardly had a start been made when the Wet came. The great-hearted but heavy draught horses floundered in quagmires, sank and scrambled up, only to sink again, until, exhausted, they could rise no more and were shot.

The working bullocks fared better, but only in degree. White ants fed fast on the posts. 'The malarious mist' of the jungle took toll of men camped on swamps, or beside swollen rivers. Their clothes wet night and day, and often short of food, 'fever and ague' were their constant companions. The worst cases were returned to the Camp doctor for attention; medical advice for others was tapped out across the wires, strung up as the poles were set in position.

Two hundred and twenty miles were covered under these conditions, then, with most of the men sick and nearly all the horses lost, the contractor threw in his hand and sought release from his obligations.

*   *   *

It is difficult to believe there was no gossip among the small group packed closely together on the fringe of the continent, but Harriet did not reveal it. Her reporting breached no holes in the bulwarks of personalities, and the events she described are those which interested the Camp, but did not set it by the ears: the numerous snakes which wriggled across the Territory; the grisly note struck by a crocodile (always alligator to Harriet) fatality; the expedition sent to the Roper which crossed explorer Stuart's tracks, and returned with three horses he had abandoned. (Strangely, Harriet 'saw' the arrival with these horses in a dream which she related at the breakfast table before the expedition came back.)

Building a permanent Residency gave everyone occupation, either as workers or advisers. The chosen site was the flat-topped hill overlooking the south, east and west arms of the harbour. Then came the search for building materials. Stone, used for the main building, was easily obtained, but timber worried the builders. Ironbark lived up to its name and defied the saw. Other ant-resistant wood was scarce, until a stand of cypress pine was found at Byrnie Harbour. Crushed coral, kiln-burnt, took the place of lime.

The men worked steadily on the job, the Camp noting and commenting critically on each day's performance, inspecting every inch added to the 'bungalow-style' house. Its flat roof gave the builders their greatest problem. They tried timber, but this was unseasoned. It warped, and rain poured in. They stretched painted canvas across it, but the sun dried out the oil and blistered the paint. Concrete was the solution, to Harriet's surprise. It roofed the building efficiently, gave the family a dress-circle view of the harbour and a unique place to entertain friends at night.

In the new Residency the family had a laundry and drying ground where the girls worked in privacy, and hung out the linen and smalls without the Camp's supervision.

Nine months without a ship. Supplies were running short. The Resident's secretary went to Dutch Timor with a list of urgent requirements. He returned with pins, needles, cottons, tapes and buttons, a sackful of mail and papers. To the Camp, starved of southern news, 'the very advertisements in the Adelaide papers seemed like meeting old friends' and were greeted with affection.

No clothing for European women in Timor's shops, and everyone's shoes were now in a sad state. One of the teamsters, Charlie Fry, turned shoemaker, and fashioned new ones from canvas and leather, unpicking a pair of old shoes for a pattern. What a treat, commented Harriet: they were 'not works of art or things of beauty ... but I remember how glad we were to get them, and how wonderfully useful they were.'

In September 1871 Harriet went south to marry Dominic Daly in Adelaide. The south-east monsoon held back her ship, coal ran short, the ship's boats were broken up for fuel and the voyage took six weeks instead of three.

Brisbane's 'crisp fresh morning air . . . after seventeen months' tropical warmth', its carriages, daily papers, postmen, butchers' and bakers' carts'—Harriet felt like Rip Van Winkle returning to another almost forgotten existence.

The Dalys spent their first months of married life at Narracoorte, S.A., but kept in touch with the Territory. The Overland Telegraph was now marching steadily south under the management of Charles Todd, South Australia's Postmaster-General, who went north to carry on the project himself, and saved miles, and time, by using the Roper as a waterway to the construction camps.

Month by month, in the face of countless difficulties, the working parties doggedly closed the gap between north and south till the wires were joined—strung across a continent, destined to carry rumour, scandal, and news of war—and save many a life in the wastes where the wires alone held man in touch with his fellows.

One of the early announcements flashed from the north told of gold turned up by 'construction parties' in the tropical bush. A rush started, companies were formed, ships chartered, and diggers by hundreds headed north. The compass of the Dalys' fortunes felt the pull. Soon they, too, were on their way, by the *Omeo* out of Melbourne, executing commissions received by telegraph to choose 'a dinner service or to select a sewing machine . . . some cases of oranges . . . when, only a few months before, Port Darwin was more isolated than any part of the known world.'

Harriet found many changes in Darwin (Palmerston) after fifteen months: younger brothers and sisters had shot up like saplings, the town had spread and grown, with a new stone dwelling, headquarters of the Overland Telegraph and Cable Company, dominating the scene from the heights above the harbour. Bark huts and log shanties in every direction, and what had once been Sleepy Hollow had become an active, buzzing mining town.

Vessels arrived daily, pouring a stream of miners through the doorway of the Territory for the hundred-and-ten-mile trek to the fields. Gold fever at its most intense. El Dorado like a mirage in the warm sky, but with as flimsy a foundation. The only roads inland were the tracks made by the Telegraph drays, the only guide was the thin wire. Men tramped with swags on their backs, carrying pickaxe, cradle and shovel, or pushed their belongings in a wheelbarrow. Felled trees made a corduroy causeway over bogs and swamps. The hazards of haulage sent foodstuff prices rocketing upward, gruelling weather and terrain claimed victims among men constantly 'swimming rivers . . . and sleeping in wet clothes', and the inevitable 'fever and ague' reduced them to hollow-eyed copies of themselves.

Harriet saw the gold gradually trickle into Darwin:

pickle bottles full of nuggets . . . calico bags . . . disclosing small quantities of water-worn, flaky gold . . . sacks of quartz . . .
. . . (to be) sent down to Melbourne to be properly tested . . .
even the children were seen groping among the rocks on Fort Point, picking up quartz.

Harriet's baby was born at the height of the gold fever, and her husband went prospecting, pegging a claim ninety-nine miles from

Palmerston. While Harriet was busy with household chores and baby-tending, an epidemic (was it malaria or 'flu?) hit diggers and almost everyone else. Some new arrivals went down so badly that they took the first ship south, leaving the gold of the north undisturbed by their picks or efforts. No hospital, an overworked doctor, and little food other than 'the hideous brown tin of canned meat to turn into soup'. Darwin was hardly geared for sickness on a large scale.

The Residency family produced a concert to boost morale as soon as enough performers were off the sick list. The audience, mostly diggers, thundered their applause of N.'s singing 'Oft in the Stilly Night', but the comics really won them, and the house rocked over the woes of 'Betsy' and the misdeeds of 'Kafozilum'.

The alluvial soon cleaned up, and the exodus of diggers increased. Dominic Daly went south in the *Springbok* for machinery to work the deeper deposits. Weeks went by without news until it was assumed his ship had gone down with all hands, and everyone carefully refrained from discussing it in Harriet's presence.

Then, one hundred and eighteen days after sailing, the *Springbok* was reported safe, mainly through the efforts of Daly and the mate, who took over from the drunken skipper and brought the ship to port, in spite of lack of provisions and fuel and an orgy of drinking by diggers convinced they would never see land again.

But the delay in consolidating his claim cost Daly a chance of fortune on the northern goldfields, so he cut his losses, sold the ready-to-build house which he had brought to Darwin but never erected, and with Harriet and the baby left for Adelaide.

The first available vessel was a very small schooner of eighty tons. Harriet, priding herself on her pioneering ability to rough it, insisted they take it. She did not bargain for a complete absence of awnings, 'no proper accommodation for ladies', and provisions that ran shorter and shorter till the menu was exclusively salt meat, biscuit and duff. Commented Harriet: 'The rum, somehow, held out to the bitter end. I notice it always does.'

> Two days before Fremantle was reached nothing was served but flour and water with a few raisins thrown in. No meat, and no tea or sugar, no water for drinking purposes, instead ale for breakfast, dinner and tea.

* * *

Harriet Daly never went again to the north, but her interest in it remained. Newspapers and official papers gave her its history after she left: the depression following the bursting of the gold bubbles, her father's trip to Singapore to bring back the first Chinese to the Territory, the Queenslanders' overlanding, accidents and 'perishes', the gold rush to Margaret River, coffee planting in Rum Jungle in 1882, and the railway from Palmerston to Pine Creek.

The first of the great grazing holdings had come to the Territory when Mrs Daly wrote her book. So had the first mission to the aborigines, pearling schooners, horse-and cattle-duffing and Chinese villages. These and much more she reported to a world largely unaware of Australia's tropical north. Two of the problems she saw and discussed, the status of the aborigines and the presence of the Asians who came to trade or work, remain to challenge us. Harriet Douglas Daly told the world of their existence when she set down in mid-Victorian wording a picture of Darwin's colourful beginning. In one other way she also forestalled us. Her book is a declaration of faith in the high potential of the Territory, and that faith is something the rest of Australia is only now beginning to share.

Junketings of the 'Seventies

Narracoorte was the great coursing centre of the district and, I believe, of the colony. There was a coursing club, of which my husband was slip-steward. . . . Squatters came from far and wide, many from over the border. We were within twelve miles of the Victorian boundary, and the excitement on the different matches and seeing the ties run off towards the close of the meeting was intense. The week wound up by a ball, which was invariably kept up not only into the small hours of the morning, but until the sun was far up in the sky. My husband and I were indefatigable dancers, and thought nothing of a sixty-mile drive in order to go to a dance. We were, however, not singular in this respect, for we frequently met others who had come on horseback or in their American buggies over a hundred miles for the same purpose. No one went home until morning, and the scene of the returning revellers was at times an amusing one—tired dancers getting on to their horses; dress-suits changed for ordinary riding attire; a ball dress, neatly folded away and put into a valise, strapped to the saddle, and the belle of the evening starting away in the early morning for her long homeward ride; buggies full of sleepy girls, wrapped in shawls and with programme and fan in hand, drove quickly away through the bush tracks, disturbing the kangaroos, wallaby, and emu over their early nibble at the short, sweet dew-laden grass.

In the Wet

To watch the clouds gathering over the opposite shore was really a grand and imposing spectacle. The sky became almost black, and lurid flashes of lightning, miles and miles away, played incessantly in the heavens. Gradually the storm approached, rising like an inky arch, sweeping across the harbour, and as it touched the water cut it up into wreaths of foam . . . every moment the thunder became louder and the lightning more vivid and alarming. The trees, which had before been motionless, now began to quiver, and the leaves rustled in a dazed and troubled manner. The birds ceased flying, and took refuge till the storm should have spent its fury and all was peace and quietude once more.

When the squall was fairly overhead, the din and noise were almost bewildering. The sea was lashed into foam, the suddenly raised surf broke angrily on the beach. Doors slammed and windows were hastily shut, people hurried hither and thither to a place of safety, while the thunder and lightning roared and flashed simultaneously. This lasted perhaps twenty minutes; then followed the rain, which came down thick and straight, when the squall itself, as if tired of being stationary, gradually rolled over and away to a further scene of action.

Tropical Mothercraft

We had a sort of dish-cover made on an enlarged scale, the framework was covered with mosquito net, and it fitted over baby's paraphernalia of mats and pillows. Over her head we put a cunningly devised creation of red, blue and yellow wool, which fluttered in the wind, and kept her attention in a most satisfactory manner. In the intervals of laundry and household duties we all played with her, and then she returned to her mosquito-proof house. As time went on and she grew old enough to sit up and take an interest in playthings, she was brought into the laundry in a nice clean American flour-barrel in which she played for hours, while I washed and ironed our clothes.

Harriet W. Daly, *Digging, Squatting and Pioneering Life in the Northern Territory of South Australia.*

30
Paddles on the Murray

DUNDREARY WHISKERS quivered and spreading crinolines trembled with excitement as their owners stood at vantage points round Sydney Harbour. The *Sophia Jane*, first paddle-wheel steamer to voyage from England to the colony, entered the Heads, and the press of the day (1831) almost ran out of adjectives in praise of the vessel and its prodigious speed.

Transportation had taken a step forward, and by 1853 the step reached the inland, when *Lady Augusta*—'a noble little craft' carrying 16 cuddy and 16 forecabin passengers—made an experimental trip on 'a hitherto unnavigated river (the Murray) through the immense Australian wilds'.

By the 1880s stations and runs were strung out through the land watered by the Murray and its tributaries, and paddle-wheelers ran regular services on the waterways. Their barges towed bolts of calico, saddles, horse-shoes, jam, currants, bonnets and bustles, on the up trip, and returned with fleece, tallow and hides.

The ships' fires were stoked with wood, and many a boundary rider or stockman added something extra to his weekly wage by spare-time timber-cutting. Log stacks were piled at stated places along the banks. One was Berri-Berri Bend, Cobdogla Station.

In 1884 a lanky stockman, 'Major' Holden, made timber cutting his responsibility at Berri-Berri, built a hut there for himself and Mary, his bride. The station homestead was well back from the river, so the crew and passengers of passing paddle-steamers were about the only white people the Holdens saw on the fine stretch of Berri-Berri Bend, where wild duck nested along the shores, fish were plentiful,

Paddles on the Murray

kangaroos abounded, vegetables throve in the clearing near the hut, and there were goats for milking.

Day after day, week after week, Holden was away to his tree-felling sawing, chopping and shaping the logs which he chained behind a pair of horses for the homeward drag.

Mary worked in and around the hut, worried and anxious in spite of her baby and the idyllic setting of the home at Berri-Berri. Holden was too thin, coughed too much, and tired too easily. But some feeling of urgency, of time running out, drove him to attempt one more load, then another, until he had his last coughing spasm, and Mary was alone with her baby and her grief.

No neighbours to turn to, and whatever must be done Mary must do. She launched the small rowing boat, placed in it food and a keg of water, set her baby's crib on a seat, sheltered it from the sun, then wrapped her dead in blankets and somehow got him aboard.

It was a long pull from the hut and its garden to Overland Corner, the nearest township, and Mary could expect no help along the empty stretch of river unless a paddle-steamer chanced along.

None came, and Mary, tending her baby, eating when she must, rowed until she was too tired to think.

In two days she reached Overland Corner, and kindly hearts and hands reached out to help her. But still along the river they tell the story of Mary Holden's ordeal when she rowed with the Murray running silently beside her and the red gums' shadow falling on her as she passed.

Retold from facts supplied by Mrs Lochee M. Andison,
Berri, S.A.

Traders on the Murray, about 1910

On the goldfields, Western Australia

31
Along the Golden Miles

YEARS BEFORE they found it, men swore there was gold in the sands of the West. When they struck it in the 'nineties, the population of Western Australia rocketed, and the trail inland was crowded with men carrying swags to the fields. Canvas and hessian humpies went up, and a few women appeared.

One was Clara Saunders of Brisbane, who was in Southern Cross the day Arthur Bayley rode into town, hitched his packhorses to the post outside the bank, and carried in their burden: 550 ounces of gold. Like a fire through grass the news spread through town. All available horses were rounded up and sold for a minimum of £40. Men hurried in all directions, buying picks and shovels, water-bags and tucker. A dray loaded with provisions and swags took off, the men walking in its wake. Within a few hours 'the Cross was a woman's town'.[1]

Bayley's Find was surveyed and laid out as a township. They re-christened it Coolgardie. In a few years it was filled with iron-roofed hessian buildings, tents and bough sheds, dust, heat, flies and dirt.

Excitement was the normal mood of its inhabitants. At any moment Fortune might, and often did, appear under the searching pick in a man's hands. Years later Clara remembered the bellringer moving down Bayley Street announcing Paddy Hannan's strike, thirty miles farther out. Again there was the rush of men, the loading of teams and the taking off, the same hastily erected shelters, the same dust and sand, the same flies.

Clara was wooed and won on the fields. A young man, Arthur

Williams, courted her with fruit (when available) and cool drinks on hot days. He had strong competition to face at the ball held on Boxing Night, when every woman had at least three partners during each dance.

Clara's marriage (at sixteen) was the first celebrated in Coolgardie.[2] Arthur had a wayside hotel licence, and Clara went with him to the Ninety Mile. They had two tents, and Clara cooked out of doors in the broiling western sun, baking bread in camp ovens. She could never recall the number of burns sustained in the process.

Almost all other food came from tins, 'even potatoes were pressed dry like a packet of hops'. Cartage from Perth was £60 a ton. None of the stores carried women's clothing, and shoes were esteemed next to water and gold where the ground heat scorched flesh even through leather.

A few years later, Mrs Arthur Garnsey (Sister Ann Bird) reached Coolgardie from Tasmania, via Rockhampton. The change from the soft green State of her birth and the tropics with their multi-coloured crotons, bougainvillea and riot of flowers to the stark towns of the golden miles with never a garden between them was a startling contrast.

Her introduction was a 'long weary journey' inland.

> The sand blew in at the train windows, although they were shut, and made our faces sting. We often had to stand up and shake ourselves and scrape the sand off our tongues. We felt that we were part of the desert. . . The water in the water bottle had a thick film of dust. We tried to strain it through our rather black handerchiefs before venturing to sip the hot, pestiferous stuff. It didn't seem safe to swallow it. We just rinsed our months and spat it out.[3]

Her first impression of Coolgardie was thunderous noise. 'Old Bailey's batteries talking', the hospital orderly informed her. 'You get used to it.' She did.

The town was well laid out with wide main streets, footpaths and bicycle tracks at each side. But the streets were little more than sandy spaces and the houses coated with dust. 'Most of these houses, or shacks, were canvas over a wooden framework and made so that they could be moved at any time . . . it was no uncommon thing to see houses travelling across country, fixed on rollers and drawn by camel teams.'[4]

Mrs Garnsey had no doubts about the land's real ruler: 'Over all reigned supreme the great King Dust—a mixture of the desert sand

and the mining 'dumps' stirred up and whisked together by those boisterous willy willys.'[5]

Dust penetrated everywhere. It showered out of women's hair under the brush, it made clothes washing a mockery. Mrs Garnsey mentions the local laundries

> where clothes were thoroughly ruined by the method of steam cleaning with condensed water and chemicals, after which they were hung out to dry in dust storms—red dust storms—so that every garment which had once been white very soon became pinky-red. . . . We soon learnt to wear only coloured clothes, and as few as possible.[6]

Again there is a record of the feeling which pervaded the diggings, an atmosphere of restlessness which came from the diggers who were either elated at success or depressed by ill-luck.

Beside the diggers, in whose ranks all classes were represented, there were natives wandering through town, squatting down to play euchre, or begging for 'bacca. Afghan teamsters who supplied the towns camped on the outskirts with their camels, often as many as a hundred, loaded for a haul farther inland.

Fresh food was scarce and expensive. 'We get used to eating eggs of the third degree. There were five degrees in eggs—new laid (?), fresh, case, cooking and eggs! They were arranged in these divisions in the shop windows.'[7]

The difficulties of keeping a house clean, of laundry, of providing adequate meals must have daunted the most stout-hearted.

Old-timers of the field argue whether there was more or less water, but the women who have recorded their impressions are not of two minds. It was scarce, they declared flatly. Mrs Williams says it was often carried fifty miles on camel-back. Mrs Garnsey recalls it was salty when pumped up from the mines. It was distilled for use, but nothing disguised its taste, and often the supply failed completely. This and the lack of proper sanitation resulted in periodic typhoid epidemics when every woman became a nurse.[8]

But when the Helena River was dammed in the Darling Ranges, and the pipeline carried water hundreds of miles from the Mundaring Dam, a new era dawned for the golden towns. Within a few months there were flowers in the gardens and a fresh light in women's eyes. Critics of the scheme might have held back their attacks which drove the engineer in charge to suicide had they seen the new hope and heart the pipeline they so greatly deplored gave to the harassed housewives and mothers of the towns on the Golden Way.

A Goldfield Wedding

On 4 July 1894, Miss Clara Saunders married Mr Arthur Williams at Coolgardie. This was the first wedding in the township, and great were the celebrations thereat. The local press was represented, and published the following report in the *Miner*.

On Wednesday evening last, the Reverend Mr. Frestrall, Wesleyan Minister, joined in Bonds of Holy Matrimony—the first couple that have decided to peg out life's lease together in Coolgardie. Miss Clara Saunders was the lady who acted as Pioneer in the Matrimonial market for her sweet sisterhood, and Mr. Arthur Williams was the first gentleman who paved the way, that . . . hundreds of other men will surely follow. The bride looked very nice in her Robes of Sacrifice, and the groom looked resolutely nervous. After the ceremony the newly married couple entertained a number of friends in John De Baun's Dining Room, the yellow wine flowed freely and dancing was joyously engaged in. Some of the ladies' costumes would have done credit to a Melbourne Ballroom. The bride wore rich cream quartz coloured silk with Orange Blossom outcrops, Miss Hickey was dressed in a reddish substance with greenstone coloured leaders running round the main body looking very nice indeed, so much so that many a male animal wished for a miner's right, so that he could apply for a perpetual lease. Mrs. Faahan wore a pale pink milk quartz combination with gold outcrops running across the full breadth of the face, a most stylish looking dress in every way, the whole outfit suiting her slight and elegant figure to perfection. Miss Burns appeared in a charming outfit, the main body being blue, trimmed all down the footwall side with laminated leaders of dark shale colour, the dancers immediately showed their appreciation by prospecting round and filling in her card for the evening. Miss Brennan set envious teeth on edge when she waltzed round in a slate coloured robe, the principal outcrop being decorated with Diorite coloured stringers, and other surface indications of a highly pleasing nature, she moved with the grace and freedom of an adept in the most joyous of all pastimes and more than one poor Dry Blower as he panted round the room with a less accomplished partner envied those who for the time being owned so good a claim. Miss Kennedy wore a Kaolin coloured silk . . . There were quite a number of other pretty dresses, but as the editor has just remarked, the Writer has to go and report on a mine and the rest be left over suffice to say that the first wedding in Coolgardie was an unqualified success, and the 'Miner' wishes Bride and Bridegroom no end of happiness and good luck. The happy couple were the recipients of a goodly number of beautiful presents, and are now settled in their little three-roomed cottage in Sylvester Street.

> Mrs Clara Paton, 'Early Days of Coolgardie', Western
> Australian Historical Society Journal and Proceedings,
> vol. 4, pt. 2 (1950).

Homes of the early settlers

32
Nurses of the Inland

WHEN THEY broke open the Golden Mile in the 'nineties and started the rush to the Western Australian fields, the crazy, feverish drama of digging was enacted in sands of the semi-desert. Lack of water, poor diet through the scarcity of foodstuffs and the long distances they had to come, dirt, primitive sanitation, heat, dust, flies were breeding grounds for epidemics. Dysentery was bad, typhoid worse.

Clara Saunders was little more than a child (she was fifteen) when an outbreak of dysentery at Coolgardie made her nurse to stricken miners. They lay in tents, on beds that were merely a bag or two, with a pair of old dungaree trousers rolled up for a pillow. Clara and her employer made soup and barley water, prepared sago and gruel to feed them. But bathing the sick was beyond the women; the best they could manage was to sponge face and hands. For this they cut towels in half, even then there were not enough.

Further out, at the Ninety Mile, Clara (now Mrs Williams) was at first the only woman on the field. Time and again she coped with emergencies: a fever patient in delirium, prospectors speared by blacks at a water hole and suffering with scurvy. Treatment was simple: water boiled in kerosene tins, a handful of Condy's crystals added for hot foments to wounds. 'Epsom salts was the only medicine I had', said Clara. 'I gave them plenty.'[1]

Every woman on the goldfields acted as nurse in emergency. No one knows just how many lives their devoted care saved, says Malcolm Uren.[2] But in 1895 the few women could not cope with typhoid raging in the construction camp of the men laying the rails to Coolgardie. An S.O.S. call went to Perth, and the Methodist

People's Mission opened a hospital at Woolgangie, railhead between Southern Cross and Coolgardie. Sister Gertrude came from Melbourne in January 1896 to take charge.

Her first patient was a boy lying 'on a few old rugs and chaff bags under the counter of a lemon squash shop. There was no ventilation and the boy was delirious', his temperature 103·6 degrees. Sister Gertrude took him to her own tent, a miner gave up his bed, and for weeks the boy, delirious and unconscious with a severe attack of typhoid, was nursed under nightmare conditions. It was two months before the fever left him.

A government hospital was established at Coolgardie. The first two nurses had a mammoth job to make anything of the hessian tents with little or no equipment. In one tent a miner had lain dangerously ill with rheumatic fever for weeks. When the nurses arrived, he was still lying fully clothed on his miserable bunk.

A working party gave the place some sanitation, installed a few amenities, even lent a hand with nursing.

The hospital grew with the town, but there was still plenty of room for improvement when Sister Ann Bird (Mrs Arthur Garnsey) arrived in January 1898.

'The most sadly busy place . . . was the hospital—a scattered collection of odd buildings with no surrounding fence',[3] standing on a rise to the east of the town overlooking the Golden Mile. The dispensary, theatre and morgue were stone, the wards corrugated iron set on piles, and a few others of canvas.

> The nurses' quarters were . . . hessian stretched over wooden framework and lined with cretonne. . . The loosely woven hessian gave us very little protection from the dust storms, and the heat inside . . . was at times so suffocating that it was no unusual thing to throw the mattresses aside and lie on the bare wires of the spring bed, with an umbrella open over our heads as a slight protection against the dust and sand, and a bottle of water and sponge beside us to mop our hot, dusty faces. Often . . . the sponge had to be damped in lemonade or soda water.[4]

When the rail reached Coolgardie, ice was brought from Perth, but the only water was salt, pumped from the mines, then distilled. It was scarce, expensive, and its taste was vile. Often there was not enough to sponge the patients. 'In despair, when the water supply ran out, nurses often tried to cool burning bodies by damping a sponge in whisky or brandy, two liquids of which Coolgardie never ran short.'[5]

Beds were made up with grey blankets and pillow cases of turkey red twill. Surgical instruments were in short supply, and carpenters' tools (sterilized as well as could be managed) were sometimes called on. Sterilizing before an operation usually meant the nurses dipping 'hand and arms up to the elbows in strong Condy's fluid till they were nearly black', then scrubbing 'in very strong, hot brine'.

Uniforms and aprons were three inches off the ground, but the conventional cap was not worn. For some protection from sun and sand, nurses wore 'any old hats and the bigger the better' as they passed between the scattered wards. Under the hats was 'long hair coiled on top of our heads . . . like a wet cushion—it was never dry'.[6]

Typhoid epidemics, mine accidents, burns, falls—any and everything that can happen to man living under such conditions came to the hospital and the nurses. What their care meant to the men living in those stark, uncomfortable tents is not hard to imagine. The term 'ministering angel' is out of use in our modern idiom, but not a miner of the 'nineties would have denied it to the nurses who worked in those early goldfield hospitals.

To north and east of the western goldfields lay the lonely, neglected, little-known Inland—a country without roads or fences, over which lay the brooding quietness of unused land, of untravelled distance.

Its real texture can only be felt by taking sound out of the air waves, for wireless had not arrived; by removing all cars, their day had not yet come; and by silencing the roar of planes in flight, their wings had not been spread in the Inland skies. Reduce the telegraph wires, and take away most of the phones. Push the frontiers closer to town, spread out the empty miles, space out its few people.

The Inland then was vaster, its dangers greater, but in its distances a few women were rearing—and losing—children where no doctor practised, no church spires stood, no school bells rang.

The century was little more than a decade old when the first recruits to the army of aid were mobilized, the initial contingent to reinforce the frontiers.

One of the earliest movements was the nursing service of the Australian Inland Mission, brought into being by John Flynn, who, says the Reverend Fred McKay, who ultimately succeeded him, was given his charter by two women.

The first is a rather shadowy figure, described as the wife of an official in Darwin. In 1908 she wrote to a friend in the south asking where was the missionary zeal of her church that left the North deprived of help and comfort.

The letter interested many Presbyterians but none more than young John Flynn. Chosen to survey the needs of the neglected North, he paid a visit in Melbourne to a woman who had lived and suffered in the Territory, where her own husband had died. She was Mrs Aeneas Gunn, once of Elsey Station, Northern Territory, author of *We of the Never Never* and *The Little Black Princess*. Mrs Gunn told Flynn that the Inland people's most pressing needs were, first, medical help; then social contact. If these aids to living were established, the Church could proceed to spiritual matters. But the country itself was the challenge, and success could only come by first solving its two major problems that stemmed from isolation.

With these words in his ears John Flynn went out to survey the country where some of the loneliest women in Australia lived. What he reported led to the founding of the Australian Inland Mission, and the system of hostels where medical help could be obtained.

Darwin in 1912 had less than four hundred Europeans in a population of about a thousand; Pine Creek and Alice Springs were not large enough to be called townships. Three hundred and twenty miles south of The Alice, where the train panted in once a fortnight, was Oodnadatta, the southern door to the Inland, the town which faced the outback, from which the camel teams started, the last place the prospectors saw before they melted with their packhorses into the distance of the gibber plains. Beyond lay the vast area bisected by the Overland Telegraph, and the wind which twanged its wires only accentuated the isolation of those who lived or moved in the Inland emptiness.

> If we want to go to the train at Oodnadatta, we have to drive by buggy for two weeks. It is nearly three hundred miles and there are no fences to go through and only eight houses to pass. We make a campfire at night and bake a damper. Sometimes we sleep near the buggy, sometimes on the sand in the creek. Sometimes we have to dig a hole in the sand ... to get water for ourselves and the horses.[7]

The first A.I.M. hostel was based at Oodnadatta. Nurse Main, the first nurse, worked for months in makeshift quarters, until, on a day of fierce heat, high wind and dust, followed by thunder, lightning and torrential rain, the official hostel opened.

For years it stood like a beacon in the sea of Inland isolation, its nurses often alone but for their aboriginal maids, with little to do but give lessons to children from the fettlers' camp and hold Sunday School and a service at the week's end.

But then would come the call for help, galloping hooves by day or night, and a breathless messenger telling of a mate ill or injured; a desperately sick man arriving on camel-back from a four-hundred-mile journey, three weeks on the road, with the thermometer reading between 118° and 123°; distraught parents travelling eight days to place their sick baby in the nurse's care. What would they have done without the hostel? John Flynn knew the answer to that. On his patrols he had seen the many small graves that dotted the Inland.

Sometimes the hostel nurse went out to bring in her patient. One journey to a stockman with several broken ribs took place on a night so dark that the horses' heads were invisible from the buggy seat. Jolting forced the pin from the swingle bar, the horses bolted and almost tipped the buggy into a quarry. Five or six times in the rain the sketchy track was lost, and the nurse climbed out of the buggy to search for the path by lantern. At 2 a.m. she reached her patient, having taken six hours to cover twenty miles.

By 1920 A.I.M. nurses were staffing hostels in other areas—at Port Hedland, Western Australia, to serve the pearlers of the coast and the cattlemen of the spinifex plains; at Maranboy, where a tinfield mushroomed; at Hall's Creek, where gold brought diggers to the volcanic hills.

Sister Francis went to Birdsville, south-west Queensland, in 1924, to open another A.I.M. hostel on the gibber plains, in sight of the lazy, yellow Diamantina. In the days before the hostel, the nearest medical help was at Marree, three hundred miles away—and lucky to reach it if the floods were out.

Sister Francis could count on goods arriving twice a year by camel train, bacon and butter for a few weeks in winter only, and always a scarcity of water. Drugs and medicines were kept in an underground room, and the sisters' skill was the solace of the people in the district where cattle stations covered thousands of square miles.

Today the nurses at the hostel have a modern building, refrigeration, and the transceiver to contact the Flying Doctor. Otherwise there are the same gibbers sharing the sandy soil with the saltbush, kittyhawks soaring in the clear Inland sky, lignum bushes along the tracks—the place looks much the same as when Sturt passed through, sunk deep in despair at the relentless rise and fall of the sandhills.

Rain garlands those sandhills with wildflowers, but rain comes seldom. When it does, it may bring floodwaters from higher upstream, and turn the ground to swamp. No landing then for the doctor's plane, and no way through for the mail van bringing stores. A plague of rats often follows in the flood's wake. Hostel sisters then sit at night with their feet off the ground, and the baby's cot is covered with wire netting.

To the A.I.M. girls it is part of their stint of duty. Their opposite numbers in the Dunbar district, York Peninsula, may be swimming a river, holding to the tail of a horse and trying not to remember the crocodiles. At Innamincka, in the Burke and Wills country, they may be setting the table in an 'Alice in Wonderland' way, for 'when the dust storms rage, the table cloth goes on last', they report cheerfully.

Today other church organizations work with the same aim: to bring help and comfort to the Inland. The earliest lay movement was born after Lady Dudley, wife of the Governor-General, returned from touring the outback, filled with admiration and pity for the courage of its women and the hardships they endured. She asked for a service to help homemakers on the frontiers, and sympathetic supporters established the Bush Nursing Association.

In spite of opposition from those who hinted darkly that a host of Sairey Gamps would take over the organization, certified nurses with a sense of vocation came forward to man the little outposts of help and comfort. Today most Bush Nurses hold three certificates.

New South Wales put its first Bush Nursing Home at Jindabyne in the shadow of Kosciusko—a lonely little end-of-the-road village serving sheep and cattle breeders of the Monaros. The first (1912) Annual Report lists nurses at three other centres. Victoria also adopted the scheme and other States followed, their history full of epic trips, in ' "bitzer" cars, trucks, waggons, milk floats, trikes, horseback, camel hump and rowing boats'.[8]

The Bush Nurse's job may have its quiet spells, but she cannot count on them. A polio victim whose limbs require manipulation, a mother brought to premature childbirth, a boy wounded shooting foxes, may all receive attention in one day. At night, the nurse may be giving consultations in the surgery, or driving out to a patient through pelting rain, with men waiting at places along the way to lift her car over the worst stretches of a greasy track. Crossing a flooded creek, working through a heat wave, giving up her own bed during a 'flu epidemic—anything can happen to a Bush Nurse and usually does. She takes it as it comes, but one can sympathize with the Sister who threatened each year to go on leave during the football season. Her area took in a huge construction camp.

Making-do in the patient's own home is routine. Sister Beatrice

Purdey, Bush Nurse at Tongala (Victoria) in 1927, worked fast the night she confined a young mother in a little just-finished house with only a stove in the room which would one day be the kitchen.

Some centres are not far from a town and a doctor. Others are over a hundred miles away. All areas could be in danger without the nurses. A severed artery or absence of snakebite serum can kill as quickly today as when the first settlers were founding the land.

An Australian dairymaid

33
A Pepper Tree at Tarella

THE HOMESTEAD stood on a stony rise and that gave it an advantage when dust storms blew. You could see the dust coming: a black wall advancing across the undulating country, bare most of the time so you wondered how the stock existed. Half an hour before the storm struck, you were conscious of a dull roar which grew louder as the wall of dust drew nearer.

You rushed to gather towels, dusters, rags, spread them on sills, and jamb down the windows tightly. Bring in the washing. Call the children. Close the doors and block up the space at the bottom. Now the house is a fortress, besieged by the army of dust.

It blows and blows. The men on the run, too far off to reach shelter in time, are crouched behind a tree, most likely, or behind the horse they have backed into the storm. Hats well down on their heads, eyes and mouths covered, they wait out the blow.

It grows dark when the dust hits, so dark that by four in the afternoon you light the lamps and listen to the noise of the wind. Time and again you think it is lessening, but it seems an age before you can be sure it is really lulling, that it has passed and gone. Nothing to do now but clean up. The house can be swept. Thanks to the rise and the stony ground, the dust which found its way inside—and there was always plenty—was never as bad at Tarella as on homesteads built on sandy soil. You shovel dust off the verandah and cart it away in barrows, and for days all the food is gritty, and you taste the dust, feel it in your hair, in your eyes, and your white clothes are a deeper tinge of red than they usually are through chemicals in the water and the western dust.

The children soon forgot, and Mrs Quin was used to it. She has seen many dust storms since 1872 when John Quin brought her, a bride of a year, to Tarella, fifty-six miles from Wilcannia, to the small four-roomed pisé house with its log kitchen and its doors in two pieces, upper and lower—stable doors. For two years she saw no white woman, and drought stalked the land. But drought was almost the usual state of the country, the creek was dry more often than not, and water was carted long distances. 'Shall I wash up or make tea? There's only one kettleful left', asked the cook on one occasion. Afterwards there were large tanks, and a dam filled with water pumped up when the creek filled.

The children remembered the country as always dry, but Mrs Quin had seen it in the early years when there was plenty of mulga. That was before the rabbits took over and denuded the ground. One of the daughters (now Mrs Hazel Stafford of Northbridge, Sydney) saw the rabbits arriving—a great wave flowing over the country. In drought time they suffered, too. Thousands of dead furry bodies round a waterhole or tank, too weak to outlast the dry spell.

But somehow in that bare-looking land the stock survived. Saltbush and mulga sustained them, and in bad seasons they turned to pigface, a fleshy-leafed plant sometimes called wild spinach. Occasionally it was served at table. The children hated it.

In spite of drought the wool clip increased annually and was loaded on to the waggons with their team of horses. Camel teams came later—the smell of the old-world beasts, Afghan drivers and the shouted 'Hooshtas!' By the time they arrived, Tarella's family had grown and so had the homestead—now three separate cottages set at right-angles, three sides of a square, a trellis on the fourth side. In the centre of the courtyard so formed, the book-keeper, their great confidant and friend, blasted out the rocky ground and planted a pepper tree. It grew and spread, a green oasis in that water-starved land and the favourite gathering place for family and friends.

The original little home housed the younger children and their governess. There were always governesses of varying degrees of proficiency. One was a pretty girl who used to sing and dance to amuse the grown-ups, and had an urge to write. Her first literary work appeared while she was at Tarella. It was *Letters from the Bush*, and the name on the title page was Katherine Susannah Prichard.

Black nurses and housemaids 'thoroughly spoiled us', declares Mrs Tetley, remembering her childhood at Tarella and the kindness of the dark people.

Mrs Tetley's soft-sounding Christian name is a native word. 'You no tell 'em truth', one of the whites might say, and a dark face would screw up earnestly, a dark head nod vigorously. 'Merita—Merita—it is true, true,' they would answer. So one daughter was named Merita; another, called Tarella after the station, was born on the day a small sister died. Diphtheria was the dread scourge. It carried off three of the family, too far from medical aid in their need.

The great standby in sickness was the household 'Doctor's' book, and the medicine chest. What did it hold? Beecham's pills, castor oil, liniments for rheumatism and Gregory's Painkiller. The station workers drank bottles of the painkiller. No one knew why until it was found to contain an appreciable amount of alcohol.

'I was eight years old before I left the station', Mrs Tetley said. 'I often think how lonely it was for my mother'—rarely a white woman to speak to, alone for weeks while the men mustered at the outer camps, gins to help her through confinements, and the ever-nagging thought: 'What to do if the children become ill.'

The children did not notice the loneliness, especially while they were small and had the aborigines' camp to visit, games to play and dolls to look after. 'Our dolls were carved from wood, with painted faces. We loved them. They were heavy, but that made them more real. They had the weight of a real baby.' Mail-day meant stir and excitement (mails came first by camel team, later by coach en route to Queensland): something was always happening in the yards: branding, drafting, a new horse being broken to the saddle. Horse-breakers came and went, though not all departed voluntarily. An entry in the bookkeeper's log reads: 'Kidman fired.' Only a minor episode in the life of the man later called 'The Cattle King', whose stations ran for hundreds of miles across several States.

On the flats above the creek a Chinese gardener grew vegetables for eight months of the year, turning the handle of a water-wheel made to the pattern used in his old country. He worked at night lifting buckets of water from the creek to spill into gutters for the crop, his thin, high voice singing through the hours to keep away the evil spirits that go abroad in the night. But that was only in the cooler months. Even John Chinaman could not coax the soil to productivity when summer ruled the land west of the Darling.

When they were old enough, the children in turn said goodbye to the governess and lessons in the little pisé house, and went away to school. Three days' ride into Broken Hill by Cobb & Co. ('Many a time I've driven the five horses through the night while the driver dozed,' remembered Mrs Stafford, and Mrs Tetley recalled trips when the way was lost and passengers spent the night in the sandhills.) Train to Adelaide and another to Melbourne, the whole trip took five long and very wearisome days.

In later years the family went each summer to a home purchased at Lysterfield Valley, four miles from Fern Tree Gully—unbelievably fresh and green after the dry land of the far west. But it was always good to return to Tarella, to the carriage and team waiting at Wilcannia, and the 'Welcome Home' banner hung out by the staff.

Sometimes the route varied, and the family caught the paddle-wheeler from Swan Hill up the Murray and Darling to Bourke. A leisurely three-week journey in the little vessel's tiny cabins, tying up at night at a jetty and visiting stations on the way. Leaning over the side watching the river slide by under the tall red gums, and the emerald flash of parakeets; the barge towed behind, laden with stores for the stations, gradually becoming lighter and ready for the wool it would haul back on the return trip.

The girls rode round Tarella (side-saddle until they were adult and the divided skirt arrived), but did not work on the run.

As more stations came in the district there were more **companions**, and visits to other properties. ('We always drove four in hand on such trips.') But the distances were still great and the trips always events. So were the dances held on the long verandah John Quin built on to Tarella, and the picnic races. Sewing, crochet, riding, birthday parties under the pepper tree—the weeks worked up to the district's annual climax, the Show at Wilcannia. The girls in new dresses, young men calling to escort them to dances and picnics.

The shearers' strike of 1902 brought drama to the outback. Pickets camped at strategic points and wire strung across the river prevented paddle-wheeelers bringing in strike-breakers.

It passed and routine returned. The long heat of summer (118° indoors at 11 a.m.). Killing for the family table, dead beasts hanging in the round, brush-roofed meat house. A new shed built with a lookout on top. Come mail-day, there was constant going up and down to watch for the coach. It stopped fifty miles off, unloaded the mails and someone from Tarella rode over for the bag.

Water was an endless topic for conversation. The children, reading books from England (few books for children were published in Australia then), marvelled at characters who were impatient with rain. Rain—why, it was the greatest of all gifts in that sun-scorched country. Even when the creek flooded, as it did every couple of years, no one grumbled seriously. The men's quarters across the stream were cut off, but a native would tie food and provisions in a handkerchief, place it on his head and swim across. And after the rain the country smiled under a carpet of white and yellow everlastings, blue vetch, billy buttons, and lightning grass which grew and seeded in a week.

Opals on part of Tarella, and the White Cliffs mines began. It was another place to visit, a Sunday afternoon ride over rising ground and down into the dip where the glare from dazzling heaps of white gravel hit the eyes. Women and children came to live at White Cliffs, and a school was opened. Great interest at Tarella the day the teacher rode over on a queer contraption. Work stopped in the house and yards, and everyone gathered to stare and prod. Pedals and pneumatic tyres; this works so and that goes thus. Once you get your balance it's easy. Anyone can ride a bicycle. Soon all the family did. John Quin bought them one apiece and they rode and rode.

Sister Tarella wrote children's books, Ida Rentoul illustrated them. Tarella and Miss Prichard, the governess, were literary rivals for a time, but Tarella married and moved to a station farther out. Somehow writing became less important. Station life ate into the hours and gave another kind of satisfaction.

'My brother-in-law arrived one day at "Tarella" in a snorting, noisy vehicle—it was the first motor car in the district. We never thought they would come to anything, the camels spent too much time hauling them out of the sand,' remembered Mrs Stafford.

But a new age was coming, the era of mechanization was on the way. The family did not see it arrive at Tarella. In 1914 John Quin sold out, took the family to Europe and returned to settle near Wangaratta, Victoria.

The 'children' married and scattered. Hazel went to a property at Tibooburra with her husband, Alec Officer. 'Of course I shan't be lonely,' she assured those who offered sympathy. 'I've always lived in the bush.' She did not realize that Tarella was not just 'the bush' but a self-contained community surrounded by empty miles, but with group interests and companionships inside its own circumference. The place at Tibooburra was far different—on the 'back road' and alone in a way Tarella was not. From its boundary right through to Western Australia not a fence stood. In that isolation, occasional visits of a half-caste drover taking sheep to the railhead were important. And there was dust such as Tarella had never seen, and restless, shifting sandhills—outside the window when one went to bed, round the back of the house in the morning.

It is an old story now, as we count time in this old-new land. Tarella still stands on the rise above the creek, and other children have played and grown there since the Quins sold out. But 'I feel a great nostalgia for it still', remarked Mrs Stafford, who had been one of the first children there, remembering where the camels came, the pepper tree in the courtyard, and the everlastings thick after rain. Dry seasons or good, Tarella was where the roots went down.

Inside the squatter's hut

34
Past the Farthest Fence

Into our varied frontier places have gone the cattlemen to settle by billabongs with their chattering birds, or on silent plains with their dreamy distances. Through sweltering summer days of the north, blistering drought seasons of the centre, and cold biting times of winter in south lands along the Bight, they tend their herds. . . . With these pioneers have gone brave women . . . who live among wild blacks, fifty miles from the nearest neighbour.

John Flynn, *Inlander*, vol. 3, no. 1 (1916).

IN SPITE OF Harriet Daly's faith in the Territory and the hardihood of a few overlanders and prospectors, the native people faced little competition for the land north, east and west of the Centre for more than a century after the first settlement.

A trickle of settlers came over the border from Queensland and South Australia, and faced into the distance where mails came seldom and news reticulated slowly—a thin trickle going where there was room for a river in flood. The few who went into the emptiness soon dispersed, and were lost to sight where the elephant grass or spinfex grew, where the Wet was a seasonal deluge, or miles lay endlessly without sign of water.

Why did they go? For grazing land, for distant pastures where stock could graze and roam across areas as large as an Old World country, or in search of Lady Luck, who lives underground in places where picks may turn up gold or wolfram, tin or gems.

The Bush. The Inland. Back o' Beyond and past the farthest fence. Two million square miles of country—big enough to put most of Europe inside and still have plenty left over. It runs up and down and across Australia, by mountain ranges, gibber plains, places where monsoon rains flood the rivers regularly as clockwork, places where rain sometimes is not seen for years. *That* was the country they entered.

How did they reach it? Some, like the Sam Pickers, overlanded by buggy—one vehicle, two horses and three humans—father, mother and ten-year-old daughter—joined on the way by a fourth, a son, whose birth caused some delay along the track. Everything somehow went on to the buggy—'water, food, swags, clothing, cooking utensils . . . the few tools required to carve a living and build a home in a new land: axe, shovel, saw, hammer, shoeing tools and those necessary to mend the harness and their own boots'.[1]

The Wet and other seasonal conditions slowed progress, and the destination, Arltunga and its gold, was not reached until December 1905—almost two years after setting out.

Another two years and the Arltunga episode was over. In that time Mrs Lizzie Picker bore two more sons, and acted as midwife and nurse for the camp. Then the alluvial petered out, crude hygiene made sickness too common, and the miners and their families began moving out, the Pickers with them.

They settled eventually at Eringa, north of Charlotte Waters—five-inch annual rainfall, one large waterhole and a few 'soaks'. It was 1914, aerial medical service was then not even a dream, and no doctor, school or church closer than Port Augusta, six hundred miles south. But many an expectant mother had reason to be glad of the family at Eringa, for at a call for help Mrs Picker would be up and away, travelling hundreds of miles if necessary, to help with the household, deliver the baby, and see the mother back on her feet.

When Japanese bombs fell on the north in World War II, elderly civilians were offered free passage south, but Mrs Picker refused to go. Droughts, floods, bad seasons and hard times had not driven her from the Territory; she was not going to let the Japs do it, she said.

So she stayed and lived out the rest of her eighty-one years in the land of her choice—almost half a century of life and action in the land where the overland buggy and the clopping hooves of two horses had brought her.

*   *   *

The century was less than ten years old when William Crook arrived in Australia, land of opportunity to William, with a wife and three children under five to keep.

There was little gold lying about in the streets of Adelaide, but a chance to work on Glen Helen, ninety miles west of The Alice, might lead along the road to fortune.

It was summer when the train set the family down at Oodnadatta —blazing sun on the gibber plains, and the flies in possession. Soon there wasn't an uninfected eye in the party; Crook himself could not see, and an old native drove the dray most of the way.

To the children, life in the Centre spelt novelty and freedom. They did not share with their mother, the one white woman of the station, the feeling of aloneness when the men were out mustering, leaving the family and the dark women behind. Not that the lubras stayed. Wallabies on the range at night, sending rocks and stones tumbling and crashing down the hillside, were more than the dark women could stand. Swearing that 'the wild and savage tribe to the West hurled the rocks and would creep in at night to kill us all', they were off at daylight after their men in the mustering camp.

A year at Glen Helen, and the family moved on to Hermannsburg Mission Station, where dedicated German missionaries and their wives worked among the aborigines. William Crook looked after the mission stock, and his children gazed with envy on native children at drill. The white youngsters were not allowed to take part, and freedom to find their own activity seemed empty and uninteresting beside such splendid marching, halting, wheeling and forming fours.

In twelve months the family was on the track again, bound for Alice Springs: 'Our transport was, I think, one camel and a horse . . . but all I can clearly remember of the journey is having to carry a pet cockatoo which kept flying out of my arms into bushes by the road.'[2]

Memories of The Alice are clearer; its half-dozen houses and Fogarty's store the community centre; the small 'bush-built' house near the telegraph station where William Crook worked; camel teams from the south pulling in, their loading creaking, the beasts grunting, and loud 'Hooshtas' shouted by their Afghan owners.

Lessons at home until the arrival of Mrs I. Standley, pioneer teacher, whose work with the white children and young native girls won her recognition outside the Territory, and set her name on the Honours list of George the Fifth.

It was a happy childhood spent splashing among the rocks and exploring creeks and hills, and the 1914 war hardly more than a distant rumble—until it added value to the wolfram mined at Hatches Creek, three hundred miles to the north. Perhaps this was the chance for the Crooks to find their pot of gold, so a horse team and waggon took them by the rough track beside the O.T. line to the turn off at Barrow Creek. There the rains came, the ground turned to swamp, and they camped until the track dried.

The children took it in their stride; by that time they were real Australians, tough as most bush youngsters. Riding, handling horses and finding their way about in the bush was literally child's play and second nature to them. Their skill improved as they grew older.

At Hatches Creek all the best claims were gone, but the waggon and team earned the family livelihood carting ore and wood for the field. A new strike in another area and

> Once again the family and waggon set off, this time across country to Wauchope. There was a track of sorts and we had an uneventful trip. But when we arrived at Wauchope the story was the same. All the claims had been pegged . . . [3]

Almost as bad for a family with a horse team and herd of goats to consider, this was a dry field, the nearest water eight miles off. So into the waggon again, and on to Wycliffe Well down the guiding line of the Overland Telegraph.

They mounted the sandhills one by one and came suddenly on a swamp, an oasis where gums threw down their shade, everlastings smiled, and lillies floated coolly on the water. Nearby was the government well (wire ropes and buckets pulled by a horse to bail out the water). To the children it was a picture from another world. The waggon came to rest, camp was made and William Crook returned to Wauchope to work.

The stay extended indefinitely, for the family decided to settle at Wycliffe and build up a cattle herd.

> Bit by bit they did so. Every calf was carefully herded and branded, including many calves discarded by passing drovers, which were reared on goat's milk. . . . It was years before there were enough cattle for sale.

Years—lonely years, full of hard work for the fair-haired English girl who had come to Adelaide when the century was young. No white woman to leaven the loneliness—only the family for company, and the strenuous life going on and on.

For the children they were years of movement and activity, spent largely in the saddle, riding everywhere over the run.

Droughts and bad seasons took toll of the cattle, but Singleton Station, north of Barrow Creek, is the result of a family's enterprise and a woman's endurance. Had she broken or asked for a life close to other women in city or town, there might never have evolved the station which grew up in Australia's Centre on a foundation of determination and courage.

* * *

The Timothy O'Sheas entered the Territory (transport unstated) from Killarney by way of North Queensland, following the clink of picks to the tin field, Embrawarra, fourteen miles from the railhead at Pine Creek. Darwin, a hundred and forty miles away, had the nearest doctor, too far off for an emergency, and many a bushman succumbed to malaria, the common fever of the Territory. Supplies came from the eastern States by ship, and were unloaded and shunted off to the mining town by the weekly 'mixed'.

There was no fortune for the O'Sheas in the tin mines, so Timothy left the family behind and went off to Arnhem Land to look at the silver lead near Bulman. Months went by without news, then Timothy was reported killed by blacks. Anguish and despair filled the family, until the rumour was laid and O'Shea came home.

The rail now passed Pine Creek to Emungalen, and Vestey's meat-works at Darwin dealt with cattle brought by train from the new centre. O'Shea put away his mining kit and took his wife and family to Emungalen, to set up a forge and act as smithy for the area.

But the meat-works closed, and Emungalen, with scarcely any justification for existence, had only a fortnightly train from Darwin.

> Sometimes people would come to Emungalen hoping to catch the train, only to find they had missed it by an hour or so. Sometimes people would struggle in, suffering from fever, to find that the train had gone.

In the Wet, packhorses were the only reliable means of transport, and this was no tourist's excursion where rivers spilled out into great lakes and the mailman swam his horses to bring the mail through. More than one baby was born on the banks of a racing stream with a lubra acting as midwife.

'I have seen my mother with eight fever patients to attend to as well as caring for her large family,' writes Mrs Ulyatt, of Muckaty Station, via Tennant Creek. 'I often wonder how she managed.'

But manage she did, with Irish energy, wit and doses of quinine, and Territorians still remember her, though a generation has passed since she joined the dust of the land of the north.

* * *

262   *Australian Pioneer Women*

Mrs Ulyatt nominates a great old pioneer, Mrs Farrar, who

came to the Northern Territory when she was nineteen and helped her husband form several stations. At the age of seventy-two she was working in the branding yard when she was knocked down by a bull and had her nose and thigh broken. After months in Darwin hospital and months on crutches

she returned—to sit and watch the scene she had helped establish? Never a bit! She put away the crutches and was back in the saddle.

Travelling in the Northern Territory, about 1910

Red Jack

She rises clear to memory's eye
From mists of long ago,
Though we met but once, in '98—
In the days of Cobb and Co.

'Twas driving into Hughenden
With mail and gold for load
That I saw Red Jack, the wanderer,
Come riding down the road.

Red Jack and Mephistopheles—
They knew them far and wide,
From Comooweal to Charters Towers,
The route they used to ride.

They knew them round the Selwyns where
The Leichardt has its source,
Along the winding cattle ways—
A woman and a horse.

And strange the tales they told of them
Who ranged the dusty track;
The great black Mephistopheles
And the red-haired witch, Red Jack.

She claimed no name but that, they said,
And owned no things but these:
Her saddle, swag and riding-kit
And Mephistopheles.

And often travellers such as I
Had seen, and thought it strange,
A woman working on the line
That crossed McKinlay Range.

Had seen her in the dreary wake
Of stock upon the plains,
Her brown hand quick upon the whip
And light upon the reins.

With milling cattle in the yard
Amid the dust-fouled air,
With rope and knife and branding iron—
A girl with glowing hair.

'Red Jack's as good as any man!'
The settlers used to own;
And some bold spirits sought her hand,
But Red Jack rode alone.

She rode alone, and wise men learned
To set her virtue high,
To weigh what skill she plied her whip
With the hardness of her eye.

I saw Red Jack in '98,
The first time and the last,
But her face, brown-gaunt, and her hair, red-bright,
Still haunt me from the past.

The coach drew in as she rode in sight;
We passed the time of day;
Then shuffled out the mail she sought
And watched her ride away.

And oh! her hair was living fire,
But her eyes were cold as stone:
Red Jack and Mephistopheles
Went all their ways alone.

MARY DURACK

[Red Jack was a familiar but mysterious figure in Central Queensland at the end of the century. Several old-timers, reminded by Mary Durack's poem, recalled seeing her on the track. But her background was not known, or was not revealed.]

35

Women in the Surgery

THE LAST QUARTER of the nineteenth century saw the forward surge of women bent on entering professions and occupations previously considered outside their sphere. Pioneers of a new era, they struggled against hostility, public opinion and the rigid Victorian tradition that a woman could only rightfully and respectably occupy herself within the walls of her home.

In the 'eighties, several young women were fired by the example of Elizabeth Blackwell, the first woman to practise medicine in the United States, and began hammering on the door of the faculties of medicine in several Australian universities.

The first to enter was Dagmar Berne, who enrolled at the University of Sydney in 1884.

Four years study in an atmosphere of discouragement and hostility convinced her she would have little success in her native country, so she went to London and qualified there in 1893.

Two years later, this 'quiet, friendly, and sensible' woman, as someone has described her, returned to practise in Macquarie Street. But she had little time left to make her mark in the city which had discouraged her ambition. She developed T.B. and died in 1900, aged thirty-four. Sydney University perpetuates her memory with the Dagmar Berne Scholarship awarded yearly to the woman medical student attaining the highest marks at graduation.

* * *

Victoria claims the first Australian-born woman to become a doctor: Dr Constance Stone, who took her degree at the Women's Medical College, Philadelphia, U.S.A., and confirmed it with a

British degree in Toronto. She worked in the New Hospital, London, and later returned to practise in Melbourne. A colourful personality, she threw herself heartily into the battle for women's rights which raged fiercely through the close of the last century until the end of World War I.

Soon after Constance Stone went overseas, Melbourne University opened its doors to women medical students, and from Wilson Hall in 1891 passed out Margaret Whyte, M.D., first in the Honours list of her year. Normally such distinction placed a graduate automatically on the resident staff of Melbourne Hospital, but the Board flatly refused to appoint Dr Whyte. Long discussions and arguments used up valuable time. Dr Whyte grew tired of waiting and joined the Women's Hospital.

She had, however, blazed the trail. The next time women graduates headed the year's Honours list, the Board had not the same sense of unfamiliarity with the situation. It was five years later, in 1896, when six residents were to be appointed, and 'Dr Freda Gamble and Dr Janet Lindsay Greig were among the leading group. As Dr Janet Greig was seventh, the committee of the Melbourne Hospital would have had to pass over three women to obtain six men'.[1]

Once again there were heated debates and strenuous opposition, but the women graduates had high recommendations from the medical staff, and were determined as a matter of principle to stand firm. When the matter came to the vote they were elected residents by a 13-5 majority. The minority's distrust was evident in the warning which accompanied their appointment that it was purely an experiment and 'their conduct would decide whether or not it could ever be repeated'.[2]

Whatever the Board feared or expected in behaviour or practice did not occur, and from that time the door so grudgingly opened to women medical graduates was never closed.

Naturally the situation was discussed beyond the walls of the committee room and the hospital grounds, and aroused much interest. The Melbourne *Argus* of 25 April 1896, published a rhyme written by 'Oriel' on the event:

> If you've been on a ramble
> And broken your leig,
> 'Twill be fixed by Miss Gamble,
> Or set by Miss Greig.

35
Women in the Surgery

THE LAST QUARTER of the nineteenth century saw the forward surge of women bent on entering professions and occupations previously considered outside their sphere. Pioneers of a new era, they struggled against hostility, public opinion and the rigid Victorian tradition that a woman could only rightfully and respectably occupy herself within the walls of her home.

In the 'eighties, several young women were fired by the example of Elizabeth Blackwell, the first woman to practise medicine in the United States, and began hammering on the door of the faculties of medicine in several Australian universities.

The first to enter was Dagmar Berne, who enrolled at the University of Sydney in 1884.

Four years study in an atmosphere of discouragement and hostility convinced her she would have little success in her native country, so she went to London and qualified there in 1893.

Two years later, this 'quiet, friendly, and sensible' woman, as someone has described her, returned to practise in Macquarie Street. But she had little time left to make her mark in the city which had discouraged her ambition. She developed T.B. and died in 1900, aged thirty-four. Sydney University perpetuates her memory with the Dagmar Berne Scholarship awarded yearly to the woman medical student attaining the highest marks at graduation.

*   *   *

Victoria claims the first Australian-born woman to become a doctor: Dr Constance Stone, who took her degree at the Women's Medical College, Philadelphia, U.S.A., and confirmed it with a

British degree in Toronto. She worked in the New Hospital, London, and later returned to practise in Melbourne. A colourful personality, she threw herself heartily into the battle for women's rights which raged fiercely through the close of the last century until the end of World War I.

Soon after Constance Stone went overseas, Melbourne University opened its doors to women medical students, and from Wilson Hall in 1891 passed out Margaret Whyte, M.D., first in the Honours list of her year. Normally such distinction placed a graduate automatically on the resident staff of Melbourne Hospital, but the Board flatly refused to appoint Dr Whyte. Long discussions and arguments used up valuable time. Dr Whyte grew tired of waiting and joined the Women's Hospital.

She had, however, blazed the trail. The next time women graduates headed the year's Honours list, the Board had not the same sense of unfamiliarity with the situation. It was five years later, in 1896, when six residents were to be appointed, and 'Dr Freda Gamble and Dr Janet Lindsay Greig were among the leading group. As Dr Janet Greig was seventh, the committee of the Melbourne Hospital would have had to pass over three women to obtain six men'.[1]

Once again there were heated debates and strenuous opposition, but the women graduates had high recommendations from the medical staff, and were determined as a matter of principle to stand firm. When the matter came to the vote they were elected residents by a 13-5 majority. The minority's distrust was evident in the warning which accompanied their appointment that it was purely an experiment and 'their conduct would decide whether or not it could ever be repeated'.[2]

Whatever the Board feared or expected in behaviour or practice did not occur, and from that time the door so grudgingly opened to women medical graduates was never closed.

Naturally the situation was discussed beyond the walls of the committee room and the hospital grounds, and aroused much interest. The Melbourne *Argus* of 25 April 1896, published a rhyme written by 'Oriel' on the event:

> If you've been on a ramble
> And broken your leig,
> 'Twill be fixed by Miss Gamble,
> Or set by Miss Greig.

If you're brought down a peig
In a scuffle or scramble,
Just creep to Miss Greig,
Or else to Miss Gamble.

Queensland's first woman doctor was a tall figure who dressed plainly, drew her hair back from a wide forehead, spoke in a deep voice and strode through the streets of Brisbane, to which she came at the close of the century with an Australian friend.[3]

Dr Lilian Violet Cooper was the child of a conventional middle-class English family. Her father was a retired Colonel of the Royal Marines, her mother cultured but orthodox, and three brothers followed acceptable middle-class professions (one became headmaster of a large boys' school, one went into the Army, and the third became a judge). Of the five daughters, Lilian was the only one who stepped out of the pattern of her time. Two of her sisters married young, two others filled their days with 'home pursuits and their dogs' and never queried the way of life prescribed for them.

But quite early Lilian made it clear such occupations were not for her. Her statement, 'I'm going to be a doctor', threw everyone into indulgent laughter. Just a girl's fancy, they said; it would pass. It did not pass, and many battles were joined before she attained her ambition to begin studying medicine.

Her first appointment was as assistant to the local doctor in a little bleak Essex village, where she walked over snowy fields and roads to the homes of her patients.

Dr Cooper came to Australia as assistant to a Brisbane physician. The arrangement did not last, and she soon set up her own practice.

The country was still close to the city at the turn of the century, and Dr Cooper became used to visits that required a train trip, then a journey on horseback, often at night and over rough mountain roads, to some remote farm. There she was frequently faced with a confinement or an operation to be performed urgently, the patient's husband usually the only available surgeon's aide.

Afterwards, Dr Cooper returned along the same track probably to find a room full of patients waiting in her city surgery. On these occasions she ate when she could and did without sleep for a night.

Her sulky and horses were familiar in Brisbane streets on her daytime rounds. She made local calls at night by bicycle. Later she drove a car, one of the first in the city.

As Brisbane's first woman doctor she encountered prejudice and hostility, some of it inside her own profession. (A common criticism of the time was that medical practice 'unsexed' a woman.) But others praised and encouraged her, her skill and devotion to duty won increasing recognition, and she was elected to the staff of several hospitals.

In World War I, Dr Cooper served in Macedonia in charge of forward dressing stations. For her work she received the decoration of St Sava from the Serbian government, a deserved recognition.

In 1941 she retired from practice and died in 1947. Her work and character had done much to advance the cause of other women doctors in her adopted country.

* * *

Western Australia's first woman medico was Dr Roberta Jull, who made up her mind on her future career very early. She has written: 'I remember well standing on the small lawn in front of the house (in Perthshire) and saying "When I am big I am going to be a doctor".' She was then eight years old.

Her parents encouraged her ambition, and after she had nursed her mother through the last stages of tuberculosis, Dr Jull began work for her entrance examination before entering on her studies at Queen Margaret College, Glasgow.

When she enrolled, Dr Jull declares,

> there were no mixed classes. I was told none of the professors would lecture to the women, so the Committee who ran the College arranged for a number of young men to lecture. The term before I began studying, it was the custom for some older woman to act in the classroom during lectures as chaperone. However, by the time I went to Q.M. this stupid and unnecessary arrangement had been dropped.

The thirteen women of Dr Jull's year faced a strenuous schedule. They travelled three miles from Queen Margaret College to the Royal Infirmary and must be ready to go through the wards at 9 a.m. A bus took them back to the College for lectures (11-1), they made their own way to the Royal casualty ward in the afternoon (2-3.30) and returned to college for lectures at 4.15 p.m. Men students of the period attended the Western Infirmary in the same grounds as their university. Fourth-year women students began work at the Royal at 8 a.m., which meant rising at 6 o'clock to catch a train—a grim stint as anyone knows who has endured Glasgow's winter.

In 1895 Dr Jull obtained her degree, and with her father and younger brother, also a doctor, went to Western Australia, where her elder brother was Government Medical Officer at Guildford. Eight miles from Perth, Guildford was at the time a country town, and the oil lamps used for street lighting went out about 1 a.m. Anyone abroad after that hour, as a doctor often was, carried a lantern.

Dr Jull assisted both her brothers with their practices, usually travelling in a hooded buggy or a sulky for out-of-town visits, and making most of her town calls on bicycle. She found a sulky uncomfortable, even dangerous, and recalls that only the groom's skill prevented a serious accident on one occasion when the horses shied at a passing camel on the road. (At that time, the 'nineties, camel teams were used for haulage to the goldfields.)

Although some people looked on a woman doctor as a curiosity, and came expressly from Perth to see what kind of a person she was, 'On the whole, my brothers' patients received me well, even the men seldom refused to accept my visits, while sometimes a woman would ask for me', says Dr Jull.

When she began to practise in Perth, her colleagues received her kindly.

> One of the oldest sent me a message by his wife: 'Tell her not to be depressed if she doesn't make money quickly. I made only £50 in my first year.' I was more fortunate, as I made double that amount.

After her marriage to Martin E. Jull, Under-Secretary for Works, she did not practise again until 1914, when the shortage of doctors took her to the Perth Public Hospital, and later the Eye Department of the Children's Hospital. When more doctors became available, Dr Jull retired once more, until on her husband's death she entered the government service, and pioneered medical inspection of pupils in Western Australia schools.

In 1925 the newly-developed infant welfare work was begun, and Dr Jull was chosen to launch this in the West. In spite of opposition, much of it within the medical profession, the work progressed and is now so much part of our lives that the generation which has grown up since that time knows nothing of the battle pioneers like Dr Jull fought to establish a service of such importance to the nation.

* * *

South Australia put the first woman doctor into the air—Dr F. E. Gibson, O.B.E., M.B., B.S.

With her husband, the late Dr Roy Gibson, she began aerial

medical work in 1937, only two years after John Flynn had brought into being the Flying Doctor Service at Cloncurry, spreading what has come to be called 'a mantle of safety' over outback homes and workers.

Dr Gibson worked alone during the three and a half years her husband was in the Army. Now another woman, Dr Merna Mueller, helps her in the work she carried out voluntarily for the Bush Church Aid Society's Flying Medical Service, based at Ceduna on the farthest coast of South Australia. Together they cope with their medical tasks.

Dr Gibson declares it is a rewarding job,

> well worth while and full of interest. It sometimes taxes one's ingenuity, and one must certainly stand alone or fall, as there are no consultants within hundreds of miles. Decisions for diagnosis and treatment must be made instantly over the flying network. Sometimes the condition is a minor thing, and instructions to Sisters or lay relatives are given. Certain medical drug boxes are kept at most of the station homes. These drugs are all numbered to make it simpler for the doctor to prescribe, and the patient to understand his directions. If the case can be treated thus, instructions are given over the Transceiver network, the base of which is situated at Ceduna. Each station, township or hospital with which we are in radio contact has a transmitting and receiving set for this purpose. If the case requires a doctor, we fly to it or send a nurse to fly the patient to the base hospital if it is wise to have him near for observation or treatment.

Calm, cool words, but they cover a work of passionate importance when read against the country Dr Gibson serves. It covers 200,000 square miles and from any point inside that area may come a call for help at any time. A stockman has spilled from a horse and 'he looks pretty bad, doc'. A child's temperature is dangerously high. A baby is coming unexpectedly. What do they do? Get on the transceiver and send out the call signal. In a matter of minutes an authoritative professional voice may speak and prescribe. It sounds so simple that one has come to take it for granted.

But talk to women who knew the area before the service operated and pity those who did not have it.

'Mother somehow lifted my injured father on to the floor of the buggy and drove fifty miles from our farm to a doctor. It was too late. If only she could have got him there earlier', said one woman of the outback.

What happened in the case of sudden illness or injury is summed up by an old-timer of the Birdsville Corner. To the question, 'What did you do before the days of the Flying Doctor?' he answered: 'You looked for the nearest sensible woman.'

On the 'sensible women' of the outback (too few and too scattered) rested too much responsibility in such emergencies. Flying Doctors like Dr Gibson now take much of the weight of their burden, boosting what the women must still give—good nursing—with professional advice, visits and conveyance to hospital if necessary.

Dr Gibson answers emergency calls several times daily over the network. Anyone possessing a transceiver may then seek advice. In addition, routine flights are made weekly and monthly to outlying places. 'Commencing from Ceduna, we fly West well over the border, North to Oodnadatta, East to Adelaide.' Two planes are used—one carries two stretchers and can seat three additional patients; the other, one stretcher and one sitting patient.

Patients are brought in to hospitals in the area—at Ceduna, Penong, 45 miles west, Koonibba (for native patients) and Cook, 270 miles north-west of the Transcontinental Railway in the centre of the great Nullarbor district, and at Tarcoola.

Some stations in the area have quarters known as 'the doctor's rooms' equipped with a table and 'the necessities for consultations, minor surgery with general anaesthesia if necessary.'

Emergencies (and there are many) do not hold the terrifying aspect of fatality when the doctor's plane can be called.

A car accident on the Nullarbor Plain, two hundred miles from Ceduna, brought Dr Gibson and two planes to the nearest landing strip, then by truck to the scene. The injured were taken to a small shack and emergency treatment given there overnight. 'The next morning all hands cleared a landing strip and the two planes were brought there. We loaded them both with the injured and flew back to Ceduna.'

Routine flights give ante-natal care to expectant mothers, check workers on the Transcontinental outside the area of the railway doctor's visits, and inspect children at little outback schools.

Sometimes emergencies demand night flying, although officially the planes are not equipped for this; and occasionally an improvised landing strip must be called into being. From the Transcontinental to the opal fields of Coober Pedy, where housekeeping takes place in homes built underground, to assist a new Australian to premature birth or cope with a ruptured ulcer in a migrant who does not speak English—wherever and whenever the call comes, Flying Doctor Gibson goes calmly to meet it. As new areas are opened up, the work grows. 'Worthwhile and full of interest,' says Dr Gibson, woman pioneer of air medical aid to one of Australia's areas of isolation.

A miner's hut in the Lithgow Valley, New South Wales, 1899

36

Sandhill Homestead

SAND—SHIFTING, drifting, relentlessly invading sand. Piled into hills and ridges that rise and fall with the rhythm of a gritty sea. Spread over thousands of square miles of country east of Lake Frome (South Australia) and west of the New South Wales border. Average rainfall: four inches a year. Never enough water; always too many flies. Fourteen hours of blazing summer sunshine with a guaranteed temperature of one hundred degrees by 8 a.m. Where the wind, blowing for days on end, was laden with 'blinding, stinging, infinite specks (that) sear the flesh with a million hot pin points'.[1]

In the 'eighties, cattlemen tried this land of the sandhills as relief winter country for their stock. It was not worth the heartbreak of fighting the lack of water and the utter isolation, so they drove out the cattle, and almost overnight the wind and the sand wiped out all signs of their middens.

In 1912 the South Australian government sank bores to tap the artesian water and give the country another chance. Even then, 'wild dogs and poor country made settlement slow', wrote Dame Mary Gilmore in a foreword to Myrtle Rose White's *No Roads Go By*.

A few hardy hopefuls tried it, among them Mrs White's husband ('The Boss'). Mrs White ('The Missus') followed him with their five-year-old daughter ('Little 'Un') into the land of sand, to the 8,000-square-mile property, Noonameena, and what she called its 'appalling loneliness' and 'menacing silence'.

It was a world roofed with an 'immensity of sky', served by a fortnightly mail service which ended thirty-five miles from Noonameena, at the home of their nearest neighbour ('who might as well have lived one hundred and thirty miles distant, so seldom did we meet'); the Afghan camel train which brought stores twice a year (flour and sugar by the ton, jam by the case, dried beans and peas by the bag, compressed potatoes by the dozen tins); and an occasional teamster, one of whom cast a sardonic eye over the country and asked: 'Where's Burke and Wills buried?'

The pedal wireless was years away, telephones were few and distant, cars new and uncertain. Most of the time 'The Boss' rode camels; other transport was a buggy drawn by four mules or two camels. Horses were used over long distances and changed at intervals.

For the first few months the White family lived in the depot dwelling with its 'uneven, humpy wall', and floor of 'Mother Earth wet and hard packed in some previous century, but now dotted over with miniature volcanoes'. The bathroom, four feet by four feet, had

> a queer contrivance attached to the roof, something like a huge colander in shape, and hip bath in size. It worked with a pulley. One lowered it to the floor and filled it with water, and got one's bath while frantically pulling it back to place. Needless to say, it was quite empty when it reached its roost in the roof.

In her first months at Noonameena, Myrtle White cooked for the men on the station, and wrestled with bread-making. She found batches of dough temperamental.

> They refused to respond to all my coaxing and pampering—blankets, hot bricks, hot bottles—nothing would persuade them to rise an inch. But as soon as the sun shone on them! No matter how deeply I buried my secret, it always rose again to confront me and shout my guilt abroad. Then men learnt early to avoid these volcanic upheavals in the ground, but there was one exciting occasion when a goat had to be rescued from the tenacious grip of a rising batch.

Mrs White's book lays bare the lot of women in the sandhill country, and their grim trials and isolation before the Flying Doctor Service established its bases of relief.

In the long summers, heat struck through shoe leather, the morning's milk was sour by nightfall, and butter was 'a hope of the future and a thing of the past'. During dust-storms one lit the lamp at two in the afternoon, ate dust-flavoured food and lived with the wind blowing unceasingly for day after day, night after night. One storm completely covered a six-foot fence.

There were long droughts when the cattle wasted pitifully away. After a drought, rain often wrought ironic devastation. Once water invaded the store-room,

> washed out great chunks of earth from the walls to mingle with currants, raisins and packets of cornflower . . . Bottles left their shelves to chase each other round and round. Sauce sailed after pickles and pickles after vinegar with a few dozen of olive oil to smooth the course.

Mrs White went to town for her second confinement. A cyclone broke soon after she left the station, the ground turned to mud and slush through which she walked to relieve the horses, then drove through the night with water often up to the horses' knees.

Her baby contracted the dreaded 'summer sickness' at Noonameena and, late at night, went into convulsions. The distracted mother called loudly to sleeping stockmen for a tub, mustard and hot water from the bore head. 'Three very scared, generous-hearted bushmen' came to her help, while the fourth rode fourteen hours to bring 'The Boss' from an out-station.

For a week the thermometer bulb registered terrible temperatures.

> Canvas blinds were soused with buckets of water, but they dried faster than one could wet them under the intense, still heat . . . in that oven in the sandhills; whilst all around, birds and animals panted their lives away . . . Boy's cot was moved to the verandah and a wet sheet placed over the rails.

When a 'cool change' came (a fifteen-degree drop from an over-the-century reading) the child was taken into town in an open car for which 'The Boss' made a cover with wooden uprights and a marcella quilt. Four stockmen rode with them over the first twenty-five miles, the stretch of the big sandhills where most trouble occurred. Here the men pushed and lifted the car up and over the hills, but at the last—and largest—even their combined efforts failed. Mrs White sat under a tree cooling the sick child with cloths wrung out in water from the canvas bag, while men twisted fencing wire into traces and hitched the horses to the car. At the engine's roar the terrified animals reared, jibbed, and fell in a struggling, kicking heap. Skilled handling quietened and steadied them and eventually they took the car over the rise.

Further on, the family sat out a two-hour dust-storm with the air full of choking grit and visibility reduced to nothing. It was night before they reached the depot with the small patient clinging frailly to life, and fourteen hours' jolting ride next day in a crowded mail car before they reached town and medical help.

Months of nursing and unending care restored the child's health, and Mrs White returned to the sandhills, to the flies which brought disease (sore eyes, dysentery, barcoo) and ants which defied all traps and burrowed into the food.

'Little 'Un' fell on a piece of sharp-edged iron and was gashed from neck to shoulder. Mrs White drew the gaping wound together with sticking plaster; she could not bring herself to stitch it.

In the short inland winter, sandhills glittered on frosty nights under a cold moon and a huge belor log burnt in the fireplace. A native station worker was found milking one morning with his feet in the bucket to keep them warm!

Rain was a wizard that worked magic on the country. Overnight, it seemed, flowers came—bluebells, wild geraniums, candytuft, native pansies, ham and egg daisies. Birds and butterflies hovered above them. Teal and divers, black duck, black swans nested on the swamp, kangaroos camped under shady trees.

It is a happy note to close on. When 'Little 'Un' was twelve years old, the White family left the sandhill country. Arid and heart-breaking, it had its own strange beauty, but it made cruel demands of women and children held within the fortress of its isolation.

View of an Australian farm, about 1880

Junior Stock Worker

I received a . . . shock to see the 'Little 'Un' and the pup she was breaking in, bringing between five and six hundred cattle along the fence. She was only nine years old, and looked a terribly small mite on her pony. She moved about behind the cattle gently flicking along the refractory stragglers with her tiny whip. She was very proud of that whip. Her father had carved the handle from a gidyea and plaited the thong from kangaroo hide, and had given it to her . . . There was no fuss, no noise, beyond the uneasy murmur of the herd, as she drove them; just quiet co-operation between girl, horse, and dog . . .

Time after time during that long summer, she helped her father move cattle off the bore on which we lived. A new one with a small flow had been put down twenty miles east of us. Small numbers of cattle were mustered off the water in the late afternoon; the Boss and the 'Little 'Un' would start them, and the 'Little 'Un' would push them along whilst the Boss came back for his evening meal. It meant an all-night job for him, as the cattle they were moving were too weak to travel in the heat of the day, but the 'Little 'Un' returned home at dark, or soon after, a matter-of-factness about her that was rather amusing.

Myrtle Rose White, *No Roads Go By.*

37
Pisé Homestead

'CATTLEWOMAN PASSES' was the headline[1] announcing the death in July 1955 of Mrs Laura Duncan of Mooraberrie Station, eight hundred miles west of Gayndah, Queensland.

Daughter of Charles Davis, solicitor, of Sydney, Mrs Duncan grew up at the family home, Llewellyn, on the Parramatta River. In the 'nineties she accompanied her sister and brother-in-law to Daroo Station near Birdsville, and from there married Scottish William Duncan, manager of Mooraberrie.

Soon after they bought the station, William Duncan died leaving Laura Duncan with three daughters and the management of Mooraberrie and its cattle.

For years she and the girls ran the station, 'through droughts, slumps and wars'[2] and a famous law suit occasioned by government action in taking over six hundred head of Mooraberrie stock.

> Miss Laura Duncan took over the management of 'Mooraberrie' from the elder Laura just after World War II began. Between them they have probably created an Australian record for far-back cattle station management, for 'Mooraberrie' has been managed by them for half a century.[3]

Mooraberrie (or Moora-pi-ee-ree: Our Sandhills) homestead is pisé built. The preparation of the building material has been described by another daughter, Mrs A. M. Duncan-Kemp, in *Our Sandhill Country*, an account of life in Queensland's far west.

> The walls of the house, some two feet in thickness and twelve in height, are of pisé brick (ant-bed clay), built by the owners ... with the aid of black labour.

The clay was carted in from the run by drays and dumped into a prepared hollow near the building site. Water was poured upon the clay to render it soft and pliable. It was then 'puddled,' trodden by the blacks, until it was the consistency of modelling clay; straw or grass was then mixed with it . . . Specially prepared moulds made of board and shaped like oblong boxes were filled with the pugged mixture, turned out on to a smooth, cleared space of ground and left to dry in the sun . . . When the pile of five to six thousand bricks were dry they were gathered into a mud brick kiln or wall, firewood was laid in cleared spaces within, a fire lighted, the kiln sealed with mud, and kept sealed for ten days or a fortnight until the outside felt warm. The bricks when opened up were 'fired' to a smooth, shining red, and, if the work were carefully carried out, beautifully even . . . A few buildings were built of indurated sandstone, grey or reddish brick-like slabs cut from the sides of hills, or from the beds of dry creeks and rivers. These slabs were gathered with the aid of blacks and plastered together with pisé to form walls; left-overs formed flagged verandahs. Some paint, sheets of galvanised iron (or cane grass) and cane-grass verandahs supplied the final trimmings.

From this homestead, the Duncan women ran the station and all its enterprises. Practising pastoralists, they took part in every aspect of cattle raising, although in Mrs Duncan-Kemp's book the main character is not the family but the country—spell-weaver of many moods, sullen under drought, but exhilarating in good seasons.

'First and last, outdoor interests absorbed most of our time', says the author and tells of cattle camps, mustering, and long days in the saddle. For pages there is scarcely a hint that women were part of this active pattern, hunting scrub cattle, branding, drafting; but then comes the kind of sequence men writers rarely mention: long trips with soiled clothes to find water for laundry during drought, or a description of a mother and her young son, 'a sinewy youngster of six', both mounted on camels, on a hundred-and-fifty-mile ride to Boulia for the mother's approaching confinement.

Mrs Duncan-Kemp wrote another book about the Corner country of Western Queensland. *Where Strange Paths Go Down* tells something of the pioneers, and describes with sympathy but no sentimentality the natives of the area, many of whom served the remarkable women who ran the station so efficiently for so long.

38
The Frontiers of Misfortune

MOST OF our present-day forms of social help and service began through the work of one or more individuals. In the list of those who championed the lonely, the underprivileged and the handicapped are the names of many women. Only a few can be given here, and they must serve as symbols for the many who carried out the initial work on the frontiers of human unhappiness.

Australia's first recorded piece of social welfare was a scheme begun by Lieutenant King on Norfolk Island to look after neglected children of the convict population. When King became Governor of New South Wales he described the children of the mother State as the finest but most neglected in the world. He outlined their condition in a despatch dated July 1800:

> Finding the greater part of the children in this colony much abandoned to every kind of wretchedness and vice, I perceived the absolute necessity of something being done to withdraw them from the vicious examples of their abandoned parents.

He met this necessity by acquiring Captain Kent's brick house and its 2½ acres of garden near the Tank Stream to make an 'Orphan House'. The committee he formed to run it included Mrs Edith Paterson, wife of the Lieutenant-Governor, and his own wife, Anna Josepha. The place was often called 'Mrs King's Orphanage'. Marnie Bassett has stated 'it was one of her greatest interests and absorbed most of her time.'[1]

Funds to support the orphanage were made available from shipping fees, fines and other public revenue. One hundred girls were housed and taught to sew, spin and read. A visiting missionary, impressed with the orphanage, wrote:

> The Reverend Mr. Marsden conducted us to the Orphan House (which is the best house in all Sydney, none excepted) where we were highly delighted with seeing the girls in the greatest order feasting on excellent salt pork and plum pudding, and seemed very happy in their new situation. The daily visitors are Mrs. King and Mrs. Paterson, the two first ladies in rank in the colony.

It appears a genuine attempt to improve conditions of a group of innocent victims whose lot, otherwise, would have been squalor and degradation. Many an Australian-born girl of the early years must have been grateful for her stay in the house by the Tank Stream and the interest taken in its running by the Governor's lady.

* * *

Welfare work on the grand scale first found a place in the colony under the driving force of Caroline Chisholm, who 'was not only a reformer but a female reformer in an age when fearless thinking and independent action were not generally considered desirable, or even quite respectable, attributes of womanhood.'[2]

The need which set her dynamic energy to work was the position of young female migrants landing without funds in the colony where there was no organization to ease them into the new life. As a result, for too many the way into the country was the path to prostitution.

Caroline Chisholm was born in Northamptonshire, England, in 1808. Her marriage with Captain Archibald Chisholm took her to Madras, India, where she undertook her first piece of social work—a school for the daughters and orphans of English soldiers. This had several features towards which modern education is still groping, one being a committee of management formed by the children themselves to roster their duties to the school.

The government took over the school when the Chisholms left India to spend their leave in New South Wales. They arrived in 1838 when Caroline was thirty, and took a house at Windsor. How and when Caroline first became aware of the plight of the migrant girls is not clear, but more and more it tugged at her mind.

These were the days of the 'bounty' system when the British government paid shipowners a sum for each migrant conveyed to the colony. The ships were ill found, the rations poor, life on board led to immorality, and deaths were frequent.

When the ships arrived in Australia, the girls were kept on board for ten days, in which period they could be 'hired' by those who cared to visit the ship. Those who were not so disposed of were then landed. The girls had little money (on one occasion Mrs Chisholm reported that a group of sixty-four possessed 14s. 3d. between them), there was no hostel to receive them, and no work to which they could be directed. Hundreds of them drifted round the city by day, and slept at night in rocks and caves around the waterfront.

Caroline Chisholm began visiting the wharves, a stately figure in dark silk, to talk to and advise the girls of the perils they faced and what they might do. Some she took into her own home at Windsor, others she persuaded friends to employ. It was not enough, and Caroline knew it, knew too that she could, if she would, help them to a better life. It was an urge which at first she resisted.

> For three weeks I hesitated and suffered much . . . as a female and almost a stranger in the country I naturally felt diffident . . . my delay pressed on my mind as a *sin*, and when I heard of a poor girl suffering distress and losing her reputation in consequence I felt that I was not *clear of her sin* for I did not do all I *could* to prevent it.[3]

The period of hesitation passed, and on Easter Sunday Caroline made her decision.

> I was enabled at the altar of Our Lord to make an offering of my talents to the God who gave them. I promised to know neither *country nor creed* but serve all justly and impartially. I asked only to be enabled to keep those poor girls from being tempted by their need to mortal sin, and resolved that, to accomplish this in every way, sacrifice my feeling, surrender all comfort—nor, in fact, consider my own wishes or feelings but wholly devote myself to the work I had in hand. I felt my offering was accepted and that God's blessing was on my work; but it was His Will to permit many serious *difficulties* to be thrown in my way and to conduct me through a rugged path of deep humiliation.[4]

One of the 'difficulties' was the lukewarm attitude of Governor Gipps, who received her testily, expecting an elderly, bespectacled crank, and was astonished to find himself confronted by a handsome, intelligent young woman armed with well-marshalled facts. Later he admitted generously that he had thrown cold water on her scheme, and praised her work and its results.

Caroline Chisholm began her work without funds, and opposed by employers, officials, even co-religionists and friends. She has written of the mental distress much of this caused her, but her faith in the cause she espoused and her own ability did not falter.

The work gave her little time for family life, apart from one day each week which she set aside for that purpose. She seldom allowed anything to interrupt it. She had three children on arrival in Australia, and tried to keep the two youngest with her. But caring for them divided her mind from the cause she had undertaken, so she returned them to the Windsor home and channelled her great industry to helping those whom she believed to be in greater need. In the active years which followed, she bore three more children, but was with them for only short periods, a fact which brought her much acid criticism.

In spite of opposition and hostility, veiled or overt, Caroline Chisholm pressed forward with her work.

She met the basic need for shelter by cajoling the Governor into allowing her the use of an old wooden shed. Draughty and rat-infested though it was, Caroline shared it with her girls, just as she later shared with them the discomforts of rough tracks, flooded streams, wind and weather encountered on journeys to places far from town.

The problem of employment she tackled by organizing committees in country districts to inform her on prospects in their locality. Then she began the removal of girls from the overcrowded town to distant areas. Some of the opposition she faced on this move came from the girls themselves. Terrified by tales of bushrangers and hostile blacks, the first party refused to mount the dray brought to convey them to their new homes.

But the plan snowballed until the party of unemployed young women going to domestic service at settlers' homes became a cavalcade of men, women and children advancing on the inland under the mantle of Mrs Chisholm's scheme.

These parties became known and talked about up and down the colony. Mrs Chisholm, on her white horse, Captain, trained to swim flooded rivers with children clinging to the saddle flaps, was a familiar and respected figure. Innkeepers would take no payment when she slept under their roofs, and settlers of all classes gave her help and encouragement. From Parramatta to Maitland, from Liverpool to Bathurst, and on to the rolling country around Yass and Gundagai, she journeyed in the interests of the young women whom government indifference left without a future.

During her trips she talked with free settlers and freed convicts about their experiences in Australia, and learnt of many families who had been separated without hope of being reunited. Here was another side to migration Mrs Chisholm felt should be reformed, another problem to challenge her crusading spirit.

With her family she left for England in 1846, determined to restore faith in migration among the people of Great Britain, and force officialdom to action. Letters from settlers and emancipists, couched in their own simple, often illiterate, phrasing, were her best arguments with the people. For officials she produced piles of neatly documented facts. With this and the support of an admiring press, the doors of workhouses were opened, and children, separated from their parents by transportation, were soon voyaging to Australia.

Mrs Chisholm carried the battle into other fields—to the banks, for a better system of meeting orders sent by settlers to their English families, and to shipowners, reluctant to surrender profits made out of sub-standard accommodation on their vessels.

By 1850 an influential committee worked with her to help conscientious migrants set sail for Australia. Conditions in ships improved and the tide of migration steadily increased.

Mrs Chisholm's part in all the activity was colossal, and her working day frightening. She lectured interested groups, interviewed officials, bankers and shipowners, advised intending migrants on all matters affecting their journey to Australia, wrote, organized and planned. Little wonder that in 1853 her health broke down and she was ill for some weeks.

When the discovery of gold made her campaign for migration unnecessary, the Chisholms returned to Australia (1854). There, Caroline visited the diggings, slept under drays or in waggons, to study at first hand the conditions of people on the fields.

She set up a chain of shelter sheds on the route to Castlemaine, and supported the diggers in their aims to secure land of their own.

For a few years the Chisholms lived at Kyneton, near the Campaspe River, then returned to Sydney. To eke out her small income Mrs Chisholm opened a school, but after five years retired to England. Her physical strength gone, she spent most of her last years in bed, in a small room with no view. The State granted her a pension of £100 a year, a poor reward for a woman who had given security and full life to so many.

Her death in 1877 was the end of a life of vision and sacrifice, devoted to those she had vowed to help without heed for her own comfort or welfare.

* * *

Another great figure in the work of social service is Catherine Helen Spence. She did not move about like Caroline Chisholm; her work was carried out in the city rather than spread over the miles of scarcely developed country where Mrs Chisholm made her way. But the work she did to improve the position of her city's unfortunates was far-reaching and important.

Catherine Spence arrived in Adelaide a year after Caroline Chisholm landed in Sydney. It was 1839, and Catherine was fourteen.

She has recorded that she sat on a log in Gilles Street and cried with disappointment at her first sight of Adelaide under the hot summer sun. It was a sad beginning to three years of poverty and unhappiness, when the family ran a small dairy and lived mainly on half a ton of rice which they had bought at bargain rates.

At seventeen, Catherine had acclimatized, and was rooted in the colony. She began writing verse and letters which occasionally appeared in papers. But it was not enough to net her a regular income, so she became a governess at sixpence an hour.

The gold rush, which drained men from the colony, gave her the theme of her first novel, *Clara Morison*, for which she was paid £40, less a £10 editing fee.

For a time she was correspondent for the Melbourne *Argus*, signing articles with her brother's name in deference to the prejudice against women journalists.

In 1859 she became interested in electoral reform, and carried on the campaign for this over many years.

But Catherine Spence was too alert, too active, to narrow her interests to one field. Children, deserted and neglected, aborigine and half-caste, stirred her to pity; conditions in Destitute Asylums, where no attempt was made to separate children from the sick, the old and the insane, aroused her crusading spirit. With Caroline E. Clark, she began bombarding the press to awaken the public conscience, while urging officials to improve conditions.

It was a long fight, but the two women were sturdy and resilient and slowly they gained ground. The government was persuaded to finance the upkeep of children in homes of approved foster parents. In 1886 a State Children's Council was formed, a tremendous forward step which affected the attitude and treatment of young delinquents, blind, deaf and mentally defective children, education at kindergarten and pre-school level, and other pressing social matters relating to child health and welfare.

Catherine Spence used her pen, energy, and her tongue to further these and other needs of the unfortunate and unhappy.

When she died in 1910 she had pioneered many activities for women. She was an early Australian novelist, pioneer newspaperwoman, lecturer, and lay preacher (often heard in the pulpit of the Unitarian Church). Practical but broadly sympathetic, she gave unstintingly of her energy and time to further the causes of the unhappy and destitute, and awaken public opinion to the social problems which the community alone could better.

In 1894 the State of South Australia pioneered the granting of franchise to women. Other States followed, and today the battles which ended with victory are almost forgotten, or smiled on indulgently. But they were very real to the women who fought them—for that matter, to the opponents against whom the fight was waged.

Many women took part in the struggle. New South Wales especially remembers Lady Windeyer, who, before her marriage to young lawyer, William Charles Windeyer, had been Mary Bolton. She had many public interests, mainly concerned with women and children. Women's hospitals, babies' homes, State aid for foster parents, kindergarten work were but some of the causes for which she laboured. Sincere and capable, her eloquence eventually was turned to gaining votes for women. Her outstanding character and her ability in reasoning and debate won many an adherent for the cause.

Under her tuition another famous worker in the field of women's problems, especially the struggle for franchise, was Miss Rosa Scott, a gracious, feminine personality whose bonnets delighted Sydney, says Miles Franklin, and whose wit, energy and skill in debate furthered the causes for which she worked.

With the right to vote established, women's part in public affairs increased tremendously, although few have contested parliamentary elections, and a large proportion of their work has been in the areas where women and children are at a disadvantage.

It was women's insistence which brought in such reforms as the rights of minors to special courts, the establishment of women police, of national playgrounds for children, the betterment of education —in these and many other areas women have pioneered. Their strength and endurance were pitted not against nature, flood, drought and climate, but against apathy, ignorance and outright hostility.

In the sum total of effort by which Australia has achieved her high living standard, women were everywhere among the pioneers. And when the march of years brought us as a nation to the wider fields of international service, there was no lack of women volunteers. The hunger of children in other lands could not go disregarded by those whose great-grandmothers helped to harvest the wheat of infant

Caroline Chisholm

colonies. The hunger of women in far-off communities for education, for social contacts, for medical aid would not be pushed lightly aside by the daughters of the pioneers. We who have come so recently from our own frontiers can have nothing but sympathy for and an urge to help those who are still living on the outposts.

39
Pioneering for Tomorrow

So THE YEARS PASSED turning settlements into States, States into a federation, and Australia into a nation. Histories recorded the names of lawmakers, explorers, scientists and public men, but few of the women who stood beside them or created the background behind them. Pioneer women were shadowy figures, vaguely known. Sometimes one or two were drawn out of obscurity. Sometimes they were stacked together and praised briefly for their endurance. More than once they received attention from a scornful pen out of patience with the phrase 'pioneer women'. But unrecorded and unassessed though it was, their contribution to the making of Australia was considerable. They had churned butter when the bush was part of Hobart Town, made cheese when settlement was new along the Swan, tied their bonnet strings and faced inland from Adelaide, Sydney, and Moreton Bay; had their babies along the way as the waggons rolled north, poured wax into candle moulds while Queensland became a State, kept house where the communication lines were thin and chancy, and knew the loneliness of the steamy Gulf, the country of sandhill and gibber, and the land where the spinifex grew. Their children played in stockyard and sheep pen when the pastoral industries were beginning, and out of camp oven and colonial stove pioneer women brought magnificent meals to hearten travellers on their way to open a new district or set the basis for a new era.

Later generations of women pioneered in new fields: in universities, professions, the arts, commerce and trade. Some few went into politics, some into the new areas of aviation, science, radio and television. For each age has its pioneers; but the first, the lonely ones, are still the symbol of high courage and endurance.

And where is the modern pioneer? Some will direct you to

Woomera, where the first women kept house in galvanized iron homes baked to a heat so fierce under the desert sun that thinking was a burden and coolness a remembered dream. The reason for their presence is the same as that which took Isabella Sim out of Adelaide to Gawler, and brought Georgiana Molloy from Roseneath to Augusta. But this time their menfolk work not with stock, but on scientific processes which may bring space travel closer, or harness the atom to serve humanity in peace.

Others will tell you that today's pioneer women stand behind the dam-makers, who are moving rivers and tunnelling through mountains above the snow-line along the Monaros.

To women in both these places, amenities come faster and aid in an emergency arrives in time that would have seemed a miracle to Mary Costello on the dry inland trail, but for the other contemporary pioneer who comes in the migrant ships from Europe and Britain there is often heavy sledding. For these women, housekeeping too often means, not isolation, but overcrowding; their pioneering is done in dwellings they share with others while working, saving and making adjustments to life in an alien land as Bridget Durack did, so that their children may know its security by right of birth or adoption.

But those who know the North declare the real pioneer of today is the woman of the area where the white men's dispossession of the native tribes has brought changes and problems. To these women, still few and scattered (though many have modern homes of grace and distinction), has fallen the task of building new lives and better relationships among the dark people of their district. Not all of them have a show-place homestead like Fossil Downs, which Mrs Maxine MacDonald runs on the Fitzroy River plains in the Kimberleys, with its twenty-thousand-gallon swimming pool, electric fans in every room of the modern homestead, and a village of small cement brick homes for the aborigines. But many of the North's white women have her feeling of compassion for the native people, a sense of urgency to improve their lot, and give them back some of the dignity as human beings of which loss of their tribal life has bereft them.

Now that the frontiers have been pushed further out, perhaps that is the work which awaits the descendants of the pioneers—to consolidate by science what the first settlers won by hard work and endurance, and to improve human relationships among all who share the continent.

To us who stand on the threshold of a new age, the stories of those who built the land we have inherited may give us fresh heart to face the challenge of that which still remains to be done.

References

Stone Age Women

[1] A. P. Elkin, *The Australian Aborigines* (Sydney, 1938).
[2] K. Langloh Parker, *The Euahlayi Tribe* (London, 1905).
[3] R. and C. Berndt, *The First Australians* (Sydney, 1952).
[4] Daisy Bates, *The Passing of the Aborigines* (London, 1938).
[5] K. Langloh Parker, op. cit.
[6] Ibid.
[7] Ibid.
[8] Ibid.
[9] Phyllis Kaberry, *Aboriginal Woman, Sacred and Profane* (London, 1939).
[10] K. Langloh Parker, op. cit.
[11] Phyllis Kaberry, op. cit.
[12] Ibid.
[13] William Dampier, *A New Voyage Round the World* (London, 1698).
[14] Ibid.
[15] Journal of the Rt Hon. Sir Joseph Banks, *Historical Records of New South Wales*.
[16] J. White, *Journal of a Voyage to New South Wales* (London, 1790).
[17] W. Tench, *A Narrative of the Expedition to Botany Bay* (London, 1789).
[18] Ibid.
[19] J. Hunter, *An Historical Journal of the Transactions at Port Jackson . . .* (London, 1793).
[20] Ibid.
[21] Ibid.
[22] James Backhouse, *A Narrative of a Visit to the Australian Colonies* (London, 1843).
[23] Ibid.
[24] Catherine H. Berndt, *Women's Changing Ceremonies in Northern Australia*, Actualités Scientifiques et Industrielles 1108 (Paris, 1950).
[25] Ibid.
[26] K. Langloh Parker, 'Our Witch Woman', *The Euahlayi Tribe*.
[27] Ibid.
[28] A. M. Duncan-Kemp, *Where Strange Paths Go Down* (Brisbane, 1952).
[29] Mary Durack, *Keep Him My Country* (London, 1955).

Enter the European Women

[1] Hartog's west coast landing was preceded ten years earlier in the north. In 1606 a Dutch vessel, *Duyfken* (Little Dove), visited the Gulf of Carpentaria. It returned to Java with little to report except the murder of several crew members by natives, and no other European ship followed *Duyfken's* course for many years.

Women in Chains

[1] The figures given by various sources vary. Even Phillip seems uncertain of the exact number of his charges.
[2] Journal of Lt R. Clark of First Fleet. (MS. in Mitchell Library, Sydney.)
[3] Diary of Surgeon A. Bowes of First Fleet. (MS. in Mitchell Library, Sydney.)
[4] Quoted from Lt R. Clark's Journal by M. Barnard Eldershaw, *Phillip of Australia* (London, 1938).
[5] M. Barnard Eldershaw, op. cit.
[6] G. Holford to Secretary of State, 1827.
[7] Macquarie to Earl Bathurst, 3 March 1818.
[8] Rev. Samuel Marsden to Macquarie, 1815.

Historical Records of New South Wales, vols. 2 (1893), 3 (1895).
Louisa Anne Meredith, *My Home in Tasmania* (London, 1852).

Keeper of the Keys

[1] *Historical Records of Australia*, series 1, vol. 12 (1919).
[2] Much of the material used in this chapter is based on *Some Early Records of the Macarthurs of Camden*, by Sibella Macarthur-Onslow (Sydney, 1914).
[3] M. Barnard Eldershaw, 'Elizabeth Macarthur, The Happy Pioneer', in *The Peaceful Army*, ed. Flora Eldershaw (1938).

Over the Hills to Goshen

[1] Goshen was the land given to Joseph's family by the King of Egypt. It was more fertile than any they had known, and it came to mean the Land of Promise.

Pioneers Farther South

[1] From *Notes by C. Craig on 'Entally House' Catalogue*, Scenery Preservation Board, Tasmania.
[2] *The Journal of Mrs Fenton: A Narrative of Her Life in India, the Isle of France, and Tasmania during the years 1826-1830* (London, 1901).
[3] Ibid.
[4] Ibid.

Swans on the River

[1] H.M.S. *Challenger*, under Captain Fremantle, arrived ahead of *Parmelia* on 2 May, anchored off Garden Island, and took possession of the west coast in the name of Britain.
[2] *Western Australian Historical Society Journal and Proceedings*, vol. 1, pt. 1 (1927).
[3] Mrs J. Cowan, 'Some Pioneer Women', *Western Australian Historical Society Journal and Proceedings*, vol. 1, pt. 10 (1931).
[4] Ibid.
[5] Mrs J. B. Roe, 'Some Old-time Memories', *Western Australian Historical Society Journal and Proceedings*, vol. 1, pt. 1 (1927).
[6] Ibid.

Flowers in the South

[1] 'The Letters of Georgina Molloy', prepared by W. G. Pickering from material supplied by Mrs J. M. Drummond, *Western Australian Historical Society Journal and Proceedings*, vol. 1, pt. 4 (1929).

Women in the Fields

[1] Beryl Burton, South Australian Country Women's Association.
[2] J. W. Bull, *Early Experiences of Colonial Life in South Australia*, (Adelaide, 1878).
[3] Ibid.
[4] Ibid.
[5] G. Sutherland, *The South Australian Company* (London, 1898).

Home-makers Go Inland

[1] *Burra Jubilee Year Souvenir*, 1951.
[2] Ibid.
[3] Facts supplied by Mrs Helen Symonds, Jamestown, S.A.
[4] From Mrs T. W. Kealy's letter.
[5] Facts from Mrs S. Parnell, Orroroo, S.A.

The Pathfinders

[1] J. J. Pascoe (ed.), *History of Adelaide and Vicinity* (Adelaide, 1901).
[2] Ibid.
[3] Now a well-known Dorset ram stud.
[4] Mrs A. L. Jeffries, Mt Bryan.

Where the Red Cedar Grew

[1] From Journal of Commissioner Parry (arrived Sydney 1829), quoted in 'First Decade of the Australian Agricultural Company, 1824 to 1834', *Royal Australian Historical Association Journal* (N.S.W.), vol. 9, pt. 3 (1923), p. 131.
[2] Mary McMaugh, 'The Days of Yore'. (MS. in Mitchell Library, Sydney.)
[3] Ibid.

Pioneer on the Move

[1] Louisa Anne Meredith, *My Home in Tasmania* (London, 1852).

Home at World's End

[1] The Wife of an Australian Pioneer, *Memories of Days Long Gone By*.
[2] Mary Macleod Banks, *Memories of Pioneer Days in Queensland* (London, 1931).
[3] Ibid.
[4] Ibid.
[5] Ibid.

Mary of Maranoa

[1] Mary A. McManus, *Reminiscences of the Early Settlement in the Maranoa District*.

Beyond the Nineteen Counties

[1] Letter from Mr John Everett to his brother, Rev. T. Everett, of Fordenbridge, Hants; printed in *Inverell Times*, 1 December 1954.

Homes South of the Murray

[1] Margaret Kiddle, 'Vandiemonian Colonists in Port Phillip, 1834-50', *Tasmanian Historical Research Association Papers and Proceedings*, vol. 3, no. 3 (1954).

2 Thomas Walker, A Month in the Bush of Australia (London, 1838).
3 R. V. Billis and A. S. Kenyon, Pastures New (Melbourne, 1930).
4 J. Sadlier, ed. from family papers and accounts, 'How We Settled at Bontherambo', Victorian Historical Magazine, vol. 8, no. 1 (1920).
5 Ibid.
6 Ibid.
7 Ibid.
8 H. J. Samuel, A Saddle at Bontharambo (Melbourne, 1950).

Pastoral Partners

1 She was a skilled artist and had a charming singing voice.
2 Hugh McCrae (ed.), Georgina's Journal (Sydney, 1934).
3 Ibid.
4 Ibid.
5 Ibid.
6 Notes on Ann Drysdale and Caroline Newcombe from newspaper cuttings in Mitchell Library, Sydney: Geelong Advertiser, 3 August 1934; Australasian, Melbourne, 27 July 1935; Herald, Melbourne, 19 January 1935.
7 R. V. Billis and A. S. Kenyon, Pastures New (Melbourne, 1930).

Observer in Blue Serge

1 Charles Barrett, Gold: The Romance of its Discovery in Australia (Melbourne, 1944).
2 Ellen (Mrs Charles) Clacy, A Lady's Visit to the Gold Diggings of Australia in 1852-53 (London, 1853).

Pioneer in Disguise

1 Ellen (Mrs Charles) Clacy, A Lady's Visit to the Gold Diggings of Australia in 1852-53 (London, 1853).

Childhood of a Pioneer

1 Mrs Campbell Praed, My Australian Girlhood (London, 1902).

No Medals for Mary

1 From a letter by Mrs E. Arrow of Bathurst, daughter of Mrs Blattman.

Spinifex Pioneer

1 Miss V. H. Ferguson, 'The Late Mrs John Withnell', Western Australian Historical Society Journal and Proceedings, vol. 1, pt. 3 (1928).

Reporter of the North

1 'The Founding of Darwin', North Australian Monthly, August 1955.

Along the Golden Miles

1 Mrs Clara Paton, 'Early Days of Coolgardie', Western Australian Historical Society Journal and Proceedings, vol. 4, pt. 2 (1950).
2 Ibid.; see below, 'A Goldfield Wedding'.
3 Mrs A. H. Garnsey, Scarlet Pillows: An Australian Nurse's Tales of Long Ago (Melbourne, 1950?).
4 Ibid.
5 Ibid.
6 Ibid.

⁷ Ibid.
⁸ See chapter 32, 'Nurses of the Inland'.

Nurses of the Inland

¹ Mrs Clara Paton, 'Early Days of Coolgardie', *Western Australian Historical Society Journal and Proceedings*, vol. 4, pt. 2 (1950).
² Malcolm Uren, *Glint of Gold* (Melbourne, 1949).
³ Mrs A. H. Garnsey, *Scarlet Pillows: An Australian Nurse's Tales of Long Ago* (Melbourne, 1950?).
⁴ Ibid.
⁵ Ibid.
⁶ Ibid.
⁷ Letter from a Northern Territory child to the *Inlander*.
⁸ *Country Guardian* (official journal of the N.S.W. Bush Nursing Association), April 1955.

Past the Farthest Fence

¹ Facts supplied by Mrs D. Treloar (née Picker).
² The facts recorded were supplied by Mrs W. W. Braitling (née Crook), Mt Doreen Station, via Alice Springs.
³ Ibid.

Women in the Surgery

¹ Gwendolen H. Swinburne, *Queen Victoria Memorial Hospital: History, the First Forty Years* (Melbourne, 1934).
² Ibid.
³ Miss M. J. Bedford, on whose notes this sketch is based.

Sandhill Homestead

¹ Myrtle Rose White, *No Roads Go By* (Sydney, 1932).

Pisé Homestead

¹ *Queensland Country Life*, 4 August 1955.
² Ibid.
³ Ibid.

The Frontiers of Misfortune

¹ M. Bassett, *The Governor's Lady* (Oxford, 1940; Melbourne, 1961).
² Eleanor Dark, 'Caroline Chisholm and Her Times', in *The Peaceful Army*, ed. Flora Eldershaw (1938).
³ Quoted by Eleanor Dark, op. cit.
⁴ Quoted by Margaret Kiddle, *Caroline Chisholm* (Melbourne, 1950).

PUBLISHER'S NOTE

Most of the illustrations in this edition have come from private collections. Grateful acknowledgement is also made to the following sources for permission to reproduce the illustrations on the pages listed: Latrobe Library pp 4, 72, 206, 256, 276; Mitchell Library pp 12, 104, 202; New South Wales Government Printing Office p 272; National Library (Nan Kivell collection) pp 42, 62, 80; *Catering* Magazine p 127 (bottom).

Acknowledgments

The list of those who helped shape this book is long, and with deep gratitude I acknowledge some whose assistance was indispensable. My thanks go to the staff of the Mitchell Library, especially for the help given by Miss S. Muorot; the Public Libraries of Queensland, South Australia and Tasmania; Mrs Chas. Young of the Queensland Women's Historical Society, and the Royal Historical Society of Victoria; the Western Australian Historical Society, for permission to use and quote from its journals; the Bush Nursing Association; Mrs Alice Shann, for permission to quote from the late Professor E. O. Shann's *Cattle Chosen*; Dame Mary Gilmore, who allowed me to use her poem, 'Ode to the Pioneer Women'; Lindsay Gordon, for allowing me to quote from his poem, 'Beaufoy Merlin'; the late Mrs P. C. McConnel, who gave her blessing to the chapter, 'Home at World's End'; Mrs E. N. Butler, for permission to use *My Australian Girlhood* by Mrs Campbell Praed; Major-General Denzil Macarthur-Onslow, for permission to use *Some Early Records of the Macarthurs of Camden* by Sibella Macarthur-Onslow; Mary Durack and the *Bulletin*, for permission to include the poem, 'Red Jack,' by Mary Durack; Douglas Stewart, for the poem, 'The Maids of the Mountains', included in the anthology, *Australian Bush Ballads*, edited by himself and Nancy Keesing; and to those authors who generously allowed me to use and quote from their books: Mrs Myrtle Rose White (*No Roads Go By*), Mrs A. Duncan-Kemp (*Our Sandhill Country*), and Mrs A. H. Garnsey (*Scarlet Pillows*).

I am also deeply in debt to Mary Durack, Mrs N. Tetley, Mrs Hazel Stafford, Lady Crofts, Mrs S. Coad, Mrs E. Arrow, Mrs T. V. Healey, Miss Winifred Lawler, Mrs Florence Stacey, Miss B. Dulhunty, Mrs M. Macdougall, Mrs Beatrice Purdey and many others who supplied me with material for chapters or incidents, or pointed out a fruitful source; and to Kay Kinane, who read and advised on the draft manuscript, and Donald McLean, who helped over the hurdle of the galley-proof stage.

My special gratitude goes to the Country Women's Association, to those branches which organized committees to collect material, and those members who supplied it; and to Mrs Ida Spencer, Mrs Barbara Cullen and Miss Dorothea Baltzer, whose encouragement and help was a prop and an inspiration on many occasions.

EVE POWNALL

Longueville, Sydney